D0303559

Heroic Leadership

Heroic Leadership is a celebration of our greatest heroes, from legends such as Mahatma Gandhi to the legions of unsung heroes who transform our world quietly behind the scenes. The authors argue that all great heroes are also great leaders. The term "heroic leadership" is coined to describe how heroism and leadership are intertwined, and how our most celebrated heroes are also our most transforming leaders.

This book offers a new conceptual framework for understanding heroism and heroic leadership, drawing from theories of great leadership and heroic action. Ten categories of heroism are described: Trending Heroes, Transitory Heroes, Transitional Heroes, Tragic Heroes, Transposed Heroes, Transparent Heroes, Traditional Heroes, Transfigured Heroes, Transforming Heroes, and Transcendent Heroes. The authors describe the lives of 100 exceptional individuals whose accomplishments place them into one of these ten hero categories. These 100 hero profiles offer compelling evidence for a new integration of theories of leadership and theories of heroism.

Scott T. Allison is Professor of Psychology at the University of Richmond. His research program focuses on human belief systems about heroes, villains, legends, leaders, underdogs, and martyrs. He has served on the editorial boards of the top empirical journals in experimental social psychology, including the *Journal of Personality and Social Psychology, Personality and Social Psychology Bulletin*, and *Group Dynamics: Theory, Research, and Practice*. With George Goethals, he is author of *Heroes: What They Do & Why We Need Them* (2011). He is the recipient of the University of Richmond's Distinguished Educator Award and the Virginia Council of Higher Education's Outstanding Faculty Award.

George R. Goethals holds the E. Claiborne Robins Distinguished Professorship in Leadership Studies at the University of Richmond. Previously he taught at Williams College where he was Chair of the Department of Psychology, founding Chair of the Program in Leadership Studies, Acting Dean of the Faculty, and Provost. Goethals explores leadership from psychological and historical perspectives. His recent research focuses on presidential debates, the presidency of Ulysses S. Grant, and the role of biography in shaping our understanding of leadership. With Scott T. Allison, he is author of *Heroes: What They Do & Why We Need Them* (2011).

LEADERSHIP: Research and Practice Series

A James MacGregor Burns Academy of Leadership Collaboration

SERIES EDITORS

Georgia Sorenson, Ph.D, Research Professor in Leadership Studies, University of Maryland and Founder of the James MacGregor Burns Academy of Leadership and the International Leadership Association.

Ronald E. Riggio, Ph.D, Henry R. Kravis Professor of Leadership and Organizational Psychology and former Director of the Kravis Leadership Institute at Claremont McKenna College.

Scott T. Allison and George R. Goethals, *Heroic Leadership: An Influence Taxonomy of 100 Exceptional Individuals*

Michelle C. Bligh and Ronald E. Riggio (Eds.), *Exploring Distance in Leader–Follower Relationships: When Near is Far and Far is Near*

Michael A. Genovese and Janie Steckenrider (Eds.), *Women as Political Leaders: Studies in Gender and Governing*

Jon P. Howell, *Snapshots of Great Leadership*

Aneil Mishra and Karen E. Mishra, *Becoming a Trustworthy Leader: Psychology and Practice*

Heroic Leadership

An Influence Taxonomy of 100 Exceptional Individuals

Scott T. Allison and
George R. Goethals

Routledge
Taylor & Francis Group

NEW YORK AND LONDON

First published 2013
by Routledge
711 Third Avenue, New York, NY 10017

Simultaneously published in the UK
by Routledge
27 Church Road, Hove, East Sussex BN3 2FA

Routledge is an imprint of the Taylor & Francis Group, an informa business

© 2013 Taylor & Francis

Library of Congress Cataloging in Publication Data
Allison, Scott T.
Heroic leadership : an influence taxonomy of 100 exceptional individuals / authored by Scott T. Allison and George R. Goethals.
  p. cm.
  Includes bibliographical references and index. 1. Leadership. 2. Heroes. 3. Leadership–Biography. 4. Heroes–Biography. I. Goethals, George R. II. Title.
  HM1261.A47 2013
  303.3′4–dc23
                                                                                    2012039022

ISBN: 978-0-415-62778-8 (hbk)
ISBN: 978-0-415-62852-5 (pbk)
ISBN: 978-0-203-10088-2 (ebk)

Typeset in Garamond and Optima
by Wearset Ltd, Boldon, Tyne and Wear

SUSTAINABLE
FORESTRY
INITIATIVE

Certified Sourcing

www.sfiprogram.org
SFI-00555

The SFI label applies to the text stock.

Printed and bound in the United States of America by Walsworth Publishing Company, Marceline, MO.

To the memory of two of our most cherished heroic leaders, Roberto Clemente (1934–1972) and Abraham Lincoln (1809–1865).

Contents

Series Foreword by Georgia Sorenson and Ronald E. Riggio   xi

About the Authors   xii

Preface   xiii

1   Introduction: Leadership and Heroism   1

2   Trending Heroes: Gaining or Losing Heroic Status   28
    Lady Gaga: A Hero in the Making?   30
    Ulysses S. Grant: The Reappraised Hero   31
    Sigmund Freud: The Vindication of a Battered Theory   33
    Drew Barrymore: The Heroic Story of the Little Girl Lost   34
    Woodrow Wilson: A Hero Trending Downward   35
    Arnold Schwarzenegger: The Downward Spiral of a Hero   37

3   Transitory Heroes: Hero Today, Gone Tomorrow   39
    Joe Darby: The Heroic Whistleblower of Abu Ghraib   41
    Mae Jemison: Living Heroic Dreams   43
    Heart-wrenching Heroism at the Fukushima Nuclear Power Plant   44
    Randy Pausch: The Hero Who Dared Us to Live Our Dreams   45
    Gabrielle Giffords: Heroic Recovery From Trauma   47
    Benjamin "Beast" Butler: Hero for a Moment   48
    Liu Xiaobo: An Emerging Hero of Peace   49
    Christa McAuliffe: Lost Hero of the Space Shuttle *Challenger*   51
    The Heroism and Leadership of Fred Korematsu   52
    Ephemeral Heroes and Villains: A Tale of Two Stevens   53

4   Transitional Heroes: Those Whom We Outgrow   55
    Justin Bieber: Heroic Pop Star   57
    Fred Rogers: Love, Wisdom, and Compassion for Children   58
    Reed Richards: Fantastic Family Man   60
    Captain James T. Kirk: The Hero Who Treks the Stars   61
    Iron Man: A Classic Superhero in the Modern World   63

5 Tragic Heroes: The Self-Destruction of Greatness   **65**
Oedipus the King: The Classic Tragic Hero 67
Tiger Woods: The Ebb and Flow of Fame and Fortune 68
Coming to Terms with Richard Nixon 70

6 Transposed Heroes: The Fine Line Between Heroism and Villainy   **72**
Harvey Dent as Two-Face: The Hero Turned Villain in *Batman* 75
John Edwards: The Modular-Minded Transposed Hero 76
Jack Nicklaus: The Villain Who Became a Hero 77
Joe Paterno: Discerning the Legacy of a Transposed Hero 78

7 Transparent Heroes: The Unsung Heroes Among Us   **81**
Montgomery Meigs: A Transparent Hero of the Civil War 83
John Wooden: Heroic Teacher and Mentor 84
Accidental Sidekicks: Marion Keisker's Moment to Help Elvis 86
Those Whom We Forgot: The Makers of Fire 87
The Supporting Cast in Heroes' Narratives: Sidekicks and Others 88
Why Our Parents are Our Heroes 89
Edith Wilson: An Unsung Hero or Villain? 91
Bayard Rustin: Peaceful Advocate of Human Rights 92
Rick Rescorla: The Hero Who Saved 2,700 Lives on 9/11 94

8 Traditional Heroes: The Classic Hero's Journey   **96**
Traditional-Moral Heroes
The Dalai Lama: "My Religion is Kindness" 98
Pat Tillman: The Consummate War Hero 100
Irena Sendler: The Hero Who Stood Up to Evil 101
George Bailey: A Hero's Wonderful Life 102
Confucius: The Master Hero of Virtue 103
Mother Teresa and the Call to Love 105
Lois Wilson: The Hero Who Helped Families of Alcoholics 106
Nathan Hale and the Powerful Heroic Script 107
Dana Reeve: The Unsung Selfless Hero 108
Groundhog Day's Phil Connors and the Heroic Theme of Redemption 110
Rabbi Israel Spira: A Hero of the Holocaust 111
Rosa Parks' Transforming Act of Civil Disobedience 112
Corrie ten Boom: The Holocaust Hero with a Hiding Place 114

Traditional-Competent Heroes
Marie Curie: Trailblazing Scientist Who Paid the Ultimate Price 115
Tina Fey: An Uncommon Celebrity Hero 116
Ellen DeGeneres: Heroic Comedienne and Underdog Advocate 117
John Nash: A Hero's Brilliant Triumph Over Mental Illness 119

Althea Gibson: Barrier Breaker and Way Paver 120
Monica Seles: Tennis Hero and Tragedienne 121
Daniel Anderson: The Hero Who Redefined Alcoholism 122
Tough Without a Gun: Heroic Portrayals by Humphrey Bogart 124
Edgar Allan Poe: American Literary Giant 125
Secretariat: The Hero Who Obliterated Triple Crown Records 126
Go Ahead, Make My Day: Clint Eastwood as Contemporary Hero 127
Lucille Ball: A Heroic Comic Genius 129

Traditional-Complete Heroes
Terry Fox: The Audacious Modern-Day Pheidippides 130
George Marshall: The Hero With a Plan 132
Florence Nightingale: The Heroic Lady With the Lamp 133
Oprah Winfrey: The Hero with Talent, Resilience, and Charisma 134
Winston Churchill: The Resilient Hero 136
Roberto Clemente and the Night that Happiness Died 137
George Washington Carver: The Humble and Ingenious Hero 139
Warren Spahn: The Greatest Left Hander Ever 140
George Washington: The Indispensable Man 141
Mikhail Gorbachev: A Revolutionary Hero in the Kremlin 142
Twelve Angry Men: A Most Unlikely Hero 144

9 Transfigured Heroes: The Cognitive Construction of Greatness   145
Robin Hood: The Thief Who Became a Hero 147
Big Iron: A Western Hero Narrative 148
Willie Mays' Catch: The Iconic Image of a Hero 149
Sherlock Holmes: An Enduring Fictional Hero 151
Amelia Earhart: Bold Achiever of Mystery 152
Merlin: Supporting Hero of Myth 153
Heroism in the Darkness: The Anonymous Navy SEALs 154
The Chilean Miner Rescue: Protecting a Heroism Narrative 156
Constructing Heroic Associations: Making a Good Line Better 157
Saint Patrick: The Construction of a Legend 158
Hub Fans Bid Kid Adieu: Ted Williams 50 Years Later 159
Betsy Ross: The Hero Who (May Have) Sewed the First American
    Flag 160
Pretty Boy Floyd: An Outlaw Hero 161
Jack is Back: The Kennedy Administration, 50 Years Later 162

10 Transforming Heroes: Those Who Forever Changed Our World   164
Transforming-Global Heroes
Muhammad Ali: The Odyssey of a Heroic Champion 166

Christopher Columbus: A Globally Transforming Figure 168
Mahatma Gandhi: The Hero of Truth and Peace 169
Nelson Mandela: The Ultimate Underdog Hero 170
Martin Luther King, Jr.: The Hero of Interracial Peace 172
Thomas Jefferson: We Hold These Truths to Be Self-Evident 173
Albert Einstein: The Hero Synonymous With Genius 174

Transforming-Specific Heroes
John Lennon: The Hero Who Gave Peace a Chance 176
Buddy Holly: The Day the Music Died 177
Bill Cosby: The Hero Who Broke Racial Barriers 178
Myriam Merlet: The Lost Hero 179

11 Transcendent Heroes: Influence at its Deepest Level   **181**
Harry Potter: The Archetypal Hero 184
Jesus of Nazareth: The Born Hero 185
Abraham Lincoln: A Transcendent Hero 186

Conclusion: Leadership, Heroism, and Heroic Leadership   **188**

References   **199**

Author Index   **206**

Subject Index   **209**

Series Foreword

In many ways, this book brings us full circle in our quest for understanding leadership, or, should we say, *leaderships*. That is, in the abandoned tradition of studying leadership sideways—by studying greatness in individuals (known as the Great Man Theories)—we are returning a century later for a second look at the traits and qualities embedded in great leaders.

To that end, this volume is a treasure trove of fascinating subjects from Helen Keller to Mother Teresa to Ulysses Grant. But they're not sitting around being dead—they are trending hot on the leadership charts (think Freud and Grant) or trending cool (think Woodrow Wilson). And Lady Gaga and Justin Bieber? Thermonuclear and trending off the charts. Arnold Schwarzenegger? Not so much.

Psychologists Scott Allison and George Goethals have taken us deeper than the usual hagiography and shown us how we understand leaders and heroes, and how that understanding is continually being reappraised, and what that reappraisal means. Their aim is to highlight the conceptual link between leadership and heroism and to settle into the space between leader and hero ("All heroes are leaders," they claim, "but not all leaders are heroes"). In short, they demand that the scientism attendant to the study of leadership yield to a more artful sentiment to "get real."

Confused? You won't be. Allison and Goethals' research with students and others helps to clearly delineate the clusters of behaviors common to all leaders. These five factors focus on the *persona* of the leader; the *vision* of the leader; the *ethics* of the leader; the *actions* of the leader; and the *influence* of the leader. Heroes are *sui generis*—a unique subset of leaders who demonstrate achievement, competence, and moral behavior that involves challenging circumstances.

As the authors attest, the bulk of leadership is more mundane than heroic. Focusing as they do on heroes and heroism contributes to a broader and more refined understanding of leaders and leadership, and makes for a highly readable and artful work.

Georgia Sorenson
University of Maryland

Ronald E. Riggio
Claremont McKenna College

About the Authors

Scott T. Allison is Professor of Psychology at the University of Richmond, where he has been on the faculty since 1987. He received his B.A. in Psychology from the University of California, San Diego and his Ph.D. in Social Psychology at the University of California, Santa Barbara. His research program focuses on human belief systems about heroes, villains, legends, leaders, underdogs, and martyrs. He has served on the editorial boards of the top empirical journals in experimental social psychology, including the *Journal of Personality and Social Psychology*, *Personality and Social Psychology Bulletin*, and *Group Dynamics: Theory, Research, and Practice*. With George Goethals, he is author of *Heroes, What They Do & Why We Need Them*, published in 2011 by Oxford University Press, and "Making Heroes: The Construction of Competence, Courage and Virtue," published in 2012 in *Advances in Experimental Social Psychology*. He is the recipient of the University of Richmond's Distinguished Educator Award and the Virginia Council of Higher Education's Outstanding Faculty Award.

George R. Goethals holds the E. Claiborne Robins Distinguished Professorship in Leadership Studies at the University of Richmond. Previously he taught at Williams College where he was Chair of the Department of Psychology, founding Chair of the Program in Leadership Studies, Acting Dean of the Faculty, and Provost. Goethals graduated with a B.A. from Harvard College and holds a Ph.D. in social psychology from Duke University. Goethals explores leadership from psychological and historical perspectives. With Georgia Sorenson and James MacGregor Burns he edited the *Encyclopedia of Leadership* (Sage, 2004), with Sorenson, *The Quest for a General Theory of Leadership* (Elgar, 2006), and with Crystal Hoyt and Donelson Forsyth, *Leadership at The Crossroads: Leadership and Psychology* (Praeger, 2008). His recent research focuses on presidential debates, the presidency of Ulysses S. Grant, and the role of biography in shaping our understanding of leadership. With Scott Allison, he is author of *Heroes, What They Do & Why We Need Them*, published in 2011 by Oxford University Press, and "Making Heroes: The Construction of Competence, Courage and Virtue" published in 2012 in *Advances in Experimental Social Psychology*, Volume 46.

Preface

This book is the latest product of a collaboration that started almost 30 years ago when Scott Allison was a graduate student at the University of California, Santa Barbara, and Al Goethals was on sabbatical there, visiting from Williams College. Looking back on some of our earliest collaborative work, we should have realized that at some point we would surely write about heroes. The first paper we published together, along with David Messick, was inspired by one of our heroes, the boxer Muhammad Ali. We were always fascinated by his influence and leadership outside the ring, particularly his role in changing race relations in the United States. Ali was always his own man. He insisted on being called Muhammad Ali rather than what he referred to as his slave name, Cassius Clay. At first the media refused to go along. But as we know from his long boxing career, Ali never quit. Eventually sports writers and broadcasters recognized that he was right to insist that they call him what he wanted to be called. He led the way for many, many more African-Americans to use names that reflected their pride in their racial identity. There was no doubt that he was the first, and that he led the way.

As we tried to identify the qualities that made Ali an effective leader to a largely hostile white establishment, we focused on his wit and his obvious linguistic intelligence. We remembered that when Ali was once asked whether he had deliberately faked a low score on the US Army mental test, so that he could avoid the draft, he mischievously quipped, "I never said I was the smartest, just the greatest" (McNamara, 2009). That self-characterization led us to researching some of the limits on people's self-serving biases. The result was our *Social Cognition* paper, "On being better but not smarter than other people: The Muhammad Ali effect" (Allison, Messick, and Goethals, 1989).

At that point neither of us had turned to studying heroism or leadership or the connections between them. But we were inching slowly in that direction. Allison's research began to focus on pro-social behavior in groups, examining the conditions under which people place their group's well-being ahead of their own individual interests. Goethals, meanwhile, was publishing work on group goals, social judgment processes, and eventually leadership. Circumstances eventually brought us both to the University of Richmond, where Allison is in the Department of Psychology and Goethals is in the Jepson School of Leadership Studies. At Richmond we began collaborating again, on both rooting for the underdog and positively evaluating people who have died. This research raised more general questions: Why do I like or admire certain people, what leads us to elevate our estimates of particular individuals? These concerns led to our first book on heroes, *Heroes: What They Do & Why We Need Them*. Although work on leadership, particularly Howard Gardner's (1995) *Leading Minds*, was always important in the way we thought about heroes, our general exploration of the psychology of heroism diverted us from focusing on the connections between leadership and heroism. Those connections are explored more fully in our recent paper in *Advances in Experimental Social Psychology* (Goethals and Allison, 2012).

But there was clearly much more to consider. This became increasingly clear in 2010 when we started to blog about heroes, particularly heroes who had clearly been leaders (blog.richmond.edu/heroes). Within two years we wrote more than 150 hero profiles and attracted over 150,000 visitors to the blog. One hundred of those hero profiles are included in this book. Profiling so many great individuals made it increasingly clear that in fact *all* of our heroes were also leaders. They might not fit traditional leader schemas, or people's implicit theories of leadership, but they were clearly leaders in the sense that Gardner defined it. Either directly or indirectly, through face-to-face contact or through their accomplishments, products and performances, they influenced and led significant numbers of other people.

Our purpose in this book is to continue exploring the various ways heroes influence us, and thereby lead. We hope to succeed in more fully developing the taxonomy of heroes that we introduced earlier, and in illustrating each of its ten types of heroes. Those types are Trending Heroes, Transitory Heroes, Transitional Heroes, Tragic Heroes, Transposed Heroes, Transparent Heroes, Traditional Heroes, Transfigured Heroes, Transforming Heroes and, finally, Transcendent Heroes. The influence and leadership of each of these types of heroes is distinct. Thinking about the different ways heroes lead helps us think more carefully about different kinds of leaders, and the many different ways that each kind has an impact on followers.

We should add a word about the heroes we have selected for this volume, and their assignment to one taxonomy category or another. All of them were suggested in formal surveys or in focused discussions. However, we used our own judgment in assigning them to hero types. At times the two of us did not completely agree on where to place certain individuals. It turns out they influenced different people in different ways, at different times in their lives. While we acknowledge that there might be disagreement as to who really is a heroic leader, and what type of heroism they best exemplify, our overall goal is to illuminate as carefully as we can the many ways different heroes influence those who admire them.

Finally, we wish to thank the many people who have helped along the way. First, we are indebted to the many colleagues at the University of Richmond, both in the Department of Psychology and the Jepson School, who have supported, or at least indulged, our interest in heroism and particular heroes. We thank Shannon Best, Joanne Ciulla, Dick Couto, Don Forsyth, Doug Hicks, Gill Hickman, Crystal Hoyt, Peter Kaufman, Pam Khoury, Gary McDowell, Jack Mountcastle, Sandra Peart, Terry Price, Thad Williamson, Tom Wren, Craig Kinsley, Jane Berry, Beth Crawford, David Landy, Laura Knouse, David Leary, Cindy Bukach, Andy Newcomb, and Jeni Burnette. We are also deeply grateful to three friends and colleagues of ours—Rick Hutchins, Jesse Schultz, and Jeff Green—who kindly contributed five of the heroic leader profiles contained in this book.

We also are very grateful to Anne Duffy at Taylor and Francis for her encouragement during the entire course of this project. And we are highly indebted to series editors Georgia Sorenson and Ron Riggio for including our book in their series, *Leadership: Research and Practice*.

Scott T. Allison and George R. Goethals
September, 2012

Chapter 1

Introduction
Leadership and Heroism

If you are anything like our students, the term *Heroic Leadership* conjures up images of legendary figures such as Mahatma Gandhi, Martin Luther King, Jr., Abraham Lincoln, and Nelson Mandela. These leaders are judged to be heroic because they were able to move millions of people. When we say "move," we mean it in every sense of the word. These leaders became heroic by moving people emotionally, moving their beliefs, and moving them toward positive action. In 1978, James MacGregor Burns coined the term *transforming leadership* to describe the ability of exceptional leaders to move people to perform at the highest level by raising their morale, motivation, and self-identities. Heroic leaders transform their followers and their societies by moving them toward achieving their maximum potential.

But let's now consider the lives and accomplishments of heroic people whom we wouldn't ordinarily label as leaders. Below we describe four individuals who have performed extraordinary behaviors. They are Wesley Autrey, Meryl Streep, Helen Keller, and Anne Sullivan. As you read the description of each person, ask yourself whether this individual does, or does not, show great *leadership*:

Wesley Autrey was a 49-year-old African-American who lived in Harlem on the Upper West Side of New York City. One cold winter day in January of 2007, Autrey was traveling with his two young daughters, age 4 and 6, on the New York subway. He and his children stood on the 137th Street subway platform, waiting with 75 other people for the train to arrive. While standing near the tracks, Autrey noticed a young white man near him behaving quite strangely. The man was a 19-year-old film student named Cameron Hollopeter, a complete stranger to Autrey and his children. Hollopeter

Mount Rushmore's Portrayal of Four Heroic Leaders (Source: Photo by dean. franklin's photostream at www.flickr.com/photos/deanfranklin).

began having a seizure, and Autrey went to assist him. Within about 10 minutes, Hollopeter appeared to have recovered fully from his episode, allowing Autrey and his children to return to the edge of the subway platform to resume waiting for the next train. But a moment later, Hollopeter's seizure returned, and before anyone could assist him, Autrey and the other commuters watched in horror as the stricken Hollopeter staggered off the subway platform and onto the tracks below.

To make matters worse, just as Hollopeter landed on the tracks, a subway train was pulling into the station at high speed and was only seconds away from running him over as he lay motionless on the tracks. None of the 75 onlookers made a move to help Hollopeter—except for Wesley Autrey. Without hesitating, Autrey asked two women to tend to his children as he scampered down to the tracks to save Hollopeter. The train was bearing down on both men fast and Autrey realized that there was no time to lift Hollopeter up to the safety of the subway platform. Autrey knew that the only way to save Hollopeter was to do something stunningly risky—he would have to lie on top of the stricken man in-between the two train rails and allow the train to race over them. As a construction worker who was used to eyeballing measurements, Autrey made an educated guess that there would be just enough room for the train to pass above their bodies. Sure enough, after five train cars passed over the two men, only one-half inch separated Autrey from certain death. Both men walked away from the incident unharmed, and Autrey was hailed as a hero.

"I don't feel like I did something spectacular," said Autrey. "I just saw someone who needed help. I did what I felt was right." New York City Mayor Michael Bloomberg presented him with the Bronze Medallion, New York City's highest award for exceptional citizenship and outstanding achievement.

Meryl Streep is considered by most film critics and by her legions of fans to be America's greatest actress. She has received more Academy Award nominations (17) and more Golden Globe Award nominations (26) than any other actor in the history of either award. Streep has received dozens of honors, prizes, hall of fame inductions, and honorary degrees from around the world.

No one in the acting profession has greater range and versatility than Streep. During her long career she has mastered many difficult accents and dialects, including Danish in Out of Africa; *British in* The French Lieutenant's Woman; *Italian in* The Bridges of Madison County; *Minnesotan in* A Prairie Home Companion; *and Australian in* A Cry in the Dark. *She even succeeded in speaking both English and German with a Polish accent in* Sophie's Choice. *Streep's most recent tour de force was mastering Margaret Thatcher's distinctive vocal mannerisms in* The Iron Lady.

During Streep's critically acclaimed career, she held her own or surpassed the finest male actors of her generation, many of whom she has co-starred with in award-winning movies—Jack Nicholson in Heartburn *and* Ironweed, *Dustin Hoffman in* Kramer vs. Kramer, *and Robert de Niro in* The Deer Hunter.

Psychologist Dean Simonton, who has written extensively on the topic of genius, believes that Streep is probably the best actress of the sound era. "I am being cautious, because of my scientific bent," he said. "It's difficult to judge the great stars of the silent era—who only had faces. And it's impossible to evaluate the many great foreign talents who never managed or even desired to make the transition to the Hollywood world." Despite his hesitation to judge, Simonton raves about Streep's versatility. "I believe the range of roles that Streep has successfully taken on, and her ability to merge with those roles, is truly unprecedented. As much as I love Hepburn ... you see Katharine in every role."

Streep has also managed to land attractive roles despite working in an industry that typically shuts out opportunities for older women. Streep recently told NPR that she hit the same wall most actresses do at 40: "I was offered, within one year, three different witch roles." Yet Streep has shone beautifully on the screen as a middle-aged woman in such films as Mamma Mia *and* It's Complicated. *Simonton believes that Streep's talent is so great that her fading beauty is irrelevant. "She has never banked on her looks, which are not outstanding by Hollywood standards," he said, "but she's always invested in great acting—as epitomized by her preparation and hard work."*

At birth, Helen Keller was a healthy, active baby until the age of 19 months when an illness left her permanently blind and deaf. She became imprisoned in a dark, silent world, and no one in her family could reach her. Keller's parents hired 20-year-old

Anne Sullivan to perform the seemingly hopeless task of educating Keller. Sullivan was the perfect person for the job. Visually impaired herself, Sullivan was empathetic, patient, resourceful, and persevering.

Sullivan first tried to teach Keller basic language skills by using her finger to spell words on Keller's hand, but Keller did not understand that each object had a different name. A breakthrough occurred on April 5, 1887, when Keller was six years old. Sullivan led Keller to a water pump and splashed water on one of Keller's hands while spelling the word "water" on the other hand. Keller later recalled that "someone was drawing water and my teacher placed my hand under the spout. As the cool stream gushed over one hand she spelled into the other the word water, first slowly, then rapidly. I stood still, my whole attention fixed upon the motions of her fingers. Suddenly I felt a misty consciousness as of something forgotten, a thrill of returning thought, and somehow the mystery of language was revealed to me."

Sullivan next tackled Keller's atrocious table manners. Keller had the habit of eating with her hands, grabbing from the plates of everyone at the table, and throwing a temper tantrum if anyone tried to stop her. Sullivan punished Keller's tantrums by refusing to "talk" with Helen by spelling words on her hands. Soon Keller developed impeccable manners and learned how to perform everyday tasks such as getting dressed and brushing her hair.

Thanks to Sullivan, Keller was transformed into a bright, curious, lovely young woman who was destined to make a positive mark on the world. The bond between Keller and Sullivan grew into a beautiful friendship that lasted for 49 years.

Keller was the first deaf and blind person in America to graduate from college, and she later became a prolific author of many books and articles on a variety of social and political topics. Most importantly, Keller became a world-famous advocate for people with disabilities. The 1962 film, The Miracle Worker, *inspired millions of people with its story of Keller's triumph over disability and Sullivan's selfless devotion to helping Keller fulfill her vast potential.*

During her lifetime, Helen Keller was consistently ranked near the top of almost every "Most Admired" list. In addition, Anne Sullivan deservedly acquired a reputation as a legendary teacher. Keller and Sullivan are forever linked as heroes who brought out the best in each other.

Wesley Autrey, Meryl Streep, Helen Keller, and Anne Sullivan—all four of these individuals are heroes to many, but would you say they are great leaders? Intuitively, being a hero isn't the same as being a leader. Or is it? Are people who are regarded as heroes also leaders? The answer depends, of course, on how one defines both leadership and heroism. In the case of heroes, outside of a dictionary definition, the social science literature doesn't really offer a definition. We have argued that heroism is in the eye of the beholder, and that heroes are heroes to anyone who regards them as heroes (Allison and Goethals, 2011).

The situation is a little different with leadership. While the phenomenon has always defied easy description, the literature is full of definitions. Some scholars in the field of leadership studies note that there are as many definitions of leadership as there are people attempting to define it (Schein, 1992; Stogdill, 1974; Yukl, 2013). Other scholars note that the complexity and interdisciplinary nature of leadership make it difficult to pin down (Harvey and Riggio, 2011). Arriving at a consensus may always be a daunting challenge given that leadership encompasses processes involving the *individual* as the unit of analysis (e.g., attitudes, beliefs, biases) as well as processes implicating the *group* as the unit of analysis (e.g., conformity, cohesiveness, interaction). The multi-layered nature of leadership makes it the most talked about yet least understood phenomenon in our social world.

A Five Factor Model of Leadership

We decided to address the issue of whether Autrey, Streep, Keller, and Sullivan have shown exceptional *leadership* or simply *heroism* by asking over 100 of our undergraduate students to define leadership. We discovered several recurring themes in our students' responses, and we were struck by the extent to which these themes corresponded to the major theoretical approaches to leadership as developed by social scientists over the past 50 years. From our survey response data, and from our review of leadership theories, we have identified five factors that form the heart of our definition of leadership. The five factors focus on the *persona* of the leader; the *vision* of the leader; the *ethics* of the leader; the *actions* of the leader; and the *influence* of the leader.

The Leader's Persona

The first factor of leadership, which we call the *persona* of the leader, refers to the public face of the leader and the way that leaders present themselves to us. As observers of leaders, we carry expectations that they will demonstrate greater charisma, energy, and optimism as compared to the average non-leader (Bass and Riggio, 2006; Mio, Riggio, Levin, and Reese, 2005). Our survey respondents emphasized the importance of the ways in which leaders carry themselves and how the image and presentation of a leader can shape their influence. Leadership theories have also focused on the central role of image, appearance, and reputation, with physical characteristics, such as height, and personality characteristics, such as charisma, being associated with an image of leadership strength (Conger and Kanungo, 1998). The importance of the leader's persona is reflected in trait theories of leadership which underscore the myriad traits needed for successful leadership (Bass, 1998; Zaccaro, 2007). Traits correlated with effective leadership include high energy, emotional maturity, confidence, and stress tolerance (Yukl, 2013). Trust is especially important (Kramer and Cook, 2004; Kramer and Pittinsky, 2012). Bass (1998) has suggested that many of these traits, especially those relating to charisma, are the hallmark of transformational leadership.

Let's consider Wesley Autrey, Meryl Streep, Helen Keller, and Anne Sullivan. Does each of their personas match that of an effective leader? We see a very good match. All of these individuals achieved greatness, in part, because of their energy, positive attitude, and confidence. Autrey was, and is, a highly personable man with a commanding presence. He certainly needed energy and confidence to cheat death on that January day when he saved the life of Cameron Hollopeter. Days after his heroic feat, Autrey wowed audiences with his humor and charisma on the David Letterman Show. Similarly, Meryl Streep has a magnetic personality that has charmed movie audiences for decades. Her face evokes the many powerful emotions from the characters she has played in films over the years, ranging from anguish in *Sophie's Choice* to pure joy in *Mamma Mia*. Helen Keller and Anne Sullivan also possessed appealing personas that moved people deeply. For decades they drew large, enthusiastic crowds at speaking engagements and during visits with foreign dignitaries around the globe.

The Leader's Vision

Next we consider our second factor of leadership, which is the leader's *vision*. Research has shown that for a leader to have an effective vision, it should appeal to the values, hopes, and ideals of his or her followers (Kantabutra, 2009). Wesley Autrey had to craft a vision, not just to save Hollopeter, but to figure out *how* to save him. His decisive planning was bold and striking. Certainly Autrey's vision of helping a complete stranger reflects our society's most noble values. Moreover, Meryl Streep's dream of making the fullest possible use of her immense talent reflects a tremendous work ethic, one of the most cherished values in our culture. The same is true with Helen Keller's vision of overcoming adversity and leading a productive life, and with Anne Sullivan's vision of helping Keller on this quest (Kim et al., 2008). All four of these individuals fashioned some type of important vision for action that propelled them to greatness.

The Leader's Ethics

Our third factor of leadership centers on the *ethics* of a leader. Leaders must use their power wisely and in a manner consistent with the ethical codes of their group or society (Gini, 1998). Cross-cultural research has shown that integrity is viewed as one of the most essential traits for effective leadership in virtually all cultures (Treviño, Weaver, and Reynolds, 2006). Honesty is viewed as an especially important quality in a leader (Becker, 2009). When considering the ethics of Autrey, Streep, Keller, and Sullivan, we observe that none of these individuals has ever been associated with scandal or misconduct. In fact, they've all been lauded for their supreme virtue and ethical behavior. Their lifetime conduct reveals the embodiment of humanity's best moral qualities. For this reason, we believe that our fabulous foursome satisfies the criterion of good ethics in determining whether they are leaders.

The Leader's Actions

The fourth defining characteristic of leadership centers on the *actions* that leaders take in their leadership role. Good leaders perform behaviors that benefit the group, and they work hard to achieve group goals (Hemphill and Coons, 1957). Acting in the service of the group good can assume many different forms. It can involve creating new ideas, new opportunities for followers, or new environments within which group tasks can be accomplished (Richards and Engle, 1986). Effective leaders excel at communicating, collaborating, and managing. In short, they do whatever is necessary to achieve their goals successfully, and while doing so they adhere to admirable ethical codes of conduct.

We believe that Autrey, Streep, Keller, and Sullivan all performed noble actions that led to their various triumphs. It was only after Autrey made sure that his two young daughters were cared for on the subway platform that he carried out his astonishing rescue of Hollopeter. Streep has managed her career wisely and has always excelled in her performances on both stage and screen. She has also devoted significant time and money to finding cures for AIDS and cancer. Helen Keller showed remarkable determination in overcoming her visual and auditory disabilities, and Sullivan worked tirelessly to teach and mentor Keller. Keller and Sullivan also promoted many worthwhile social causes. We see then that all four of our exceptional individuals took actions that made them the extraordinary figures that we perceive them to be.

The Leader's Influence

Finally, our fifth defining feature of leadership is *influence*. Good leaders influence others in a multitude of positive ways. They communicate their vision to others, model energy and loyalty, build trust and unity, honor commitments, provide feedback, delegate effectively, and coach others to improve their performance (Yukl and Lepsinger, 2004). Most importantly, according to our survey respondents, effective leaders are able to motivate and inspire their followers to achieve their highest aspirations (Goethals and Wren, 2009; House, Spangler, and Woyke, 1991). This ability to inspire describes the kind of influence shown by Autrey, Streep, Keller, and Sullivan. These four exceptional individuals have influenced others by inspiring them with their personas, their visions, their ethics, and their actions.

After hearing about Wesley Autrey's heroic act, many people were—and continue to be—moved emotionally to a powerful degree. "His pure selfless act of heroism is something that will inspire me for the rest of my life," wrote one reader after reading our blog post about Autrey (Allison and Goethals, 2012). Similarly, Meryl Streep has inspired almost two generations of actors who are often awestruck by her talent and accomplishments. "She not only inspires me as an actress, but as a person," proclaims one of Streep's fans on a YouTube video (DeLalla, 2012). Helen Keller's triumphant story, and Anne Sullivan's loving mentorship of Keller, have been the inspiration for many films and biographies that tell their powerful tale of an individual overcoming the most daunting of obstacles.

What can we conclude about the leadership qualities of Autrey, Streep, Keller, and Sullivan? Despite never having held a formal position of leadership or having any group of people working under them to lead, all four of our exceptional individuals meet our five criteria for defining leadership. Autrey, Streep, Keller, and Sullivan may not be leaders in the traditional sense, but they have shaped the thoughts, feelings, and behaviors of others in ways that only an outstanding leader can.

Leadership, it seems, can assume many different forms, and one of the most important forms of leadership is also one of the most overlooked. The kind of leadership that our four exceptional individuals have demonstrated is called *indirect leadership* (Gardner, 1995; Hunt, 1991; Yammarino, 1994). Indirect leaders influence others from a distance, without face-to-face interactions. According to Gardner, it is the influence of an individual's work or products—what they have done or how they have done it—that defines them as an indirect leader. That indirect leaders do not interact with their followers does not deter them from having a truly profound impact on individuals and society. Some of our greatest artists and scientists are legendary in demonstrating powerful indirect leadership. Noteworthy examples of indirect leaders include Albert Einstein, Pablo Picasso, Oprah Winfrey, John Glenn, and Joan of Arc, to name but a few.

Our focus in this book is not just on leadership, but on an *exceptional* type of leadership that we call heroic leadership. The Merriam-Webster Dictionary defines *exceptional* as the quality of being superior, or of being rare. Every individual whom we profile in this book possesses one of these two qualities. Some of the leaders we discuss here will be obvious legends such as Mandela, Lincoln, King, and Gandhi. Their superior leadership is revered all around the world. But we will also focus on some obscure and unusual leaders whom you've probably never heard of, and we do so to illustrate how exceptionality in the rare sense can also leave a significant mark on society.

We think, then, that Wesley Autrey, Meryl Streep, Helen Keller and Anne Sullivan are not only heroes, but exceptional leaders who are heroic in their application of leadership skills involving their persona, vision, ethics, action, and influence. One of the central goals of this book is to highlight the conceptual link between leadership and heroism. In our previous work on heroes (Allison and Goethals, 2011; Goethals and Allison, 2012), we have argued that all heroes are leaders, but not all leaders are heroes. We want to reiterate that claim here. Heroism is characterized by great achievement in either the domain of *competence* or the domain of *morality*, or in both. We will demonstrate in this book how all heroes who excel in one or both of these two domains are either direct or indirect leaders. For example, people may disagree about whether Tiger Woods is a hero, but we can be sure that Tiger is an indirect leader for people who believe in Tiger's heroism. Not all leaders are heroes, of course. Some leaders are too inept, or stray too far from any reasonable moral code, to be considered heroic.

Leadership and Heroism as Mental Constructions

Another theme that we will explore in this book is the idea that leadership and heroism are not just phenomena that we witness in our external physical environments. They are also mental constructions inside our own heads. Leadership scholars have called these mental constructions "implicit leadership theories." Emrich (1999) has drawn attention to three elements of implicit leadership theories. People have implicit theories, or schemas, about *what leaders are like*, that is, what traits define them; *what leaders do*, that is, how they actually behave; and *what leaders cause*, or the causality of leadership (Goethals and Hoyt, 2011). People often give leaders too much credit for a group's success and too much blame for a group's failure, a phenomenon that Meindl and Ehrlich (1987) have called the "romance of leadership." We suspect there is a parallel implicit theory that heroes generally cause success and salvation, but that evil, ruin, chaos, destruction, and despair reflect the work of villains.

As noted earlier, people have a good idea about the personality profile of a good leader. Traits associated with effective leadership include charisma, surgency (or extraversion), analytical and social intelligence, kindness, emotional stability, and health. It is interesting to note that dominance is not associated with leadership (Van Vugt, 2006). To identify traits associated with heroism, we asked 75 college students to list the traits that they believed characterized heroes. We then asked 50 other students to sort the traits on the basis of similarity and differences between the different traits. A sorting analysis revealed eight different trait clusters. Below we present an alphabetical list of these traits, named for the defining term in each cluster, and several of the related traits in that cluster:

> Caring: compassionate, empathetic, kind
> Charismatic: dedicated, eloquent, passionate
> Inspiring: admirable, amazing, great, inspirational
> Reliable: loyal, true

Resilient: accomplished, determined, persevering
Selfless: altruistic, honest, humble, moral
Smart: intelligent, wise
Strong: courageous, dominating, gallant, leader

We have called these the *Great Eight Traits* of heroism (Allison and Goethals, 2011; Goethals and Allison, 2012). Note how this list of hero-traits bears many similarities to lists of traits defining leaders. One obvious point of overlap is found in the trait *charisma*, central to many conceptions of leadership. *Strong, smart,* and *inspiring* are also commonly associated with leaders. The trait *reliable* resonates to "integrity," crucially important in many studies of effective leadership, while *reliable* and *selfless* are important elements of "servant leadership" (Greenleaf, 1977), the idea that leaders act as servants to their followers and address followers' needs rather than their own. *Caring* is not frequently thought to be associated with leadership. However, "kindness" is noted in the evolutionary approach to leadership, and in studies of mate selection (Buss, 1994).

Our *Great Eight Traits* of heroes are consistent with the results of a research program on lay-conceptions of heroism recently undertaken by Kinsella, Ritchie, and Igou (2010; 2011; 2012). These investigators used prototype methodology to uncover 13 central features of heroism: *brave, moral integrity, courageous, protect, conviction, honest, altruistic, self-sacrifice, selfless, determined, saves, inspiration,* and *helpful*. Moreover, Kinsella et al. discovered 13 peripheral features as well: *proactive, strong, leader, compassionate, risk-taker, exceptional, humble, fearless, caring, powerful, intelligent, talented,* and *personable*. These features of heroism include a number of characteristics that go beyond our Great Eight, such as the traits of protection, bravery, and proactivity. Kinsella et al. also found that their participants rated heroes as more *courageous* and *self-sacrificing* than leaders or role models.

Interestingly, Kinsella et al.'s research does not identify charisma as central to leadership or heroism. But we believe that charisma, as part of our Great Eight, best illustrates the schematic nature of perceiving both leaders and heroes. The term *schema* derives from the Greek word for "shape." Our work on heroes emphasizes shaping: both the way that heroes, like leaders, shape us, and also the way that constructive social perception processes shape our images and understandings of heroes and leaders and our understanding of these very concepts. We suggest that once elements of heroism or leadership are detected in an individual, and the schema of that person and the schema of hero or leader are sufficiently matched, a hero or leader is identified. Then, following principles of schematic perception, the cognitive construction of heroes and leaders involves a Gestalt perception-like process of filling in the gaps.

Malcom Gladwell describes this Gestalt process beautifully in his best-selling 2005 book *Blink*. In a phenomenon that he calls "The Warren Harding Error," Gladwell tells the story of Ohio political operator Harry Daugherty's fascination with small-town newspaper editor Harding. Daugherty believed that Harding just "looked like a Senator." He was tall, superbly built, with a bronzed complexion. He moved with power and grace and possessed a strong, sonorous voice. In every sense of the word he was charismatic. Harding activated people's implicit theories of leadership; he matched the template to near-perfection. Once cognitive construction filled in the blanks, Harding was assumed to have other important leadership qualities, including intelligence and integrity. Interestingly, Harding himself wasn't much fooled by the image but did not have the strength to resist Daugherty's flattery or marketing efforts.

The consequences were not good for America. Harding was elected Senator in 1914, and when the Republican Party deadlocked at the 1920 convention, Harding received the presidential nomination, along with running mate Massachusetts Governor Calvin Coolidge. They were elected easily, over Democrat James Cox (and his young running mate, Franklin D. Roosevelt). Harding died after two-and-a-half years in office. He presided over a corrupt administration and is routinely at the bottom of polls of historians' ratings of presidents. He was way over his head, but for better or worse, he triggered the implicit leadership schema in the people around him.

If Warren Harding was one of America's worst presidents, Abraham Lincoln was certainly one of its greatest. People's perceptions of Lincoln illustrate schematic construction even more vividly. To the extent that good looks are important in the identification of many leaders and heroes, and are part of charisma, Lincoln would seem to start at a distinct disadvantage. He was unattractive and he knew it. His looks and demeanor led dashing Union Civil War General George B. McClellan to call him "the original gorilla." When political opponents called Lincoln two-faced, he wryly asked whether anyone could really believe that he would wear the face they saw if he had another. But Lincoln became a hero to many during the war, and in many ways benefited from heroic interpretations of his appearance. Historian Shelby Foote (1958) wrote that "thousands touched him, heard him, saw him at close range and hardly one in all those thousands ever forgot the sight of that tall figure, made taller still by the stovepipe hat and the homely shape of the shawl across the shoulders." The "impression remained ... imperishable in its singularity—and finally, dear" (p. 803). The uniqueness of Lincoln's appearance gradually became an asset. Observers and admirers worked on the image until it became iconic and heroic.

Lincoln's face, in particular, required some mental gymnastics to fit a hero schema. One Paris editor thought his widely distributed photographs were so ugly that they would set back the Union cause. But a Union soldier wrote of Lincoln's appearance in his diary:

> None of us to our dying day can forget that countenance. ... Concentrated in that one great, strong, yet tender face, the agony of the life and death struggle of the hour was revealed as we had never seen it before. With a new understanding, we knew why we were soldiers.

According to this soldier, Lincoln's appearance accommodated not only attributions of charisma, but also the Great Eight heroic traits of strong, caring, resilient, and inspiring. Lincoln's perceived heroism was also enhanced by his height of six feet, four inches, which was exaggerated when he wore his iconic stovepipe hat. Research has shown that tallness correlates highly with perceptions of good leadership (Lindqvist, 2011).

Heroes and Leaders, Scripts and Narratives

Implicit theories of leadership and heroism not only contain defining traits of typical leaders and heroes. They also contain schemas or scripts about what leaders and heroes do. These schemas or scripts often take the form of stories or narratives. Jerome Bruner (1989a, 1989b, 1991) proposed that narrative structures are children's fundamental way of understanding the world and constructing reality. He suggested that children "turn things [they don't understand] into stories, and when they try to make sense of their life they use the storied version of their experience as the basis for further reflection" (1991, p. 118). These stories play a crucial role in helping children grasp their social environment and reduce complexity. Bruner and others writing in Katherine Nelson's (1989) book *Narratives From the Crib* show that very young children's narrative language is surprisingly inventive and sophisticated. Children understand their experience through stories. Bruner notes that among other attributes, narratives are marked by events taking place over time, by characters who have goals, beliefs and values, by unusual events, and by moral implication.

Howard Gardner (1995) and Robert Sternberg (2011) have both argued that such narratives are central to leadership. Leaders influence their audiences through stories marked by dynamic tension that unfold over time, and in which leaders and followers together play a central role in achieving group objectives. In Gardner's theory, the most important leader narratives are about the identities of the leader and the followers, and the ways they must collaborate. Leaders are charged with the task of helping people understand who they are through stories that explain where the group has been, where it is going, and what obstacles lie in the path of getting there.

We turn once again to Abraham Lincoln for compelling evidence of the power of leadership narratives. Lincoln concluded his second inaugural address, often regarded as his greatest speech, by giving the nation some much-needed direction at the end of the Civil War:

> With malice toward none, with charity for all, with firmness in the right as God gave us to see the right, let us strive on to finish the work we are in, to bind up the nation's wounds, to care for him who shall have borne the battle and for his widow and his orphan, to do all which may achieve and cherish a just and a lasting peace among ourselves and with all nations.

This rhetoric was typical of Lincoln. In vivid language, he sketched a narrative of a united country working toward a common cause. In the Gettysburg Address, for example, he spoke of the nation's "unfinished work" and "the great task remaining before us." His language told stories about needing followers to perform important and noble work to achieve their future goals.

Given how much people rely on narratives to understand their worlds, it isn't surprising that there are compelling narratives about the way heroes behave. Joseph Campbell's classic *The Hero with a Thousand Faces* (1949) argues that there is a universal *monomyth* about heroes that has emerged in heroic tales told for millennia across the globe. One central element in the monomyth is the hero venturing forth into a strange and supernatural world where she or he encounters mysterious forces. There is almost always a repeated struggle against these forces. Obstacles appear in numerous and unpredictable forms to test the prospective hero. These obstacles are not only villains and monsters, fires and floods, but also internal demons. Lust is a typical demon the hero must conquer. In the *Odyssey*, the hero Odysseus asks his shipmates to tie him to the ship's mast so that he cannot be drawn to destruction by the Sirens who arouse his sexual passions.

The hero monomyth contains the idea that other characters guide or assist the hero in a range of different ways. Often an elderly person provides direction and council as the hero initiates his or her journey into the unknown. The movie *Star Wars* capitalizes on this universal mythological feature in Alec Guinness' character Obi-Wan Kenobi, the kindly white-robed elder who counsels the young hero Luke Skywalker (Mark Hamill) to "let the force be with you." In sports, manager Leo Durocher served as a veteran guide to baseball heroes Jackie Robinson of the Brooklyn Dodgers and later Willie Mays of the New York Giants. Also, along the mythological journey, other characters, often young helpers or sidekicks, help the struggling hero. In *Star Wars*, Luke Skywalker teams up with Han Solo (Harrison Ford) and Princess Leia (Carrie Fisher). Similarly, Batman has Robin, Don Quixote relies on Sancho Panza, and Ronald Reagan leaned heavily on his wife Nancy to surmount many difficulties during his presidency. She famously commented that women are like teabags; you never know how strong they are until you put them in hot water.

Toward the end of the hero monomyth, the hero enjoys a final victory over daunting obstacles, both internal and external, which have repeatedly aligned themselves against the hero. Again, some other figure may assist. And finally, in most hero stories, the protagonist returns to his or her original familiar world, forever transformed and often with a "boon" to help transform the original world. For example, Moses is transformed from a weak to a highly empowered individual who is able to lead the exodus of the Israelites out of Egypt and across the Red Sea to Mount Sinai. He returns from the mountain with the Ten Commandments, given to him by God, thereby forever changing the world's moral code. Joseph Campbell's universal narrative of heroism—the monomyth—is familiar and easy to understand. It is this universal narrative structure that makes it so easy for people of all ages to understand the concept of hero and to identify heroes of their own.

Campbell's idea of monomyth and the idea of archetype to which we turn next both suggest cross-cultural universal understandings of heroes. Different cultures undoubtedly have different heroes. Our research participants' lists of heroes described earlier clearly reflect heroic narratives of Western culture. However, while people in different societies may have different heroes, our sense is that similar dimensions of competence and morality are common across cultures. We suspect that a cross-cultural examination of hero narratives is a promising area for further research.

Archetypes and the Innate Mind

Joseph Campbell's monomyth narrative was rooted in Freudian psychoanalytic theory and Jung's theory of archetypes. For example, Campbell drew from Freud's notion of the Oedipal Complex in observing that many heroes' struggles involve confrontation with father figures. In *Star Wars*, Luke Skywalker's chief antagonist, the black-clad and mysterious Darth Vader, turns out to be his father. But Jungian influences are also prominent in *Star Wars*. The Obi-Wan Kenobi figure is Jung's archetypical "wise old man." Father figures permeate many hero myths. In our previous work on heroes, we have found ourselves unable to ignore the possibility that narrative structures around heroes, or hero scripts, reflect evolved, inherited Jungian archetypes (Allison and Goethals, 2011; Goethals and Allison, 2012).

One of the most important assumptions of Jungian archetypes is the idea that schemas, scripts and narrative structures are not based entirely on experience. Jung argued that a part of our psyche called "the collective unconscious" was a storehouse of latent or potential images based on human evolutionary history. These latent images, or *archetypes*, prepare us for frequent encounters with meaningful situations and people. By referring to these images as latent potential, Jung meant that they were not initially conscious but could be activated when experience sufficiently matched one of them.

Jung claimed that archetypes have form but not content (Jung and von Franz, 1964). This idea is probably best understood as meaning that archetypes, much like schemas, are general outlines or shapes. Hogg (2001) describes prototypes as "context specific, multidimensional fuzzy sets of attributes" (p. 187). That description aptly captures the idea of archetype. While archetypes are very similar to schemas, or prototypes, there are two important differences. Social psychologists typically think of schemas as based on individual experience, not inherited collective experience. Jung (1969) addressed the idea of collective experience as follows:

> There are as many archetypes as there are typical situations in life. Endless repetition has engraved these experiences into our psychic constitution, not

in the form of images filled with content, but … only as forms without content, representing merely the possibility of a certain type of perception and action.

(p. 48)

Another difference between schemas and archetypes is that the latter, when activated, have an affective or emotional valence. We are emotionally drawn to, or repelled by, the activated archetypical images.

Jung's *mother* archetype nicely illustrates these ideas. Human infants are prepared to see mothering figures, and will generally respond positively to these figures with a clear approach tendency. Jung claimed that people pay attention to, and are drawn toward or repelled from, objects, persons, and experiences that fit a latent archetypical image. It is important that Jung wrote about a number of archetypes relevant to understanding heroism, including the archetypes of *hero, demon, magic, power*, and *wise old man*. Jung also discussed the ways that archetypical images may be combined. For example, the hero and demon archetypes can both be activated by a leader such as Jim Jones or Adolf Hitler, or fictional characters such as Dracula. Their pull or appeal can stem from the activation of both those archetypes.

In summary, we make the claim that *hero* is an archetype that includes latent images of the looks, traits, and behavior of heroes, as well as the narrative structure of heroism outlined by Campbell (1949). Is there any evidence for such an idea? Research on the mysteries of inherited cognition and natural language (Chomsky, 1986) is extremely suggestive. Infants carefully appraise features of human faces and show a remarkable ability to discriminate emotional expression in those faces (Klinnert, Campos, Sorce, Emde, and Svedja, 1983). Shortly after birth, infants show a distinct preference for face-like shapes, and after as little as 42 minutes the ability to imitate facial gestures (Carruthers, Laurence, and Stich, 2005; Johnson and Morton, 1991; Meltzoff and Moore, 1995).

Recently, Carruthers et al. (2005) have argued for a nativist understanding of the human mind, based in part on discoveries showing that a great deal of cognition is uniform and predictable, and similar across cultures, and that the human mind shares a great deal with other species. In this same vein, Marcus (2005) observes that "dozens of experiments have shown that babies come to the world able to think and reason" (p. 23). Marcus refers to research conducted by Pinker (1991) and Dehaene (1997) suggesting a "language instinct" and a "number sense." In short, there is considerable evidence supporting the idea of inherited cognitive capacities that interact with experience to produce the ways mature humans think and construct their worlds. We believe that this growing evidence of innate mindfulness is consistent with Jungian archetypal understandings of the world. Human beings may be endowed inherited, universal hero narrative structures that provide a ready basis for adopting heroes.

Heroes as Agents of Social Influence

Social psychology has long been defined as the study of social influence (Allport, 1985; Kassin, Fein, and Markus, 2010; Myers, 2010; Taylor, Peplau, and Sears, 2006). As social psychologists, we thus view heroes and leadership from the perspective of how heroic leaders influence the thoughts, feelings, and behaviors of others. Only recently have scholars begun to address the issue of how heroes influence others (e.g., Bocchiaro, Zimbardo, and Van Lange, 2012) and in turn are influenced by others (e.g., Monin, Sawyer, and Marquez, 2008). Below we briefly describe how heroes can affect the way people *feel*, *think*, and *act*.

Influence on Emotions

Heroes move us emotionally, and this is one aspect of heroism that sets it apart from leadership. When we earlier described the *Great Eight* traits associated with heroism, we noted that an important defining characteristic of many heroes is charisma and magnetism. Some of our most inspiring heroes, such as Martin Luther King, Jr., use soaring rhetoric to dare us all to join them on their heroic journeys. Other heroes, such as the New York subway hero Wesley Autrey, move us emotionally with their actions. Still others move us with their selflessness, love, and compassion, as revealed in our large survey of people's heroes (Allison and Goethals, 2011). Roughly one-third of our survey respondents listed family members as their heroes, and when asked why, respondents emphasized the love and emotional support that their parents or siblings gave them. Heroes can lift our spirits, dreams, and aspirations. We identify with them, we want to be with them, we want to be like them, and we want to bask in their successes (Cialdini et al., 1976). Leaders, of course, can do all of these things, too, but not necessarily. Heroes and their heroic work produce a great emotional payoff.

Influence on Thoughts

Heroes, like leaders, also influence our worldviews. Leaders can also alter worldviews, of course, but they must be heroic leaders to do so. Heroes and heroic leaders challenge our conventional thinking and our traditional ways of viewing our lives, our surroundings, and our rules for conduct. Legendary spiritual and religious leaders made their mark by defying their society's prevailing mindsets. Confucius' moral philosophy 2,500 years ago challenged traditional views of Taoism and Legalism. According to Islamic theology, Muhammad received revelations from God, and these messages formed the basis of a new holy wisdom described in the Qur'an. According to Christian theology, Jesus of Nazareth was a revolutionary whose new moral doctrines challenged the existing moral landscape.

The Dalai Lama, Desmond Tutu, Martin Luther King, Jr., Gandhi, and other spiritual leaders have all defied conventional thinking by advocating peaceful solutions to difficult, violent, intergroup conflicts.

Heroic leaders suggest new ways of looking at old situations, offering new schemas and fresh scripts for people to follow. This cognitive influence is especially apparent in the sciences, where scientific heroes suggest new paradigms that bring about revolutionary shifts in scientific thinking (Kuhn, 1962). Examples abound. Copernicus offered a new heliocentric view of the universe; Darwin forever altered the way we view the origin of species; Einstein turned our views of space and time upside down; and Freud stunned the world with his visionary theory of unconscious processes. Heroes also engender new ways of thinking in the business world. Henry Ford revolutionized transportation and industrial output, and Steve Jobs made computing smooth, sleek, and stylish. In each of these examples, a bold and heroic scientist or entrepreneur dared to challenge entrenched ways of thinking by completely re-framing the nature of the world.

Influence on Behavior

Heroes show us how to behave well, and they urge us, either directly or indirectly, to follow their path. Oprah Winfrey is a striking example. Described as "arguably the world's most powerful woman" by CNN and Time.com, Winfrey devoted two decades during *The Oprah Winfrey Show* to promote books and literature, various forms of self-improvement, family values, and a stronger spiritual lifestyle. Winfrey's show helped propel non-traditional lifestyles (gay, lesbian, transgender) into the cultural mainstream. Her book club encouraged legions of Americans to read more; a book plugged by Winfrey sold a million more copies than it would have ordinarily. Winfrey's influence has been sweeping and legendary, and it has not gone unnoticed. She was named "one of the 100 people who most influenced the 20th Century" and "one of the most influential people" of 2004, 2005, 2006, 2007, 2008, and 2009 by *Time*. At the end of the twentieth century *Life* magazine listed Winfrey as the most influential person of her generation. Barack Obama has said she "may be the most influential woman in the country." In 1998 she made the top of *Entertainment Weekly*'s list of the 101 most powerful people in the entertainment industry. In 2003 Winfrey edged out both Superman and Elvis Presley to be named the greatest pop culture icon of all time by television network VH1.

Heroes do more than shape the behavior of lay-people; they also inspire the actions of other heroes as well. Elvis Presley affected the songwriting of Chuck Berry, Fats Domino, The Everly Brothers, Little Richard, and Buddy Holly. In the 1960s the Beatles built on this foundation and took rock music to a level of creativity not seen before or since. The Beatles' John Lennon admitted that "if there hadn't been Elvis, there wouldn't have been the Beatles" (Davies, 2004, p. 256). The

Beatles' groundbreaking 1967 album, *Sergeant Pepper's Lonely Hearts Club Band*, was inspired by the Beach Boys' innovative 1966 album *Pet Sounds*. "Without *Pet Sounds*," said producer George Martin, "*Sergeant Pepper* wouldn't have happened. *Pepper* was an attempt to equal *Pet Sounds*" (Davies, 2004, p. 277). Musical heroes operate much like their scientific counterparts, building on the pioneering work of their predecessors and contemporaries.

Heroes begetting heroes can also be seen in the world of sports. Tiger Woods has often attributed his success to Charlie Sifford and Lee Elder, two black golfers who broke the color barrier on the professional golf tour. Major league baseball players routinely express their appreciation for Jackie Robinson, who in 1947 was the first black player to be allowed to participate in Major League Baseball. Larry Doby, the first black American Leaguer, viewed Robinson as a hero, and always reverently referred to him as "Mr. Robinson." There is no question that in every field of human endeavor, whether in science, sports, the arts, or business, heroes exert profound effects on the behavior of others. These effects can include emotional awe, feelings of empowerment, an innovative spirit, sheer inspiration, and a drive for self-improvement.

Influence as the Basis for Our T(r)axonomy of Heroism

Heroism assumes many different forms and thus defies simple categorization. Franco, Blau, and Zimbardo (2011) recently proposed a taxonomy of heroism based on the types of risks that heroes take when they perform their good deeds. Of the 12 subtypes of heroes in their taxonomy, two describe heroes who take physical risks. These heroes include *military personnel* and *courageous civilians* who put themselves in harm's way to help others. The remaining ten hero subtypes feature heroes who take social risks. These heroes include *whistle-blowers, scientific heroes, martyrs, good Samaritans, underdogs, political figures, religious figures, adventurers, politico-religious figures,* and *bureaucratic heroes*. As these subtypes suggest, Franco et al.'s taxonomy is driven by the context in which heroism takes place, whether military, religious, scientific, political, or moral.

We propose a conceptually different taxonomical framework. We believe that the most centrally defining aspect of heroism is the nature of the influence that heroes, like leaders, have on their followers and on society. Our analysis begins with the observation that a hero's influence can differ in many significant dimensions. Influence can vary along the continua of *weak* versus *strong*; *short-term* versus *long-term*; *widespread* versus *limited*; *waxing* versus *waning*; *hidden* versus *exposed*; and *constructed* versus *authentic*. These dimensions of influence

TABLE 1.1 Our Influence Taxonomy of Heroism

Type of Hero	Subtypes	Definition	Examples
1. Trending Hero	• Upward • Downward	On a trajectory toward heroism	Lady Gaga Woodrow Wilson
2. Transitory Hero	• True • Trivial	Enjoys 15 minutes of fame	"Sully" Sullenberger Steven Slater
3. Transitional Hero		Unique to one's stage of development	Power Rangers Justin Bieber
4. Tragic Hero		Falls from grace	King Lear Tiger Woods
5. Transposed Hero	• Hero to Villain • Villain to Hero	Experiences status reversal	LeBron James Ben Wade
6. Transparent Hero		Contributes behind the scenes	Firefighters, Police, Health Workers, Parents, Coaches, Soldiers
7. Traditional Hero	• Moral • Competent • Complete	Makes exceptional contributions over time	Michael Jordan Mother Teresa Wayne Gretzky
8. Transfigured Hero		Constructed Hero	Chilean Miners Robin Hood
9. Transforming Hero	• Global • Specific	Transforms societies	Gandhi Albert Einstein
10. Transcendent Hero		Transcends categories of heroism	Jesus Harry Potter John Wooden

are reflected in the various categories of heroism contained in our taxonomy. Our taxonomic structure features the following subtypes of heroes: trending, transitory, transitional, tragic, transposed, transparent, traditional, transfigured, transforming, and transcendent. Because each of these subtypes share the same first two letters—"tr"—we're tempted to call our framework a *traxonomy* rather than a taxonomy. Table 1.1 displays our taxonomy and the ten hero categories within it. Below we briefly describe each of the hero categories in our framework.

Trending Heroes

People are highly sensitive to the changing fortunes of others. This sensitivity serves as the basis for our perception of both hero formation and hero dissolution. We naturally take notice of which people in our social environment are slowly attaining heroic status and which are slowing losing it (Allison and Hensel, 2012). Rising stars and falling giants are said to be *Trending Heroes*. For example, the perceived impact of former U.S. presidents is often in a state of flux as new information surfaces or as historians offer new interpretations of old information. Ulysses S. Grant is an example of one president who is trending upward. In a 2000 C-SPAN poll of U.S. presidents, Grant was ranked as the 33rd best president. When this poll was repeated in 2009, Grant rose to 23rd. In the world of sports, young Irish golfer Rory McIlroy has been a Trending Hero for several years. His rising fortunes are not just due to his exemplary performances on the golf course; they are also due to his ability to connect with fans, and to his charitable work with UNICEF and disadvantaged children.

Heroes can also trend downward. In the first ever poll of historians' rankings of U.S. presidents, conducted by Arthur Schlesinger in 1948, Woodrow Wilson finished fourth. In the 2000 C-SPAN poll, he was ranked sixth, and later in the 2009 C-SPAN poll he had fallen to ninth. Professional athletes inevitably trend downward as their skills erode. Similarly, aging actors and actresses discover fewer opportunities for work on stage and screen. Hollywood actors who have been judged to be on the decline include Val Kilmer, Renée Zellweger, Helen Hunt, and John Travolta (Bloch, 2009). These and other fading public figures are experiencing firsthand an inescapable law of heroic gravity: What goes up must come down.

To understand the psychology of Trending Heroes, we note that people are sensitive to change and that the direction of change appears to matter more than one's absolute position. For example, people report that they would be happier if their three dollars grows to five dollars than if their eight dollars shrinks to six dollars (Kahneman and Tversky, 1979). From an economic standpoint, this emotional response is irrational because an end state of six dollars is greater than an end state of five dollars, but psychologically we detest the trend of shrinking fortunes so much that we'd rather have less money than be trending downward. Similarly, we're more attracted to people who dislike us but are starting to warm up to us than we are to people who like us but are becoming critical of us (Aronson and Linder, 1965). Human beings show a strong sensitivity to the direction of change in many judgment contexts, and included among these contexts is our perceptions of rising or falling heroes.

Transitory Heroes

Some heroes come and go in what seems like a blink of an eye. American artist Andy Warhol once quipped that "In the future, everyone will be world-famous for 15 minutes" (Murphy, 2006). Warhol was describing what we call a *Transitory Hero*, the type of hero who enjoys a very short shelf-life. We also suggest that there are two subtypes of the Transitory Hero: the Transitory-True Hero and the Transitory-False Hero. A striking example of a Transitory-True Hero is Chesley "Sully" Sullenberger, the US Airways pilot who saved the lives of 155 passengers when he successfully landed his crippled aircraft on the Hudson River in January of 2009. Sullenberger's act was widely celebrated for a few short weeks, but soon forgotten. In our view, Sully's heroism may have been ephemeral, but he was nevertheless a true hero for showing remarkable skill and courage in saving the lives of scores of people.

A notable example of a Transitory-False Hero was Steven Slater, the JetBlue flight attendant who quit his job in frustration by screaming obscenities over the loudspeaker, grabbing a couple of beers, and sliding down the emergency chute. Slater became a folk hero to hundreds of thousands of people on Facebook and on Twitter. People resonated to the idea of quitting a thankless job in a blaze of glory. Such an act was glorified in the famous Johnny Paycheck song, "Take This Job and Shove It," released in 1977. But we call Slater a Transitory-*False* Hero because his fame was deservedly fleeting. Slater displayed neither skill nor morality in resigning his position. He simply acted out a fantasy that attracted attention.

Transitional Heroes

Human beings experience many important phases of development throughout their lifespan. As we mature, our values, emotional states, cognitive abilities, and priorities tend to shift and evolve in significant ways. With these changes come adjustments in our preferences for heroes. Our college-age students tell us that their *Transitional Heroes* from a decade ago were the Power Rangers, Michael Jordan, and the Backstreet Boys. Most of our students openly admit that they have largely outgrown these heroes. As authors of this book and products of the mid-twentieth century, we gravitated in our youth to personal heroes who were professional athletes and artists such as Willie Mays, Jerry West, Elvis Presley, and the Beach Boys. As older adults, we now choose our heroes more carefully based on different criteria. In keeping with theories of adult development (Erikson, 1959), our choice of heroes is now based less on one's ability to throw a ball or hit a note. Today our heroes are Gandhi, Lincoln, King, and others who have made meaningful moral contributions to society.

Tragic Heroes

Human beings have a breathtaking ability to self-destruct and, as stated in an old aphorism, the bigger they come, the harder they fall. Tragic Heroes are usually heroic leaders whose character failings bring about their downfall. Legendary playwright William Shakespeare was especially attuned to the psychological power of the Tragic Hero. King Lear, Hamlet, Macbeth, and Brutus are vivid examples. There is certainly no shortage of modern-day Hamlets. The story of U.S. President Bill Clinton contains some of the central elements of the Tragic Hero narrative. Clinton was a brilliant, charismatic president with superb political instincts. Even his detractors held a grudging admiration for him. Clinton's tragic flaw was his repeated philandering, and during his second term in office his sexual misconduct led to impeachment charges of perjury. Numerous other public figures have had their careers derailed by one or more of *The Seven Deadly Sins*: pride, envy, anger, sloth, greed, gluttony, and lust. Tragic Heroes attract our sympathy, and sometimes even our anger, and they remind us of just how fragile one's heroic status can be.

Transposed Heroes

Sometimes heroes unexpectedly, and overnight, become villains. In the Batman comic book and movie franchise, the character of Two-Face illustrates the concept of a *Transposed Hero*. Two-Face was once Harvey Dent, the virtuous district attorney of Gotham City and an ally of Batman. After a criminal throws acid on his face, hideously scarring him, Dent loses his sanity and becomes a crime boss. LeBron James may serve as a real-world example of this kind of transposition. A basketball great, James was the toast of Cleveland until he left the team in what was perceived to be an arrogant, disrespectful manner. Literally overnight, James was transposed from the role of hero to the status of villain (Bradley, 2010). In sporting contexts, a hero who fails to perform at a crucial moment during competition becomes what is called a *goat*. When Boston Red Sox first-baseman Bill Buckner mishandled a simple ground ball during the 1986 baseball world series, he allowed the opposing team to win the championship. To this day, almost 30 years later, Buckner is considered a goat or villain despite enjoying a long and distinguished career as a ballplayer. Footballer great David Beckham is yet another striking example of a Transposed Hero. Early in his career, Beckham was sent off in an important World Cup game and was widely blamed for his team's defeat. He overcame this villainous reputation later by evolving into one of the most admired figures in the sport.

While some villains can quickly become heroes, this status reversal is more rare than the hero-to-villain conversion. An example of an individual who changes from sinner to saint is the great Christian philosopher Saint. Augustine (Augustine of Hippo, 1998). We also see it in Russell Crowe's character of Ben Wade in the 2007 film, *3:10 to Yuma*. Interestingly, Wade later converts back to villain status, thus again underscoring the temporal vicissitudes of hero and villain status. It is important to note that there is an important difference between Tragic Heroes and Transposed Heroes. While both these hero subtypes can involve a fall from grace, the Tragic Hero is a sympathetic figure whose life or career ends in shambles. In contrast, Transposed Heroes often make calculated choices to achieve a complete status reversal, and they may actually thrive in this new role.

Transparent Heroes

Transparent Heroes are arguably our most important, most abundant, and most under-appreciated heroes. They quietly perform heroic deeds behind the scenes, outside of the public spotlight. We call them transparent because they invisibly go about performing society's most virtuous and loving actions. Transparent Heroes are our parents who make great sacrifices for us. They are the teachers who mold our minds, the coaches who teach us discipline and hard work, the healthcare workers who heal us, emergency first responders who save us, and military personnel who protect us. Transparent Heroes are paradoxically our most abundant heroes and yet also our most unsung heroes. To determine the relative abundance of Transparent Heroes, we asked 50 participants to estimate the prevalence of the hero subtypes in our taxonomy. The results showed that participants estimated that 65 percent of all heroes are transparent—the invisible individuals among us whose heroic work often goes unnoticed. No other category of heroes came close to matching this percentage; the next highest percentage was 13 percent for traditional heroes, whom we describe next. Transparent Heroes may be invisible and unsung, but they are judged to be widespread throughout our society.

Traditional Heroes

The *Traditional Hero* is an individual who closely matches our schema or prototype of a hero and who also follows the life path of the hero in classic literature.

He or she is the person whose life story parallels the monomythic hero journey as described by Campbell (1949). This journey features a hero who is expelled from her ordinary world, encounters formidable obstacles, battles a dark adversary, receives assistance from unlikely sources, returns forever transformed, and offers a boon to society. Because Campbell's model of the hero's journey is derived from mythological legends from all corners of the globe, we are more likely to find the purest instances of this Traditional Hero in fictional stories. The heroic tales of Luke Skywalker, Batman, and Harry Potter are all narratives of the traditional hero. But many real-world heroes, such as Abraham Lincoln and Oprah Winfrey, also have important elements of the Traditional Hero. It is not unusual for public figures to emphasize elements of the traditional heroic script in their own lives to engender support from the public and to further their own political causes. Individuals who have done so with some success are J.K. Rowling, Barack Obama, David Geffen, and Celine Dion.

Transfigured Heroes

People are hungry for heroes, and at times this hunger motivates people to construct heroes, to see heroic elements where none exist, or to turn a mildly heroic tale into an extremely heroic one. Heroes who benefit from these constructions or exaggerations are called *Transfigured Heroes*. One prominent example is the story of Jessica Lynch, a former private in the U.S. Army who fought in the Iraq War. Lynch was injured and captured by Iraqi troops, and she was later rescued by American Special Forces personnel. Her story was a simple one. During a battle she was wounded by a grenade and was unable to fight back because her weapon jammed. But shortly after her rescue and return to America, the *Washington Post* published an article about Lynch entitled, "She Was Fighting to the Death" (Loeb, 2003). The article reported that Lynch's unit was ambushed and that she "shot several enemy soldiers" and "continued firing at the Iraqis even after she sustained multiple gunshot wounds and watched several other soldiers in her unit die around her." The article provided a stirring account of a courageous hero performing magnificently under dire conditions.

The only problem with the *Washington Post* story is that it never happened. Lynch herself has repeatedly denied that any of these heroic events occurred. "That wasn't me. I'm not about to take credit for something I didn't do ... I'm just a survivor." Lynch blames the *Washington Post* and the military for using her to promote a false heroic narrative. "They used me to symbolize all this stuff. It's wrong. I did not shoot, not a round, nothing. I went down praying to my knees. And that's the last I remember" (Campbell, 2012).

Transfigured Heroes are credited with performing more heroic behaviors than they truly performed because of our deep-seated need for heroes and to see heroism where none exists. We are especially likely to crave heroism in difficult situations, and we will mentally create heroes or exaggerate heroism even when objective facts fly in the face of our constructions. Psychologists have long known that human beings love to embellish heroic stories and imbue them with drama, excitement, and inspiration. Moreover, people have little use for dissonant elements that might diminish the heroic narrative. Transfiguration describes the mental tricks we play on ourselves in the service of quenching our thirst for heroes.

Transforming Heroes

Our conceptualization of the *Transforming Hero* borrows heavily from the seminal work of James MacGregor Burns, who first used the term *transforming* to describe exceptional leadership (Burns, 1978, 2003). According to Burns, transforming leadership occurs when both leaders and followers engage in a mutual effort to raise levels of motivation and morality. The transforming leader is able to articulate a clear vision, offers a plan to attain the vision, exudes confidence, leads by example, and empowers followers to make the vision a reality. We believe that virtually all transforming leaders are also Transforming Heroes. Martin Luther King, Jr., is an ideal example of a transforming hero as seen in his charisma, expression of lofty ideals, and ability to stir followers to action. Heroes who are transforming can be more influential than any other subtype of hero.

We distinguish between heroes who transform entire societies (transforming-global heroes) and heroes who transform smaller subcultures within societies (transforming-specific heroes). As chief architect of the civil rights movement in North America and elsewhere around the world, King is clearly a transforming-global hero. Other globally transforming heroes include Nelson Mandela and Mahatma Gandhi. Examples of transforming-specific heroes are Albert Einstein, who transformed the field of physics; Elvis Presley, who transformed popular music; and Steve Jobs, who transformed personal computing.

Transcendent Heroes

We acknowledge that some heroes belong in more than one of the subtypes of our taxonomy. Consider Oprah Winfrey. Her life story possesses many of the elements of the monomythic hero journey described by Campbell (1949), making her a Traditional Hero. She has also transformed television, making her a Transforming Hero. Another hero who defies simple categorization is legendary basketball coach John Wooden. He, too, is both a Traditional and a Transforming Hero, and one could also argue that he is also a Transparent Hero for his behind-the-scenes mentoring of so many young men for so many decades. What are we to do with heroes who cannot cleanly fall into one category? We call them *Transcendent Heroes*. Their contributions feature a complexity or depth that transcends our taxonomic structure.

Jesus of Nazareth is most certainly a transcendent figure. The transcendent heroism of Jesus is derived from his transforming influence on western culture, and also from his life story mirroring the path of the Traditional Hero. Elements of Campbell's traditional hero's journey in the life of Jesus include a born calling, a humble birth in a manger, help from disciples, a tumultuous clashing with the status quo, the crucifixion, and the rising from the dead to save the world. Jesus may also be considered a Transfigured Hero, depending on one's beliefs about the veracity of biblical accounts of his divine nature.

Because they are able to satisfy the criteria for multiple categories of heroism, Transcendent Heroes would appear to be the most influential of all the heroes in our taxonomy. But this is not necessary the case. A hero could conceivably be both trending and transitory, as when a rock singer enjoys one hit song (trending upward) but then disappears from the music radar screen (transitory). One-hit wonders of this type could be called transcendent because they meet the criteria for more than one hero type, but they are hardly more influential than a Transforming Hero such as Martin Luther King, Jr. We thus argue that truly Transcendent Heroes must combine transforming heroism with at least one other type of heroism in our taxonomy. Thus Transforming Heroism is a necessary but not sufficient condition for transcendency. In this way Transcendent Heroes occupy supreme status of influence among all the heroes in our taxonomy.

Organization of This Book

In this book we profile 100 heroes, some of whom you probably know and some of whom you likely don't know. These heroes come from all walks of life and represent many different domains of heroic activity. Some are heroes from fiction, and others are real-life legends. Some are heroes without question, while others will leave you wondering why we included them among the 100 profiles. We assure you that all 100 individuals, even the ones that engender puzzlement, have been listed as heroes by at least some of the many people we've surveyed about heroism.

We've arranged these hero profiles by the taxonomical category in which they fall, beginning with the hero category that we believe is the least influential on society—Trending Heroes—and ending with the hero category that we believe carries the greatest influence—Transcendent Heroes. In our conclusion, we attempt the daunting task of making sense of heroism as it relates to the complex field of leadership studies. We will examine important areas of overlap between heroism and leadership, and we will also identify key areas of difference between these two important phenomena.

The 100 profiles that follow comprise the vast majority of this book. We hope you agree that the individual lives we describe are fascinating illustrations of heroic leadership in all its many forms.

Chapter 2

Trending Heroes
Gaining or Losing Heroic Status

People are highly sensitive to changing fortunes. We monitor our own changing fortunes, of course, but we also show great sensitivity to the shifting fortunes of others. We want to know who's doing better and who's doing worse than they were before. Is my favorite athlete or sports team having a good year? Is China's economy still growing rapidly? Are public schools in decline? Did my neighbor buy a new car? This sensitivity to changing fortunes is the foundation of our perceptions of Trending Heroes.

Lady Gaga: A Trending Hero

Trending heroism reflects the reality that most heroes are not created in an instant. It takes time to accumulate a resume of heroic success and accomplishment. We propose that as natural observers of human behavior, people are sensitive to cues indicating that hero formation is occurring. People take notice of the individuals around them who are experiencing rising fortunes and growing accolades. Conversely, people also show sensitivity to the reverse process, namely, heroism in decline. When heroes stumble—an all-too-frequent occurrence—people are highly responsive to the stumble and watch carefully for signs indicating whether the stumble is merely an aberration or the beginning of the end of heroism.

Why are we so sensitive to trends in heroism? We're naturally drawn to changes in our social environment because they may have implications for our own well-being. Long ago, famous social psychologist Leon Festinger theorized that our sensitivity to others' outcomes fulfills our drive to know where we stand in relation to others (Festinger, 1954). We also find changes in others' fortunes to be a source of drama or entertainment (Kim et al., 2008). Unexpected changes in fortunes can be especially dramatic, as when underdogs triumph and established powerhouses fail (Goldschmied and Vandello, 2009; Goldschmied and Vandello, in press; Vandello, Goldschmied, and Richards, 2007). Historically unsuccessful sports teams that finally enjoy some success are said to be plucky underdogs, up-and-coming programs, rising upstarts, and Cinderella stories (Allison and Goethals, 2011). We seem to have fewer labels for fallen giants. We briefly revel in their misfortune, as befitting our schadenfreudian tendencies, but our focus is usually more on celebrating the unexpected successes of the downtrodden.

Heroism can trend quickly, or it can trend slowly. Our sensitivity to changes in others' fortunes may be so great that we may rarely view anyone, especially heroes, as homeostatic over time in terms of their status or outcomes. Fortunes, it seems, are always fluctuating. People in general, but especially heroes, seem prone toward experiencing small victories and minor setbacks on a daily basis. The only exception to this rule may occur in our perceptions of dead heroes. Research has shown that our judgments and impressions of the dead tend to resist change (Eylon and Allison, 2005). Dead heroes tend to be frozen in time. Living heroes, however, are inevitably in the process of being formed, knocked down, resurrected, or dying.

In this section of the book, we discuss six Trending Heroes. Four of them are trending upward, and two are trending downward. We begin with Lady Gaga, who less than a decade ago was a quirky, unknown vocal artist with a unique look and catchy sound. During the late 2000s and early 2010s, she steadily grew an audience of followers and devotees who began to use her name and the word *hero* in the same sentence. Next we discuss the rising reputation of a nineteenth-century U.S. President, Ulysses S Grant. An increasing number of historians are ranking Grant higher than ever in polls of presidential greatness, and we explain how Grant's progressive actions in the area of race relations are largely responsible for his upward trend toward heroism. We then discuss the revival of interest in the work of Sigmund Freud, whose theories were rarely taken seriously by most psychologists of the late twentieth century. Today, many of Freud's ideas about unconscious processes are being validated by modern scientific research. The next profile is of actress Drew Barrymore, who has achieved great success as an actress despite her turbulent upbringing. Barrymore's recent philanthropic activity has been impressive and makes her a rising hero to many.

We conclude this section with two heroes trending downward: Woodrow Wilson and Arnold Schwarzenegger. First comes Woodrow Wilson, an American president who throughout most of the twentieth century enjoyed the reputation of a great hero. Historians of the current century are now less kind to Wilson, condemning his record on racial issues and speculating that his role in the Treaty of Versailles may have helped spawn Nazi Germany. We conclude this section on Trending Heroes by profiling Arnold Schwarzenegger, who was once a champion bodybuilder and film star whose movies dominated the box office. Sadly, his successful life trajectory came to a grinding halt, and even sustained a reversal, as he struggled in his role as Governor of California. All six of the heroes profiled in this section, from Gaga to Schwarzenegger, demonstrate the ever-shifting state of our perceptions of heroism.

Lady Gaga: A Hero in the Making?

Is Lady Gaga a hero? A few years ago we surveyed our students for their opinions about Lady Gaga and whether she has earned the status of hero. At the time, she was a brash new phenomenon and the jury was definitely still out. While very few of our students were willing to assign the label "hero" to her, they did concede that she was a great talent and a role model to many people. Several also said that Gaga could become a hero over time but that right now it's too early to tell. We suspect that, at this point, she has arrived at heroic status in the minds of many.

The responses from our students from a few years ago raise the question of what Lady Gaga, or any rising entertainment star for that matter, would have to do to be perceived as a hero. Possessing a great and unique talent certainly helps. In 2008 Lady Gaga's debut album *The Fame* reached number one in the UK, Canada, Austria, Germany, and Ireland, and it peaked at number two in the United States. Critics also loved *The Fame*. Her music style is said to combine the elements of many legendary rock icons, including Madonna, Gwen Stefani, David Bowie, and Freddie Mercury, whose band Queen's classic *Radio Gaga* was the inspiration for Lady Gaga's own moniker.

Lady Gaga has also won the respect of many of her peers. Said Kylie Minogue:

She's like a meteor that just came from outer space and landed on the pop landscape or pop/dance landscape. I think it's amazing. She's largely responsible for bringing dance to the kind of mainstream or pop arena in the States. She's incredibly talented. She's an absolute force to be reckoned with and I'm a great admirer.

Barbara Walters chose Gaga as one of the *10 Most Fascinating People of 2009*. Gaga also became the first living person to have more than ten million Facebook fans.

Another factor that appears to be propelling Lady Gaga toward heroism is her effort to promote positive social change, especially in the area of gay rights. She is an active proponent of gay marriage, and she revealed that her song *Poker Face* was about her bisexuality. Gaga credits her gay fans for much of her early success. "The turning point for me was the gay community. I've got so many gay fans and they're so loyal to me and they really lifted me up. They'll always stand by me and I'll always stand by them." Gaga is well aware of her impact on young people. "The truth is what I'm a role model for is the ability to change culture," she said.

Fans of Gaga have labeled her a "fashion icon" with superb vocal and performing instincts during her concert tours. Gaga's unique look is her own creation; she designs and makes her own costumes on stage. One blogger has written: "She isn't afraid to act smart, dress for herself, focus on things other than her body, be odd, and have a sick name." Critics rave that her live performances are "innovative" and "highly entertaining."

Although some may still be skeptical about Lady Gaga's heroic status, there is no denying the impact of her unique artistry on pop culture. There is something compelling about her courageous trailblazing in the areas of music, dance, fashion, and redefining sex roles. Gaga once said:

> I want women—and men—to feel empowered by a deeper and more psychotic part of themselves. The part they're always trying desperately to hide. I want that to become something that they cherish. You have to be unique, and different, and shine in your own way.

Ulysses S. Grant: The Reappraised Hero

A proposal several years ago by a number of Republicans wanting to honor Ronald Reagan by putting his image on the fifty-dollar bill might have had the unintended effect of further raising the stature of the man who is already on it. That would be another Republican, Ulysses S. Grant. People can argue about which president, Reagan or Grant, best exemplifies the principles of the GOP. But if the party is truly the party of Lincoln, it is important to remember that there is no

Republican who fought harder and more effectively for Lincoln's principles than did Grant. It isn't even close.

Lincoln's principles were saving the Union and freeing slaves. He eventually came to believe that the best way to accomplish the first was to undertake the second. He argued that freeing slaves, and arming them in the Union cause, was an indispensable necessity to winning the war and saving the country. Grant became president less than four years after Lincoln's assassination and worked hard to continue a Reconstruction policy, like Lincoln's, that protected the rights of African-Americans. He struggled successfully to secure ratification of the Fifteenth Amendment to the Constitution, guaranteeing blacks the right to vote, and in 1875 he supported a civil rights bill that anticipates in many ways the civil rights bill that was finally passed and signed into law by Lyndon Johnson, nearly 90 years later.

Besides continuing Lincoln's policies as vigorously as he could, Grant deserves credit for overseeing international negotiations which preserved the peace when the United States could ill-afford another war, and for paving the way for economic expansion in the last quarter of the nineteenth century.

At the time of the move to put Ronald Reagan on the fifty-dollar bill, Sean Wilentz wrote in the *New York Times*, "Though much of the public and even some historians haven't yet heard the news, the vindication of Ulysses S. Grant is well under way." In 2000 a C-SPAN survey of historians ranked Grant 33rd among all US presidents. That in itself was an improvement over mid-twentieth-century polls that put Grant near the bottom, with Warren G. Harding and James Buchanan. In 2009 another C-SPAN survey ranked Grant 23rd, and placed him in tenth place on the dimension called "Pursued Equal Justice For All." Some argue that he should be ranked behind only Lincoln, Harry Truman and Lyndon Johnson on that aspect of leadership.

Most interesting in the debate about Reagan and the corresponding reassessment of Grant is that our appraisals of presidents, among many other leaders, often change. A 2009 book by Joan Waugh entitled *U.S. Grant: American Hero, American Myth* shows that Grant was regarded by most Americans, in the South as well as the North, as a mythical, heroic figure for many years after his death in 1885. Then so-called "lost cause" historians elevated Robert E. Lee, denigrated Reconstruction, and turned Grant into a drunk and a "butcher." This period in history overlaps the tightening of Jim Crow laws in the South and the often overlooked segregationist policies of President Woodrow Wilson. Now people are looking at Grant through new lenses, as a result of a number of recent biographies, which themselves pick up on themes of early or mid-twentieth-century writers who were ignored during the heyday of the "lost cause" perspective.

To some extent, most all heroes and villains are the subject of myth. We construct charismatic, heroic, or villainous images of prominent people. In cases like

Grant's, their reputation rises, falls, and rises again. Many of them thus qualify as Trending Heroes. It will be fascinating to see as the sesquicentennial of the Civil War unfolds how Grant's reputation as a military hero is appraised and reappraised, and whether those reappraisals affect his standing among the nation's 43 presidents.

Sigmund Freud: The Vindication of a Battered Theory

We often look to Albert Einstein as a shining example of a hero who transformed the way we think about the world. There are, of course, other scientists as well. Copernicus forever changed the way we view our solar system, proposing that celestial objects rotate around the sun rather than the earth. Darwin transformed our thinking about the origin of plant and animal species, proposing that processes of natural selection govern the evolution of life. To this list of transforming thinkers we add the name of Sigmund Freud, one of the most controversial and divisive figures in the history of science.

Freud was the first person to offer a theory of the human personality, a theory that was viewed as provocative, perverse, and counter-intuitive. Human beings and their behavior, he said, are driven by dynamic, unconscious psychological conflicts. Our unconscious desires for sex and aggression (the id) often collide with our drive for moral perfection (the superego) and our flawed attempts to fulfill these motives within the constraints of reality (the ego). To ward off the inevitable anxiety that results from these conflicting demands, we use *defense mechanisms*—unconscious distortions of reality that keep us functioning.

Freud's theory was especially controversial in its emphasis on unconscious sexual urges, especially desires in early childhood for our opposite-sex parent. Many alternative schools of thought about human nature, such as behaviorism and humanism, were developed as a base of opposition to Freud. Over the past century, Freudian theory lost much of its luster and became a frequent source of disrespect, and even ridicule, within the academic community. A *Newsweek* article called him "history's most debunked doctor" (Adler, 2006), and W.H. Auden wrote in his 1973 poem, "In Memory of Sigmund Freud," "if often he was wrong and, at times, absurd, to us he is no more a person now but a whole climate of opinion."

But over the past two decades, Freud has seen some measure of vindication. A number of recent psychological studies have supported his idea that people's judgments occur automatically and without awareness. Drew Westen, a psychologist at Emory University, said that before Freud, "nobody realized that our conscious mind is the tip of the mental iceberg." Freud was also correct about denial and other defense mechanisms. "The research is crystal-clear that we look the other way not to see what makes us uncomfortable," Westen said.

Freud is also getting more credit for anticipating work on the role of depletion of psychic energy in everyday tasks. Psychologist Roy Baumeister and his colleagues found that when people spend time resisting the temptation to eat chocolate, they are less persistent in solving problems as compared to people who are allowed to eat chocolate (Baumeister and Tierney, 2011). Freud is also given credit for establishing the field of psychotherapy, and for being the first psychologist to recognize the importance of early childhood experiences in shaping adult behavior.

Because they dare to change the world, transforming heroes can ruffle feathers, rattle sensitivities, and become subject to the vicissitudes of public and professional opinion. Sigmund Freud's audacious theory of human nature attracted its share of critics, but it also triggered a voluminous amount of research, much of which has supported Freud's claims about the role of unconscious processes in shaping human judgments. As with many transforming figures, Freud and his reputation are likely to remain in flux for years to come. But at the present moment, his theories of the unconscious are considered prescient.

Drew Barrymore: The Heroic Story of the Little Girl Lost

When we think of the obstacles that heroes must overcome, the images that usually come to mind are great physical barriers or formidable villains. For example, Batman's obstacle is the Joker; Nelson Mandela's obstacles were prison bars; Sir Edmund Hillary and Tenzing Norgay's obstacle was the sheer size of Mount Everest. But frequently the most daunting obstacles heroes confront are unseen. They are the hero's inner demons that inflict emotional pain and trigger self-destructive behaviors. A vivid example of a hero who conquered these inner demons is the actress Drew Barrymore.

As with many people in the entertainment industry, Drew Barrymore grew up surrounded by addiction. Many of the Barrymore family members were famed actors who struggled with alcohol and drug abuse. Starting at a very young age, Drew Barrymore got caught in a whirlwind of sex, drugs, and alcohol. By the age of 11, she was a regular at the famous Studio 54 nightclub, smoking cigarettes, drinking alcohol, and experimenting with marijuana and cocaine. Her mother put her in rehab when Barrymore was 13. At the age of 14, Barrymore wrote her autobiography, aptly named *Little Girl Lost*.

Drew Barrymore's story could easily have had a tragic ending, but miraculously she turned her life around and has become one of Hollywood's most successful and sought-after actors. "I've been humbled," she explained. "That makes you grateful for every day you have." Barrymore has also adopted a very healthy attitude about her troubled past. "I never regret anything," she said, "because every little detail of your life is what made you into who you are in the end."

Most impressively, Barrymore has used her fame to make the world a better place. "I don't want to sit around and hope good things happen. I want to *make* them happen," she explained. In 2005, she was devastated to learn that there are more than 100 million school-aged children around the world who don't get enough to eat. Barrymore realized that she could make a difference by becoming a United Nations World Food Program celebrity partner. Traveling to Kenya, she witnessed the tragic conditions of hunger and poverty faced by the children of Nairobi. "Feeding a child at school is such a simple thing," she said while serving food to Kenyan schoolchildren in 2005. "But you can tell it works miracles."

In 2007, the World Food Program appointed Barrymore as their official Ambassador Against Hunger. "I am honored and humbled to accept this challenging and rewarding assignment," she said. "I can't think of any issue that is more important than working to see that no schoolchild in this world goes hungry." In March of 2008, Barrymore appeared on *The Oprah Winfrey Show* and announced that she was donating $1 million of her own money to support World Food Program projects in Kenya. "I've seen what a difference a simple cup of nutritious porridge can make in a child's life. It helps them learn, stay healthy and sets them on track for a bright future," she said.

Barrymore's life journey is not unlike that of many heroes who are able to overcome turbulent childhoods involving parental loss or dysfunction. Typically the hero on this journey leads a life of turmoil and despair until a trigger event, or rock bottom, is reached, which compels the hero to undergo a complete overhaul of his or her life. A big part of this overhaul involves the hero becoming a selfless and tireless advocate of positive social change. Many fictional and non-fictional heroes have followed this type of heroic journey, including Batman, Johnny Cash, Oprah Winfrey, Christina Aguilera, John Lennon, and, of course, Drew Barrymore. These heroes teach us that the same strength and courage we use to overcome our inner demons can also be used to make the world better for us all.

Woodrow Wilson: A Hero Trending Downward

Our evaluations of heroes are often in flux, with some heroes gaining popularity and others slipping downward in their reputations. As we've noted, heroes whose images are rising or falling are said to be *trending heroes*. We've argued that Sigmund Freud is trending up. His explorations of the unconscious and its effects on both conscious thought and overt behavior seem increasingly relevant to modern psychologists. Another individual, a hero to many in America, seems to be trending down. He is the 28th President of the United States, Woodrow Wilson.

For many years Wilson was near the top of presidential rankings. For example, in the first such poll of historians, conducted by Arthur Schlesinger in 1948, Wilson was fourth. In a 2000 C-SPAN poll he was ranked sixth, but in the 2009 C-SPAN poll he had fallen to ninth. Interestingly, one of the heroes we also discuss in this section, Ulysses S. Grant, moved by far the most in the C-SPAN ratings from 2000 to 2009, rising from 33rd to 23rd.

Why is Woodrow Wilson trending down? Will his ratings rebound back upward, or are they likely to stay depressed? Some insight comes from the leadership characteristics that historians judged in the two C-SPAN polls. Wilson improved on only one, Vision, moving from fifth to fourth. But on Crisis Leadership, Economic Management, International Relations, Relations with Congress, and Performance Within Context of Times his ratings fell. However, the biggest drop was on Pursued Equal Justice For All. He went from a not very good 20th to the bottom half, 27th.

Despite a highly acclaimed and mostly favorable biography of Wilson published in 2009 by John Milton Cooper, there seems to be more focus on Wilson's racial and segregation policies. Wilson was a southerner, the first elected after the Civil War, and only the second Democrat, and his cabinet was mostly Southern, some of it highly racist. One argument, for example, for segregating the post office during Wilson's administration was reported to have been that railroad cars carrying mail were not big enough for two bathrooms. It was unthinkable that black and white employees might use the same facilities. Wilson was certainly preoccupied by other issues, and may not have been as racist as his segregation policies suggest. Furthermore, he needs to be understood in the context of his times. He served as president during the height of Jim Crow. For whatever reasons—justified or not—his standing is slipping.

If the explanation is "Equal Justice For All," as suggested by C-SPAN, what are we to make of that? It may be that in an increasingly diverse society, which has elected an African-American president, historians and others are both more sensitized to issues touching on race, and more critical of those perceived to retard progress on that front. Consistent with this possibility is the finding that Grant's C-SPAN rating on the "equal justice" dimension changed from eighteenth to ninth between the two surveys, explaining part of his overall rise in the ratings.

Another explanation may lie in increasing debate about the wisdom of Wilson's policies in shaping the Treaty of Versailles following World War I. Did the treaty's harsh treatment of Germany make Nazism more likely? Undoubtedly these issues will be debated for years to come, and presidential ratings will rise and fall. At the moment, a president once widely regarded as "heroic" is being assessed more negatively. He is still in the top ten, but his drop in the ratings is of note. At present, he is a Trending Hero heading down.

Arnold Schwarzenegger: The Downward Spiral of a Hero

In 1767, German playwright Gotthold Ephraim composed a play in which a character, a sergeant in the army, is asked whether he'd seek promotion to a higher rank. "I don't consider it," he says. "I am a good sergeant; I might easily make a bad captain, and certainly a worse general. People have had this experience" (Powell, 2011).

With this statement, Ephraim may have been the first person to hint at the *Peter Principle*—the tendency of people to rise to their level of incompetence. Former California Governor Arnold Schwarzenegger might have benefited from heeding Ephraim's message about the importance of knowing one's self-limitations. In several ways Schwarzenegger's life has had all the markings of a tragic hero. He rose to great professional heights, but his career unraveled when he appeared to over-reach his abilities when he became Governor of California. To make matters worse, while Governor, Schwarzenegger showed poor judgment in his personal life as well.

During the 1970s, Arnold Schwarzenegger became a bodybuilding legend, winning an unprecedented seven Mr. Olympia contests. When his bodybuilding career ended, he made it his goal to become a star of motion pictures, an ambition that was met with derision by most observers. After all, Schwarzenegger sported a thick Austrian accent, was a stiff public speaker, and lacked any experience on stage or in film. With hard work and savvy, Schwarzenegger proved his critics wrong and went on to become one of the most highly sought-after leading men in Hollywood during the 1980s and 90s.

While achieving remarkable success as a bodybuilder and an actor, Schwarzenegger also enjoyed great triumphs as a businessman. He made millions of dollars from many different business ventures and in real estate investment. Everything Schwarzenegger did seemed to turn to gold. And so in 2003, when his home state of California was in political and economic turmoil, it came as no surprise that Schwarzenegger believed he could become a successful governor of the state.

Schwarzenegger announced his candidacy and easily won the 2003 California gubernatorial election. He enjoyed great popularity during the early years of his term as governor, riding a wave of economic prosperity and promising to clean up gridlock in the state's government. He earned the nickname of *The Governator*, a reference to his earlier film work in which he played the role of *The Terminator*.

Expectations were high and people seemed hopeful that Schwarzenegger's record of success would continue unabated.

But within a few years, his luster began to fade. It became clear that Schwarzenegger could not fix California's budget problems. In fact, the state's deficits and tax burden grew enormously under his administration. Toward the end of his term he drew much criticism when, in one of his final official acts, he commuted the manslaughter sentence for the son of a political ally. Then it was revealed that Schwarzenegger fathered an out-of-wedlock child, a secret that he kept from the public and from his wife during his entire tenure as governor. His marriage to Maria Shriver ended acrimoniously.

Heroes are rarely able to sustain an uninterrupted record of success over long periods of time. They are vulnerable to an array of forces that can easily knock them off their pedestals, the most common of which is their own hubris. There is no doubt that Arnold Schwarzenegger had the best of intentions when he pursued his dream of becoming an effective governor of California. In keeping with the Peter Principle, Schwarzenegger's climb up the professional ladder ended when he encountered a leadership position at which he could not succeed. His poor judgment in his personal life then compounded his troubles. The good news for Schwarzenegger is that he has returned to areas of life for which he is best suited for success.

Chapter 3

Transitory Heroes
Hero Today, Gone Tomorrow

There's no better illustration of Andy Warhol's quip about everyone's 15 minutes of fame than the concept of transitory heroes. These heroes are people whom we admire for some significant action or achievement but for only a short period of time. They don't last because their heroism has no lasting effect, other than to be a reminder of something we once applauded. Also, in many cases their heroism was created by a single act that becomes overlooked in our busy ongoing lives. They may not have demonstrated sustaining effort or commitment. One of our favorite examples is US Airways pilot Chesley "Sully" Sullenberger who deftly ditched Flight 1549 into the freezing Hudson River in January, 2009. On takeoff from LaGuardia airport, flocks of birds had been sucked into Sully's jet engines, causing each of them to fail. But his skilled handling of the large Airbus A320 brought all 155 passengers to safety. It was a magnificent performance in a most pressured situation. Sadly, our attention spans are limited, and just a few years later Sully comes to mind as a hero for just a few. Those few include, of course, the individuals he saved, but not many others remember his daring and his calm competence. He achieved something great, but that accomplishment had no impact on most people after a few months.

Former Congresswoman Gabrielle Giffords of Arizona is another example of a transitory hero. Giffords was shot by a lone gunman at a rally in her congressional district in Tucson, Arizona in January, 2011. Six people were killed. Her courageous recovery from the assassin's bullet and her struggle to regain full brain function inspired many. But her bravery and tenacity are being quickly forgotten. There is too much happening too fast in today's world for a story even as moving

Gabrielle Giffords: A Transitory Hero

as hers to retain much impact. This is particularly interesting because her struggle was not simply one of a single heroic moment. Her fight to recover continues.

Both Sullenberger and Giffords clearly acted in ways that fit people's mental lists of the defining characteristics of heroes. We have shown that those lists include dimensions of both competence and morality, and most often images of struggle and sacrifice against nearly insurmountable odds. Sully succeeded in maneuvering his large jet to a smooth water landing under the most trying circumstances. Then he made sure that all of his passengers had been rescued by boats in the Hudson before he and his crew abandoned the aircraft. He provided a perfect example of competence and self-abnegating moral behavior. Giffords' struggle to stay alive and to regain nearly normal functioning was equally impressive. She inspired her congressional colleagues and the whole nation when she went to the Capitol to cast a crucial vote and also when she appeared at President Barack Obama's State of the Union address just a year after being shot.

Even though Sullenberger and Giffords' heroism is fleeting, we regard them as true heroes. They exemplify heroism's essential qualities. In contrast, we think some transitory heroes are better regarded as false heroes. Even though they are publicly acclaimed, their "heroic" actions do not meet standards of competence or morality. They do satisfy needs we need to understand, but they do not provide genuine inspiration or authentic models of high achievement. A good example is Steven Slater, the JetBlue flight attendant who shouted obscenities at his passengers, stole some beer, and exited down the aircraft's evacuation slide. He immediately gained notoriety and celebrity, and was a "folk hero" to many. Millions know the frustrations of air travel, for flight attendants as well as passengers, and could empathize with the impulse to tell off the airlines. They'd like to do it themselves. Also, people have more general fantasies of telling off their bosses, expressed so succinctly in Johnny Paycheck's noted song, "Take This Job and Shove It." Thus Steven Slater expressed feelings many of us experience ourselves. We know that they are not particularly admirable. We know that they don't express our best selves. But they are real nonetheless. Freud would argue that naming people who vicariously express those feelings "heroes" is similar to expressing socially unacceptable feelings through jokes. Freud emphasized the ways that humor (as well as dreams and slips of the tongue) bypass normal inhibitions and allow people to express impure thoughts. Admiring and making heroes of people who express our private frustrations or unacceptable impulses seems similarly Freudian. To the extent such people are heroes, we regard them as false heroes.

The profiles to follow include a wide range of heroes, who for a short time attracted attention for their heroic acts. They come from a truly wide range of backgrounds and occupations, and underline how widespread heroism is, even when it is fleeting. We first consider Abu Ghraib whistleblower Joe Darby, who revealed sadistic torture of war prisoners by U.S. Military Police in Iraq. Next we describe the career accomplishments of Mae Jemison, NASA's first black woman astronaut; this profile was written by our good friend and colleague Rick Hutchins. We then consider the men and women who lent a hand to stem the disaster stemming from the Fukushima earthquake and tsunami in 2011, the inspiring lecturer Randy Pausch, and the courageous shooting victim Gabrielle Giffords. In the remainder of this chapter, we cover the life of Civil War general Benjamin Butler, who gave emancipation an important early nudge forward by declaring escaped slaves "contraband" of war, and refused to return them to their Southern owners; Liu Xiaobo, winner of the 2010 Nobel Peace Prize; Christa McAuliffe, the school teacher who perished in the space shuttle *Challenger* explosion in 1986; Fred Korematsu, the civil rights worker who protested the prison camp internment of Japanese-Americans living on the West coast during World War II; and two men called Steven who briefly came to the world's notice: Steven Slater and Steve Bartman. All are, in one way or another, exceptional individuals who won our acclaim, at least for the time we paid attention.

Joe Darby: The Heroic Whistleblower of Abu Ghraib

Heroes are not always admired for their actions. Sometimes a heroic act is controversial, receiving high acclaim from some but contempt from others. One type of hero that often attracts both extreme approval and extreme condemnation is the *whistleblower* (Bocchiaro, Zimbardo, and Van Lange, 2012). Joe Darby is a courageous man whose story follows the classic pattern of the whistleblower. In January of 2004, while serving in the U.S. Army at the Abu Ghraib prisoner of war camp in Iraq, Darby discovered photographs of prisoners being abused by American soldiers. The abuse was physical, sexual, and emotional in nature, and it was obviously illegal and outrageous. "It violated everything I personally believed in and all I'd been taught about the rules of war," he said. When asked what was going through his mind when he first saw the photos, Darby simply said, "Disbelief. I tried to think of a reason why they would do this."

Darby turned the images over to the authorities and wanted to remain anonymous, but his name became known after Secretary of Defense Donald Rumsfeld publicly identified him during a Senate hearing. It was at this point that things got ugly for Darby. The army decided to send him home, but a security assessment of his hometown revealed that it wasn't safe for him to return there. "There were a lot of threats, a lot of phone calls to his wife," said a local army veteran. "The overall threat of harassment or criminal activity to the Darbys was imminent." His wife Bernadette recalls that "we did not receive the response I thought we would. People were mean, saying he was a walking dead man; he was walking around with a bull's-eye on his head. It was scary." Darby and his wife now reside in protective military custody at an undisclosed location.

One of Phil Zimbardo's central tenets of heroism is that heroes have to be active when others are passive (Zimbardo, 2012). From this perspective, the opposite of heroism isn't villainy; it is apathy. Joe Darby clearly had the courage to take action while others remained silent. Human rights worker Carroll Bogert has said that

> torture flourishes in the dark, and what Darby has done is to shine a light on what was happening in a place that was dark. Darby told the truth. Telling the truth doesn't always make you popular. And I think a lot of public opposition has come down on his head for the fact that he told the truth. But I think that history will put him in a good light.

Fortunately, Darby has received some much-deserved recognition for his courageous actions. In May of 2004, he was profiled as the "Person of the Week" by anchor Peter Jennings on ABC's *World News Tonight*, and in December 2004 he was selected by ABC News as one of their "People of the Year." Darby was also featured on *60 Minutes* in 2007, and he received a John F. Kennedy Profile in Courage Award in 2005. There is no doubt that, as with many whistleblowers, Darby paid a steep price for his heroic actions. There will always be people who question Darby's motives or who believe that his whistleblowing betrayed his country. But many more will agree with what Edmund Burke is reported to have said: "All that is necessary for the triumph of evil is that good men do nothing."

Mae Jemison: Living Heroic Dreams

Not all heroes are created in a moment of crisis or deadly peril. Sometimes a life will simply grow to heroic proportions. Mae Jemison is just such a hero, a polymath who has dreamed great dreams and made them come true, and in so doing has shown us the greatness inherent in us all.

Mae Jemison, M.D., is best known as the first female African-American astronaut. In 1987, inspired by watching Nichelle Nichols' portrayal of Uhura on *Star Trek*, she joined the NASA astronaut program. For five years she trained for space flight, supported launch activities at the Kennedy Space Center, and worked at the Shuttle Avionics Integration Laboratory before flying her first and only space mission on the Space Shuttle *Endeavour* in 1992 as a life sciences mission specialist.

If this were Jemison's only notable contribution, she would still be a hero worthy of the record books. However, this Renaissance woman's life was remarkable long before her historic shuttle flight, and continues to be remarkable to this day.

As a little girl, she was enamored of the arts and sciences. As early as kindergarten, she assumed that she would one day travel in space and that she would grow up to be a medical doctor (her interest in medicine, she says, began as a childhood fascination with pus). Her love for science was equaled by her love of the arts, which manifested itself most strongly as a passion for dance. She began training in a wide range of dance styles at the age of nine, and for a time wanted to be a professional dancer (and she has indeed choreographed and produced several shows of modern jazz and African dance).

Somewhat precocious, she graduated from high school and entered Stanford University at the age of 16. Four years later, she graduated with a B.S. in chemical engineering and a B.A. in African Studies. Four years after that, she received her doctor of medicine degree from Cornell Medical College. When she completed her medical internship, she spent two years in Liberia and Sierra Leone as a medical officer with the Peace Corps.

Following her historic career at NASA, Jemison started her own company, the Jemison Group, which develops science and technology for use in daily life. She also founded the Dorothy Jemison Foundation for Excellence, named for her mother, which promotes various projects such as international science camps for children and adults. Several years later, she founded BioSentient Corp, a company which is working to commercialize a patented NASA biofeedback technology.

She has also served on the board of directors of Gen-Probe Inc; as an honorary member of Alpha Kappa Alpha, a sorority founded in 1908 at Howard University to promote scholarship among black women; as a professor-at-large at Cornell University; and a professor of environmental studies at Dartmouth University.

To put it briefly, she has lived a life devoted to the betterment of humanity through the arts and sciences.

In 1993, her interest in Star Trek came full circle when she appeared as a guest on an episode of *Star Trek: The Next Generation*. She also appeared on television in 2006 as the subject of a profile on the show *African American Lives* for PBS. Since her historic mission on the Space Shuttle *Endeavour* in 1992, Mae Jemison has touched the lives of millions of Americans and given inspiration to countless women, minorities and young people. However, just as there have been no limits in her own life, there are no boundaries to the dream she represents and she has become a role model for all people, all around the world. She is the embodiment of the spirit that will take us to the stars.

Heart-wrenching Heroism at the Fukushima Nuclear Power Plant

When terrorists struck New York's twin towers on September 11, 2001, the world witnessed extraordinary acts of heroism from emergency personnel who sacrificed their lives to save innocent civilians. A decade later, the world witnessed a similar act of heroic sacrifice, although at a much slower and more agonizing pace than seen on 9/11. Every day, 400 workers at the Fukushima nuclear plant in Japan willingly exposed themselves to life-endangering radiation levels and terrible living conditions in a heroic effort to avert a nuclear meltdown.

The nuclear plant was damaged by the massive earthquake that struck northern Japan in early March of 2011. Weeks after the disaster, nightmarish details about what was going on at the Fukushima plant began to surface. According to news reports, the workers were "furiously connecting electrical cables, repairing instrument panels and pumping radioactive water out." Some workers were accidentally exposed to dangerously high levels of radiation. All worked long shifts under extreme stress. And many of them fully expected to die as a result of their repair efforts.

The Fukushima workers ate only two meals each day—"a carefully rationed breakfast of 30 crackers and vegetable juice and for dinner, a ready-to-eat meal or something out of a can" (Lee and Hancocks, 2011). In addition, because fresh uncontaminated water was in short supply, the workers had only wet wipes to clean themselves. If this weren't enough, many of the workers lived with the burden of their own personal tragedies weighing heavily on them. "My parents were washed away by the tsunami, and I still don't know where they are," one worker wrote in an email. "Crying is useless," said another worker. "If we're in hell now, all we can do is crawl up towards heaven."

Japanese authorities did everything in their power to assist and support the Fukushima workers. The task of repairing the facility, and cleaning up radioactive spills, took many months and by necessity involved putting the workers in harm's way. The heroism of these men is being recognized around the world, especially among Japanese civilians living nearby whose lives (and livelihoods) benefited the most from the noble sacrifice being made.

Time is an important concept in understanding heroism. A heroic act sometimes requires a split-second decision, such as Wesley Autrey's decision to save a man who fell onto a set of New York train tracks. But there are times, such as in Japan in 2011, when heroism involves a long-term commitment to place the welfare of others ahead of one's own welfare. One could argue that our greatest heroes are these latter heroes—those who understand full well, after ample deliberation, that their daily actions may be costly to themselves but who plow forward because they know their actions are absolutely essential for the collective well-being.

As with many heroes, the Fukushima workers downplayed their contributions. "In reality we are not heroes," said one worker, "as we are taking turns doing the work under supervision in accordance with law." Said another: "We have the option to turn down working at the plant. My family has told me to take it. It is a very difficult decision to make." But he, like the others, remained to do the job of protecting people, a job that heroes know they must do.

Randy Pausch: The Hero Who Dared Us to Live Our Dreams

Some heroes tug at our heartstrings by the way they live, and some by the way they die. Randy Pausch was a hero who did both. Pausch lived his life to the fullest, contributing significantly to the betterment of society and creating ways to fulfill even his most outlandish childhood dreams. Told by doctors at the age of 46 that he had terminal cancer, Pausch used the same unbridled enthusiasm that served him so well in life to make his final months immeasurably rich and inspiring to us all.

Randy Pausch was a Professor of Computer Science at Carnegie Mellon University in Pittsburgh. Although a highly acclaimed faculty member, he was largely unknown to most people outside his profession and university community. In 2006 his doctors gave him the devastating diagnosis—pancreatic cancer. With only months to live, Pausch was invited by Carnegie Mellon to give *The Last Lecture*—a speech in which eminent professors impart their final words of wisdom as if it were their last chance to do so. In Pausch's case, it truly was his last chance.

The lecture was entitled "Really Achieving Your Childhood Dreams," and it vaulted Pausch into the public spotlight. He opened his speech by informing the audience of his death sentence, but he relaxed the crowd with his trademark smile, the familiar bounce in his step, and his genuine enthusiasm. His last lecture focused on his many childhood ambitions, such as experiencing zero gravity, becoming Captain Kirk, playing professional football, and designing computer-based theme park rides for Disneyworld. Pausch spoke passionately about the importance of having dreams, and of having fun in the pursuit of those dreams. "I don't know how to not have fun," he said "I'm *dying* and I'm having fun. And I'm going to keep having fun every day I have left. Never lose the child-like wonder."

Pausch also implored his audience to persevere in life. "Never give up," he said. "Brick walls are there for a reason: they let us prove how badly we want things. Don't bail. The best of the gold is at the bottom of the barrels of crap." Pausch emphasized the importance of helping others, nurturing relationships, and remaining loyal to friends. "Do the right thing," he said. "When you do the right thing, good things have a way of happening." He added: "If you lead your life the right way, the karma will take care of itself. The dreams will come to you." At the conclusion of his lecture, Pausch received a lengthy standing ovation from a tearful, grateful audience.

Pausch's last lecture found its way onto YouTube, where it quickly went viral. Millions of people were moved by his inspiring life and by the courage with which he approached his terminal illness. His remaining months were very full and rich. Oprah Winfrey invited him to give an abridged version of his lecture on her show. He co-authored a *New York Times* best-selling book entitled *The Last Lecture*. The Pittsburgh Steelers heard of his dream to play in pro football and invited him to practice with them. J.J. Abrams, the director of 2009's *Star Trek* movie, heard that Pausch wanted to be Captain Kirk and permitted him to play a small part in the movie. During these last few months, Pausch underwent numerous painful procedures and treatments in an attempt to thwart his cancer. But he succumbed to his illness in July of 2008 at the age of 47.

After he was first diagnosed with terminal cancer, no one would have blamed Randy Pausch if he had simply disappeared from sight and spent private time with his family. Heroes, however, eschew the easy path. They selflessly share their time, their wisdom, and their love for others in an effort to make the world a better place. In fact, Pausch himself admitted that his intended audience for his *Last Lecture* was his three young children, ages three, six, and seven, to whom he wanted to leave a lasting legacy about how to live a good life. He surely did that, and more.

Gabrielle Giffords: Heroic Recovery From Trauma

As college professors, we sometimes require our students to read *Into Thin Air*, Jon Krakauer's gripping account of the May 11, 1996 Mount Everest disaster in which eight climbers were killed in a blizzard during their descent. Several heroic rescues occurred on the mountain that day, but one climber who didn't save any of the others is often viewed by our students to be the greatest hero of the tragedy. The climber's name is Beck Weathers, a Texas physician who sustained severe injuries on the mountain. Weathers was left for dead by his fellow climbers, yet somehow he managed to save *himself*.

Heroes, it seems, are not always the people who save others or who perform actions that make the world a better place. Heroes can also be individuals who survive horrific ordeals and triumph over great pain and injury. Presumed to be too close to death to be rescued, Beck Weathers roused himself from his hypothermic slumber and in near blindness stumbled on frostbitten feet back to his expedition's camp. For years he endured numerous painful surgeries to treat severe injuries that left his face and limbs disfigured. Today he is back practicing medicine. There are countless other examples of heroes who prevail over personal setbacks and tragedy—people who suffer crippling injuries as victims of accidents, crimes, or illness.

The story of Gabrielle Giffords follows this heroic narrative of recovery from trauma. On January 8, 2011, Giffords, a U.S. Representative from Arizona, held an open meeting with her constituents outside a suburban supermarket in Tucson. A crazed gunman appeared from the crowd and shot her in the head. The bullet passed through the left side of her brain, but somehow it did not kill her. Giffords' intern, a young man named Daniel Hernandez, tended to her injuries and was hailed for his heroic actions after the incident.

While we applaud the heroism of Hernandez and others who come to the aid of the sick and injured, we also believe that the long, difficult journey of the sick and injured makes them heroes as well. Giffords' road to recovery has been supremely challenging and will remain so for many years. At first, simply surviving her injury was the main goal. The next huge breakthrough was responding to simple commands by moving a finger. Giffords then overcame a significant hurdle by learning to breathe again on her own, and then later being able to sit up in bed.

The long-term rehabilitation process for someone with Giffords' injuries is "grueling," according to Dr. Christina Kwasnica, director of the Neuro Rehabilitation Program at St. Joseph's Hospital in Phoenix. "It's hard work. One of the hardest parts is realizing how long the road is." More than two years after the shooting, Giffords is still bravely immersed in a rigorous program of physical therapy, occupational therapy and speech therapy. Indications suggest that she is doing remarkably well, thanks to hard work, perseverance, and a supportive family. Still, Giffords has a long way to go. Brain injuries are remarkably complex, and doctors caution that there's a strong possibility she may never recover completely. We wish her all the best.

The heroic journey can take many different forms. The conventional view of heroes is that they save others from suffering, but inevitably we all find ourselves on the receiving end of a serious setback. In these instances, the most heroic act we can perform is to save ourselves.

Benjamin "Beast" Butler: Hero for a Moment

General Benjamin Butler is described in James McPherson's masterful history of the Civil War era, *Battle Cry of Freedom*, as the "ubiquitous" Benjamin Butler. Butler was a so-called "political general" from Massachusetts who was given a military position in the Union army because of his connections in Congress and his ability to raise troops in his home state. He served in Virginia early in the war, then oversaw martial law in New Orleans after it was captured by Union forces in 1862. It was there that he acquired the unflattering nickname "Beast Butler" for his harsh treatment of civilians. He also was called "Spoons Butler," after being accused of stealing silver from the owners of New Orleans homes he commandeered during his tenure in the Crescent City.

In 1864 Butler was back in Virginia but badly bungled several critical military assignments, infuriating Union commander Ulysses S. Grant. Once Lincoln was re-elected in November of 1864, Butler's political clout no longer mattered, and Lincoln allowed Grant to sack him.

Nothing thus far sounds very heroic about Butler, in terms of either the dimensions of competence or morality that we have stressed are essential to the perception of heroism. However, Butler did take a far-reaching step early in the war that paved the way for Lincoln's Emancipation Proclamation of January 1, 1863. While emancipation was long in coming, and resulted from many forces and events, Butler's contribution was timely and crucial.

It happened in May of 1861, the month immediately following the Confederate attack on Fort Sumter. That attack opened the actual fighting, which would last for over four years. Butler was stationed at Fort Monroe in Hampton, Virginia. The fort was essentially an island in the waters of Hampton Roads, connected to the mainland by a narrow strip of sand. Three slaves escaped from where they were working on rebel fortifications and ran down the ribbon of beach to the fort. The slaves' owner was a Confederate Colonel who came to Fort Monroe under a white flag of truce, demanding that Butler return the three slaves. He argued that the Fugitive Slave Act of 1850 required that Butler do so.

You might imagine how Butler, a savvy politician, reacted. He said, effectively, now let me see. You are an officer in the army of a self-declared nation that is trying to cast off the authority of the United States, but you'd like me to apply the laws of those United States for your benefit. Butler reminded the officer that the South regarded slaves as a "species of property" and it was a long-standing principle of warfare that enemies seize each other's property. Butler then declared the escaped slaves as "contraband of war" (i.e., captured property) and kept them at Fort Monroe.

Word spread in the African-American community, and soon hundreds of escaped slaves arrived behind Union lines at Fort Monroe, now known among slaves as the "freedom fort." Similar escapes happened in other parts of the Confederacy. Union politicians, including Abraham Lincoln, did not know how to treat these individuals. Were they free? Were they now just slaves in Union forces? In short order the U.S. Congress passed a number of "confiscation acts" that regulated the treatment of escaped slaves. It was quickly recognized that they could do important work for the Union, including bearing arms. Benjamin Butler's "contraband" decision thus paved the way for the emancipation policy that Lincoln announced preliminarily in September of 1862 and formalized in the Emancipation Proclamation of 1863. Butler's crucial contribution has generally been overlooked and overshadowed by his incompetence and self-aggrandizement. But he does earn the appellation Transitory Hero.

Liu Xiaobo: An Emerging Hero of Peace

Heroic journeys can assume many different forms. People can enjoy instant heroism through a single act, as in the case of New York subway hero Wesley Autrey. Or people can, through a steady commitment of doing good works, construct a resumé of heroism that reaches a crescendo of accomplishment and acclaim. Individuals who fall into this latter category are said to have spent their lives *trending* toward heroism. Such is the case of Liu Xiaobo, a Chinese intellectual, writer, and human rights activist whose passion for peace and justice earned him the 2010 Nobel Peace Price for his long-term dedication to promoting positive social change.

Because of his strident advocacy of human rights in China, Liu has spent much of his life either in a Chinese jail or in exile abroad. The Chinese government has imprisoned him several times for participating in the 1989 Tiananmen Square protests, for expressing his opposition to China's one-party Communist system, and for seeking the release of prisoners jailed for participating in various demonstrations. Liu's latest jail sentence stemmed from his role in organizing and disseminating a document called *Charter 08*, which calls for 19 changes to improve human rights in China. These reforms include establishing an independent legal system, granting citizens the freedom to assemble peacefully, and eliminating the Communist Party's grip on the nation.

Over the years, Liu's endorsement of political change in China has attracted increasing attention and admiration both inside and outside his country. The Norwegian Nobel Peace Prize committee in Oslo, Norway, was particularly interested in Liu's career. On October 8, 2010, the committee awarded him the Nobel Prize—and 1.5 million dollars—for "his long and non-violent struggle for fundamental human rights in China."

Not surprisingly, the Chinese government took quick action to suppress any news of the award. Broadcasts of the announcement in China by CNN were blacked out, and coverage of Liu Xiaobo's accomplishment on popular internet sites was removed. Moreover, electronic posts about Liu on China's Twitter-like service were quickly deleted, and any cell phone text messages with the Chinese characters for Liu Xiaobo were removed.

These repressive actions, of course, have had the effect of earning Liu even greater heroic status. We know from our studies on heroism that among our most revered heroes are underdogs who make significant self-sacrifices in the service of helping others. Liu's life story fits this heroic script to perfection. China's attempts to diminish Liu and his Nobel Prize-winning work have only given him greater fame and highlighted the urgency of his cause. Over the past several decades, formerly oppressive governments all around the globe have steadily begun permitting their citizens more freedoms of expression. China continues to resist embracing these freedoms, but thanks to the tireless efforts of dissidents such as Liu, it appears to be only a matter of time until sweeping changes occur in China.

Since Liu Xiaobo's award was announced on October 8, 2010, France, Germany, and Taiwan's main opposition party have all urged China to free him. The Dalai Lama, also seen as a traitor by China because of his struggle for Tibetan freedom, has formally congratulated Liu and called for his release. Two other former Nobel Peace Prize winners—Archbishop Desmond Tutu of South Africa and the Czech politician Vaclav Havel—have long been calling for Liu to get the Peace Prize and to be released from prison. Liu Xiaobo's wife, Liu Xia, was grateful that her husband received the award and also said, "I strongly ask that the Chinese government release Liu Xiaobo."

Was Liu any more of a hero after having won the Nobel Prize than he was prior to winning it? In our research, we have found that most people believe that it is the heroic work that makes a hero, not societal recognition. But some people believe that a central criterion for heroism is, indeed, recognition. Certainly, after having won the Nobel Prize, Liu and his dedication to social change in China are now known to millions of more people. Today we celebrate his sacrifice and heroism, and the Nobel Committee's acknowledgment of his work.

Christa McAuliffe: Lost Hero of the Space Shuttle *Challenger*

People often report that they can remember exactly where they were and what they were doing at the time they received the news of a shocking event. Psychologists call this *flashbulb* memory. If you are an American over the age of 35, you probably have a flashbulb memory of the crash of the Space Shuttle *Challenger*, which occurred more than 25 years ago on January 28, 1986.

Any deadly accident qualifies as a great tragedy, but what made the *Challenger* crash so especially poignant was the loss of one highly acclaimed crew member, Christa McAuliffe. Even prior to the shuttle's launch, the American public had embraced McAuliffe as a bold and generous hero about to embark on the kind of adventure that is usually the stuff of dreams.

McAuliffe was a New Hampshire high school teacher selected by NASA with great fanfare to become the first civilian in space. NASA screened 11,500 applicants and chose McAuliffe because of her teaching excellence, bubbling optimism, and boundless energy. She wrote on her application, "I watched the Space Age being born and I would like to participate" (Burgess, 2000, p. 20). NASA asked McAuliffe to assume the role of teacher in space and transmit lessons back to earth about experiencing zero gravity and other space-related phenomena.

Millions of McAuliffe's fans, many of them schoolchildren, were glued to their television sets to witness the launch of her shuttle. A mere 73 seconds after *Challenger* took off into space, it exploded. The nation was in grief-stricken shock. Six other heroic crew members lost on that day were Francis R. Scobee, Michael J. Smith, Judith A. Resnik, Ronald E. McNair, Ellison S. Onizuka, and Gregory B. Jarvis.

In the aftermath of the tragedy, the best of human nature quickly surfaced. Letters, poetry, postcards, and words of sympathy flooded the mailboxes of the surviving members of the McAuliffe family. These loving words came from people from all walks of life, especially teachers and schoolchildren. The letters came from all corners of the globe: the town of Hamilton, Scotland; the Belgian town of Zele; the city of Sydney, Australia; the ancient Egyptian city of Heliopis; along with Paris, London, Athens, and Hong Kong. Many more came from around the United States. Each letter conveyed the hurt, the sorrow, and the powerful influence that Christa McAuliffe had on people's lives.

McAuliffe's husband Steven said that remembrances of Christa were "comforting and inspirational for our family." Within hours of the tragedy, President Reagan gave a moving speech in honor of the *Challenger* crew. "We mourn seven heroes," Reagan told the grieving public. He spoke especially to children: "I know it's hard to understand, but sometimes painful things like this happen. It's all part of the process of exploration and discovery."

Perhaps the most powerful legacy of Christa McAuliffe was her passion for teaching. "I touch the future," she said. "I teach." With these words, McAuliffe recognized that teachers leave their marks on the world long after they are gone. Quite remarkably, and by accident, NASA engineer Jerry Woodfill stumbled across McAuliffe's unfinished lesson plans 21 years after *Challenger* crashed. These lessons are now available online for any school or teacher to use, and for anyone to see.

Over a quarter of a century after McAuliffe's untimely end, she is still viewed as a hero to millions of people who admired her for pursuing her dream to participate in space flight and to share her knowledge with others. "She was the ultimate teacher," said Dennis Van Roekel, President of the National Education Association. "She not only engaged in this extraordinary venture to captivate the imagination of students, Christa wanted to elevate the teaching profession so students would aspire to teach" (Burgess, 2000, p. 177).

The Heroism and Leadership of Fred Korematsu

Heroes show leadership by taking steps to save or improve our lives. As stated before, a hero's leadership can be *direct*, as when the leader interacts directly with followers, or it can be *indirect*, as when the leader's works and deeds provide an example or model for others. Two of the twentieth century's greatest indirect leaders were Rosa Parks and Fred Korematsu. Parks became a civil rights hero when she refused to vacate her seat on a Montgomery, Alabama bus in 1955. Korematsu's indirect leadership is not as well known but is no less important.

Korematsu was an ordinary 22-year-old American living in Oakland, California, when Japan attacked Pearl Harbor on December 7, 1941. In the weeks that followed, Americans feared another Japanese attack on the west coast of the United States. Racial discrimination against Japanese-Americans, already a problem before Pearl Harbor, became intensified. Korematsu was fired from his job as a welder in a shipyard, simply because of his ancestry. Ten weeks after the attack, President Roosevelt issued Executive Order No. 9066, which required all people of Japanese ancestry along the entire Pacific coast, including all of California and most of Oregon and Washington, to leave their homes and report to internment camps. At the time, most Americans supported Roosevelt's decision. Even the *Los Angeles Times* defended it: "While it might cause injustice to a few to treat them all as potential enemies," wrote the editor, "I cannot escape the conclusion ... that such treatment ... should be accorded to each and all of them while we are at war with their race."

Most Japanese-Americans complied with Executive Order 9066 to demonstrate their loyalty to America and its laws. But Korematsu recognized the inherent injustice of the decree. "I was just living my life, and that's what I wanted to do," he said in a 1987 interview.

Korematsu did not turn himself in to authorities. Consequently, he was arrested, jailed, convicted of a felony, and sent to the Topaz internment camp in Utah.

While imprisoned at the camp, Korematsu appealed his conviction, arguing that his constitutional rights had been violated. The court ruled against him. In 1944 he appealed all the way to the Supreme Court, which upheld his conviction in a 6–3 decision, authored by Justice Hugo Black. The court ruled that Executive Order 9066, though constitutionally suspect, is justified during times of "emergency and peril".

After the war, Korematsu waited nearly 40 years to clear his name. In 1982 he obtained suppressed government documents indicating that the forced relocation of Americans to internment camps was motivated by racism, not military necessity. With this evidence, the courts overturned Korematsu's conviction. In 1998, President Bill Clinton awarded Korematsu the Presidential Medal of Freedom, the nation's highest civilian honor. At the ceremony Clinton said, "In the long history of our country's constant search for justice, some names of ordinary citizens stand for millions of souls. To that distinguished list today we add the name of Fred Korematsu."

Heroism can take time. Leaders know when to stay the course, and heroic leaders such as Korematsu stay the course to its triumphant conclusion. "It may take time to prove you're right," he said, "but you have to stick to it." In the face of injustice, he urged people "to protest, but not with violence, and don't be afraid to speak up. One person can make a difference, even if it takes forty years."

Ephemeral Heroes and Villains: A Tale of Two Stevens

A recurring theme in our review of heroes is the idea that heroism is in the eye of the beholder. One person's hero is another person's villain. While we acknowledge the subjectivity of heroism, there is no denying the fact that some people are much more heroic than others. Two heroes whom we profile in this book, Mahatma Gandhi and Nelson Mandela, have clearly had a far more positive and enduring impact on the world than two others we profile, Lady Gaga and Pretty Boy Floyd.

In our taxonomy of heroism, described earlier, we suggested that some heroes are ephemeral or transitory in their influence. They are at one end of the duration-of-influence continuum, with Transforming Heroes who forever change society at the other end. Interestingly, this same continuum also applies to villains and the negative deeds that they do. Ephemeral villains are bad guys whose badness is minor or fleeting, whereas transforming villains (e.g., Adolf Hitler) perform acts of evil that have truly altered the world permanently.

One Transitory Hero who received considerable media attention a few years ago is the former JetBlue flight attendant, Steven Slater. You may recall that Slater was the man who resigned his position in a blaze of glory. On August 9, 2010, after the aircraft on which he was working landed safely, Slater shouted obscenities at a customer who was rude to him, grabbed beer out of the plane's kitchen galley, and slid down the plane's emergency evacuation chute. Slater became a folk hero to millions of working Americans who admired him for acting out the famous Johnny Paycheck song, "Take This Job and Shove It." Slater attracted over 200,000 Facebook admirers, and people even composed songs in his honor.

Conversely, a prominent example of a transitory villain is Steve Bartman, a Chicago Cubs fan who tried to catch a foul ball during Game 6 of the 2003 National League Championship series. Bartman's outstretched hands deflected the ball, possibly preventing Cubs' left-fielder Moises Alou from catching it. Given new life, the batter eventually drew a walk and scored, sparking a comeback for the Florida Marlins, who won the game and the series. Bartman instantly became a target of hatred. He had to be led away from the stadium under security escort for his own safety as Cubs fans shouted profanities at him and pelted him with debris. He also received police protection after his name and address were made public on baseball message boards.

What does this tale of two Stevens tell us? It tells us that transitory heroes and villains don't enjoy the spotlight for very long. Ten years from now, most people will hardly remember Slater and Bartman. Unlike transforming heroes and villains, transitory individuals tend to perform actions that affect only a small, inconsequential slice of life. Transitory heroes and villains capture our attention for a brief while, but like a helium balloon with a slow leak, they soon sink to their former level of anonymity.

Chapter 4

Transitional Heroes
Those Whom We Outgrow

Heroes offer inspirational models of accomplished performance and moral commitment. Throughout our lifetimes, most of us have had a long list and wide range of heroes. Some may be fleeting, and some may be lasting. Some who are no longer our heroes may have been important to us at particular points in our psychological development. But they are no longer heroes because we have moved on to other aims and aspirations. The persons who inspired us at age ten, for example, might not be psychologically relevant as adults. When we were younger, baseball All Star Willie Mays was a hero known for his amazing abilities, and his cheerful athleticism and dedicated achievement. We were inspired to work as hard and happily and effectively as Willie. Internalizing aspects of his heroism helped us develop beyond the domain in which he motivated us.

But then life changes. As a Little Leaguer we needed Willie's example. As a college sophomore, his qualities no longer mattered. We had moved on to later stages of development with different concerns and priorities. Similarly, in high school, the Beach Boys mattered. As graduate students, we had moved on. Great scholars and perhaps political leaders were our heroes.

We call the heroes who helped define our identities and shape our motivations at early stages of development *Transitional Heroes*. The term Transitional Hero resonates with Winnicott's (1953) concept of the transitional object, defined as some prized, private object that gives a young child a sense of security and helps her or him take the first steps toward autonomy. An iconic example of a transitional object is Linus' dirty, well-worn blanket in the comic strip, *Peanuts*. It was his source of "security and happiness" (Schulz, 1956). As we develop, we need

Mr. Spock and Captain Kirk: Transitional Heroes

heroes as well as objects to cling to, even if they are only revealed to us through books, magazines, records, or movies. They influence us for important parts of our unfolding lives, but not as we move past those periods.

As always, heroism is in the eye of the beholder. One person's transitional hero may be a long-lasting, life-span hero for another. Country and Western singer Patsy Cline was a hero to some young women only for a time, but remains a hero much later in life for others. It's also true that some individuals may be transitional heroes during important youthful life passages, then fade in influence, and then perhaps re-emerge later in life as a heroic figure. One of us greatly admired Elvis Presley as a pre-teen. Then Elvis changed, making some truly horrible movies and becoming an almost weird, overweight, drug-addled caricature of himself. Elvis left the building, so to speak, and so did the author. Later, both of us realized the huge impact Elvis had on not only American but on world culture. Now he has regained his heroic status in our eyes. To us, he is The King.

Our profiles of Transitional Heroes begins with Justin Bieber, the young Canadian popstar, who has been rated on an online "influence" scale as having more impact than Barack Obama. As a mid-teen, Bieber tried to appear younger than he was, perhaps in an effort to capture the pre-teen and young teen audience. As he's grown into an adult, he remains a hero to many young fans, and may doubt that his hold on them will last when his admirers leave their mid-teen years. As long as he looks more like 14 than 19 (his age at this writing, 2013) he is likely to gain new admirers. If he is a transitional hero, as we suspect, even the newly inspired will move on to other heroes as they mature.

A classic example of a transitional hero is former children's television host Mr. Rogers. *Mister Rogers' Neighborhood* on PBS provided a safe, comforting educational environment for young boys and girls for over 40 years. Fred Rogers qualifies as a Transitional Hero because many of the children he meant so much to in pre-school forgot him or even mocked him during their adolescent years. But Mr. Rogers wonderfully illustrates the point that some transitional figures can become heroes at more than one stage of development. Many men and women who admired Mr. Rogers as youngsters in the 1970s likely found him heroic again in the early 2000s when he served as heroes for their own children.

Reed Richards, a.k.a. Mr. Fantastic, and Iron Man perfectly exemplify the comic book superhero. Each has a complicated and inspiring, if troubled, life history and provides pleasant and even somewhat daring escapism for boys and girls (mostly boys) of a certain age. They inspire those youngsters, but for most admirers their heroism is likely to be fleeting. Again we thank Rick Hutchins for composing a very clever profile of Reed Richards.

We find Captain James T. Kirk of the *Star Trek* series among our most interesting transitional heroes. He provided a strong example of effective and mostly moral leadership. Although he was often distracted by attractive women, when the chips were down we could always count on Kirk to do the right thing. For one of us he was "only" a transitional hero, having lost favor and influence after college. For the other, he always has been and probably always will be a hero ("Till death do us part"). The former author decided where to classify him.

As a group the heroes we describe in this chapter illustrate how our interests, motives and aspirations change over time, and with them, our heroes.

Justin Bieber: Heroic Pop Star

For many talented teens, achieving fame and fortune in the entertainment industry is a precursor to personal turmoil and self-destruction. The career paths of young stars such as Britney Spears and Lindsay Lohan are vivid illustrations of how easily a young talent can become derailed by drug abuse and criminal behavior. Success at a young age can indeed be fragile and ruinous.

With this caveat in mind, we focus on Justin Bieber, a young singer who has been trending toward heroism for several years. Some might say that he, along with Lady Gaga, is already there. As he's been trending upward, Bieber has had to face many self-defining decisions: Will he make mature choices? Will he continue to give back to the society that has given him so much? Or will he follow the sullied and chaotic paths of Spears and Lohan? Only time will continue to tell. For several reasons, it is difficult not to root for Bieber to do well. In a very real sense he is an underdog who has prevailed. As an ordinary 13-year-old living in Canada in 2004, he and his mother began loading onto YouTube a few homemade video clips of him singing. A man named Scooter Braun discovered these videos, contacted Bieber's mother, flew them down to Atlanta to record some songs, and became his manager.

Bieber's skillful vocals, humble attitude, and good looks made him an instant hit. There's no doubt that two years after being discovered, he had become a bona fide star. But most importantly, Bieber has managed to successfully accomplish two things that suggest he continues to trend favorably toward heroism. First, he has avoided displaying the personal recklessness of Britney Spears and Lindsay Lohan. Occasional missteps are to be expected, but a key to Bieber becoming a legitimate hero is to evade the embarrassing bouts of self-destruction that have beset so many teen megastars before him. Another reason we believe that Bieber's trajectory remains upward is his significant involvement in charity work. He has given much of his time and money to many good causes, including Jumpstart, Haitian relief funds, Nashville's flood fund, education, literacy, and numerous children's charities. "It's really important that I'm able to help out other kids," he said in 2010. "I'm a kid myself, so it means a lot to me."

Our research on heroes shows that people use two major criteria to label someone a hero. One criterion is having a great ability, and the other is showing great morality. From what we can see about the early career path of Justin Bieber, he is beginning to excel in both the ability and morality dimensions of heroism. A talented singer, Bieber treats his fans well and is a fine role model for young people. At the same time, he is still young and faces the many challenges of dealing with success. In the coming years he will encounter many temptations and countless crucial decision points where a disastrous choice can easily be made. We wish him well along his journey.

Fred Rogers: Love, Wisdom, and Compassion for Children

About twenty years ago, a friend of ours was in the throes of a major depression. As she lay listlessly on the couch one day, feeling the weight of the world on her shoulders, she flipped through the television channels and came across the classic children's television program *Mister Rogers' Neighborhood*. Struck by the show's gentle, loving host Fred Rogers, our friend penned a letter to him, expressing her grief and hopelessness, but also her appreciation for briefly lifting her spirits with his message of love and hope. A week later, to her great surprise, she received a handwritten letter back from Rogers, who thanked her for writing and gave her encouragement and support. To this day the framed letter from Rogers hangs on the wall of our friend's home, and she remains deeply grateful to him for reaching out to her during the most difficult time in her life.

Not surprisingly, Fred Rogers wrote many such letters to his fans. In an age when celebrity misbehavior and drug use capture most of the headlines, Rogers was a true gentleman whose primary mission in life was to enrich the lives of other people, especially children. As a young man, Rogers noticed during television's infancy how the new medium was being misused. "I went into television because I hated it so," said Rogers. "I thought there was some way of using this fabulous instrument to be of nurture to those who would watch and listen."

Rogers developed a show in 1968 that helped children build self-esteem, conquer their fears, and love others. *Mister Rogers' Neighborhood* encouraged children to become happy and productive citizens. It was the longest-running program on public television, lasting 33 years and finally ending its run in 2001. Rogers was an American icon of children's education and a symbol of compassion and morality. He became such a beloved figure that one day, when the media reported that his car had been stolen, the thieves immediately returned the car to the exact spot from which it was taken, with an apology on the dashboard. It read, "If we'd known it was yours, we never would have taken it."

While accepting a Lifetime Achievement Award at the 1997 Emmy Awards Show, Rogers approached the microphone and said, "All of us have special ones who have loved us into being. Would you just take, along with me, ten seconds to think of the people who have helped you become who you are. Ten seconds of silence." Tears began to flow from the eyes of many in the audience. Rogers finally looked up from his watch and softly said, "Whomever you are thinking about, how pleased they must be to know the difference you feel they've made." Actor LeVar Burton recalls a time when Rogers was invited to a gathering at the White House, and he asked everybody, including President Clinton, to close their eyes for 60 seconds and think about someone who had helped shape them. Again people wept. "Fred felt it was critical to acknowledge those who have helped us come into being," said Burton. "And Fred's legacy is that he is that person for so many of us."

Rogers was awarded the Presidential Medal of Freedom in 2002, and one year later, after Rogers passed away at the age of 74, the U.S. Senate approved a resolution to commemorate his life. It read, in part,

Through his spirituality and placid nature, Mr. Rogers was able to reach out to our nation's children and encourage each of them to understand the important role they play in their communities and as part of their families. More importantly, he did not shy away from dealing with difficult issues of death and divorce but rather encouraged children to express their emotions in a healthy, constructive manner, often providing a simple answer to life's hardships.

To the very end of his life, Rogers encouraged people to love one another and to appreciate the deep connections all humans have with each other. Shortly before he died, while giving a commencement speech at Dartmouth College in 2002, he said,

Our world hangs like a magnificent jewel in the vastness of space. Every one of us is a part of that jewel, a facet of that jewel. And in the perspective of infinity, our differences are infinitesimal. We are intimately related.

Reed Richards: Fantastic Family Man

Heroism is a concept that stretches from the subtle to the grandiose. Heroes come in all shapes and sizes, in both reality and fiction. From saving the Earth to toppling dictators to stopping the foreclosure on the ranch to rescuing a frightened kitten from a tree, the actions of heroes are necessary in all aspects of the human experience to cushion the wrongs that we suffer. Reed Richards is a man who is flexible enough to fill all these roles.

Demonstrating from an early age a pliable genius that was both creative and crafty, Reed used his gifts in the service of his fellow man at every opportunity. In World War II, he served behind enemy lines in occupied France, risking his life and applying his unmatched intellect to espionage and military intelligence, doing his part to bring the conflict to a quicker end. In the Cold War with the Soviets that followed, he feared that the communists would gain prestige and prominence by winning the Space Race, and so he devoted all his efforts to ensuring that the United States would be the first nation to reach the moon.

It was the urgency of this effort that led to his greatest failure, as well as the most amazing development in his life and the lives of his closest friends. Refusing to wait for official clearance, Reed decided that he must go to great lengths to ensure success in this endeavor. Accompanied by his best friend, Ben Grimm, a former test pilot, his fiancee Susan Storm and her brother Johnny, he launched his rocket into space. Unfortunately, he lacked the data to properly calculate the strength of cosmic rays and the ship was forced down to a hard landing; all aboard survived, but, alarmingly, they had been affected by the cosmic rays. Each had been endowed with a fantastic, but frightening, super power: Ben had become a misshapen monster, Johnny could burst into flame, Sue was invisible, and Reed's body had become as stretchable and moldable as plastic.

Despite the trauma of the mission's catastrophic failure and the strange changes they had undergone, Reed was resilient enough to realize that they now possessed greater power than anyone in the world—his knee-jerk reaction, and his friends agreed, was that they must use their powers to help mankind.

In the years that followed, Reed (known now to the world as Mister Fantastic) led his team on many heroic adventures. He defended the world from conquest by his arch-rival and fellow genius Doctor Doom and the prince of Atlantis, the Sub-Mariner; he continued to battle communists, such as the Red Ghost; he repelled several alien invasions, notably the recurring incursions mounted by the Skrulls; ultimately, he saved the entire planet from destruction at the hands of the world-devouring Galactus. Throughout all this, no matter what menaces were demanding his attention, he never stopped seeking a cure for the disfigurement that Ben had suffered on their initial space flight.

In 1968, he had married Susan, and she was pregnant with their first child; but he learned that the cosmic radiation in her body threatened the lives of her and the baby. The only cure lay in a dangerous alternate dimension called the Negative Zone and was in possession of a powerful, hostile creature called Annihilus. In the company of Ben and Johnny—who refused to let him go alone—he braved the deadly peril of the Negative Zone and returned with the cure. Of all the heroic actions performed by Reed Richards over the years, surely this is the one which defines him: He is a man who literally went beyond the ends of the Earth to save the life of his unborn child.

Though the influence of Reed Richards extends around the globe and reaches to the stars, he is ultimately a family man: husband, father and friend. He is the person in your life who you know won't fail you when you need to be saved.

Captain James T. Kirk: The Hero Who Treks the Stars

From surveying people's beliefs about fictional heroes, we've discovered an ironic fact. "They're the only *real* heroes," summed up one of our respondents. Why are fictional heroes seemingly so real to us, and so beloved? The reason is that creators of fictional heroes ensure that their characters embody the central elements of heroism. In this way fictional heroes serve as hero *prototypes*, unmistakably capturing our view of the ideal heroic figure.

James T. Kirk, the main protagonist from the Star Trek franchise of movies and television, is an excellent example of the perfect male fictional hero. His character was developed by Gene Roddenberry, who created and produced the original *Star Trek* television series shown on NBC from 1966 to 1969. Roddenberry conceived *Star Trek* as a cowboy western set in space, "a wagon train to the stars," combining elements of *Buck Rogers* and *Flash Gordon*. Set in the twenty-third century, *Star Trek* portrays the future as a near-utopia in which poverty, hunger, and warfare on earth have all been overcome.

In *Star Trek*, James Kirk explores the galaxy as Captain of the U.S.S. *Enterprise*, whose mission is "to explore strange new worlds, to seek out new life and new civilizations, to boldly go where no man has gone before." The show was well ahead of its time in featuring racial and gender diversity among the crew, and using dazzling futuristic technologies such as computer discs and cell phone-like communicators.

The original Captain Kirk, played by William Shatner, was the quintessential male hero of the 1960s. As a young student, his keen intellect and brashness had enabled him to win an "unwinnable" computer battle simulation called the *Kobayashi Maru*. As Captain of the *Enterprise*, Kirk cleverly thinks his way out of impossibly adverse circumstances against more advanced alien life forms. The late Randy Pausch revealed that he became a better teacher, colleague, and husband because of Kirk's leadership skills. "For ambitious boys with a scientific bent," said Pausch, "there could be no greater role model than James T. Kirk."

Shatner's portrayal of Kirk was also intended to attract the attention of female fans. Kirk was handsome and a hopeless flirt around women, both human and alien. It was not unusual during fight scenes for Kirk to have his shirt ripped off, baring his upper torso. His sense of humor, playfulness, and soft romantic side also contributed to his sex appeal.

Perhaps more than any other quality, Kirk's selflessness made him a phenomenal hero. His selfless qualities were best revealed in a highly acclaimed episode, *City on the Edge of Forever*, which won a 1968 Hugo Award for best science fiction dramatic presentation. In this episode, Kirk travels back in time to the 1930s and falls in love with Edith Keeler, played by Joan Collins. He then discovers that, in the normal timeline, Edith dies in a traffic accident; otherwise, she will lead a peace movement that delays America's entry into World War II, enabling Germany to defeat the Allies. Although Kirk has the ability to prevent her death, in a heart-wrenching scene he allows the fatal accident to occur, thereby saving the lives of millions.

In 2009 the *Star Trek* franchise received a much-needed boost with the critical and box-office success of *Star Trek XI*, starring Chris Pine as a young James Kirk. Although Pine's portrayal of Kirk was unmistakably his own, he did retain much of Shatner's brash charisma and intelligence. The success of *Star Trek XI* ensures that we'll see the character of James Kirk in the movies, and possibly on television, for many years to come. In keeping with more modern renditions of superheroes, such as Iron Man, *Star Trek XI* has given Kirk a somewhat darker edge to his character. We look forward to following the development of James Kirk's heroic leadership in future installments of *Star Trek*.

Iron Man: A Classic Superhero in the Modern World

Comic book superheroes have long captured people's imaginations. The proto-typical superhero has an extraordinary power or ability, a secret identity, a strong moral code, a striking costume, a sidekick, and a mortal enemy. The world inhabited by the superhero is typically dark and sinister, with a formidable villain posing grave danger to the general population. Only the superhero can save this world. He or she (but usually he) triumphs by overcoming three types of obstacles: family or origin issues, a unique personal vulnerability, and the fearsome villain.

The latest superhero enjoying great popularity is Iron Man, portrayed in two recent movies by Robert Downey, Jr. Iron Man made his first appearance in a Marvel Comics book in 1963, at the height of America's Cold War with the Soviet Union. Iron Man's secret identity is Tony Stark, a brilliant weapons designer who suffers a severe heart injury while being kidnapped by a foreign menace. In the original comic version, the kidnappers are Russians; in the first *Iron Man* movie, they are Afghan terrorists. To save his life and aid his escape, he constructs a powered suit of armor that transforms him into a nearly unstoppable human weapon.

What accounts for the great critical and box-office success of the *Iron Man* movies? There are several factors. First, the part of Tony Stark is played superbly by Robert Downey, Jr., who is both charismatic and likeable. Second, as viewers of Stark's remarkable accomplishments, we are especially impressed because he is a man without an innate superpower. He relies solely on his superb mind and fierce determination to overcome his enemies.

Third, the *Iron Man* movies have successfully put a modern spin on many of the classic superhero themes. For example, narcissism, rather than humility, is seen as a virtue. In place of the Cold War is the threat of terrorism, to which all modern viewers can relate. Modern technological gadgets are portrayed as the solution to the world's problems; we even witness Robert Downey, Jr. use his cell phone to hack into the U.S. government mainframe. There is racial and gender diversity, with African-Americans and women showing as much physical prowess and genius as Tony Stark himself.

But with all these modern trappings, *Iron Man* owes most of its success to its effective use of the classic elements of the heroic journey. There is a poign-ant origin story, featuring Stark's emotionally unavailable father who plants the seeds of greatness in his son. There is adversity for Stark to overcome, namely his damaged heart that is failing him and requires his genius to repair. The villain in *Iron Man 2* is an evil Russian physicist, who is nearly Stark's intellectual equal. Stark's inherent goodness is highlighted when he saves a small boy from certain death at the hands of the villain.

Iron Man 2 also emphasizes the hero's reliance on social support to achieve his noble goals. Early in the movie, Stark notes with pride that he has no sidekick, yet in the final battle with the villain he concedes that he needs help from his friend, James Rhodes. The movie ends with Stark winning the heart of his beautiful female love interest, Pepper Potts, played by Gwyneth Paltrow. Throughout the story, Stark receives important assistance from both Potts and the physically formidable Natalie Rushman, played by Scarlett Johansson.

Why are we drawn to superheroes? Put simply, we admire their ability to overcome imposing obstacles, and triumph over evil using powers we all fantasize about having. In a dark world, their actions shine the light of hope and promise for a better tomorrow.

Chapter 5

Tragic Heroes
The Self-Destruction of Greatness

As we've noted earlier, heroism can be fragile and fleeting. The pedestal on which heroes stand is not a large, stable platform, but rather a tenuous, narrow ledge from which heroes can plunge if they take one small misstep. It seems that rarely a day passes when the news media fail to report a story about a hero who has self-destructed in some way. A great hero who possesses a tragic flaw that leads to his or her self-destruction is called a *Tragic Hero*.

Great playwrights throughout history have recognized that tales of Tragic Heroes pack considerable dramatic punch. Sophocles' story of King Oedipus contains the timeless story of a great king whose pride and impulsivity lead him to fulfill a prophecy that he would marry his mother and kill his father. Moreover, the works of Shakespeare feature many unforgettable Tragic Heroes, including King Lear, Hamlet, Macbeth, and Brutus.

Hubris is the most common flaw of the Tragic Hero. Prideful arrogance has been the undoing of many leaders who allow power to go to their heads. Lord Acton was famous for saying "power corrupts; absolute power corrupts absolutely." A surprising amount of research confirms Acton's observation. Power frees people from restraint and accountability, and has the overall effect of disinhibiting goal-directed and instinctive behavior. And it sometimes leads us to disregard other people's perspectives as we focus on our own agenda. The research showing these effects is based on observations of college students in a lab setting who are made to feel momentarily more or less powerful. In one study, participants who were made to feel powerful were more likely to get up and turn off an annoying fan than others who did not feel powerful. The latter just let the fan blow on them.

Tiger Woods: A Tragic Hero

Other research has shown that people who felt powerful were more likely to eat the last cookie on a plate of shared snacks. And they were less careful about getting crumbs on the table. They went about satisfying their feeding instincts in an unrestrained way. And even sexual instincts were uninhibited. Both men and women who feel powerful are more likely to flirt. This finding underscores former Secretary of State Henry Kissinger's comment in 1973 that "power is the ultimate aphrodisiac." Support for this idea also comes from the real world as well as from the psychology laboratory. Presidential scholar Theodore H. White, in writing about President John F. Kennedy and First Lady Jacqueline Kennedy, noted that he "knew that Kennedy loved his wife—but that Kennedy, the politician, exuded that musk odor of power which acts as an aphrodisiac to many women" (White, 1978).

According to White, only three presidential candidates he had ever met had denied themselves the pleasures invited by that aphrodisiac—Harry Truman, George Romney, and Jimmy Carter. He was reasonably sure that all the others he had met had, at one time or another, on the campaign trail, accepted casual partners. "The noise, the shrieking, the excitement of crowds, and then the power, the silent pickup and delivery in limousines, set the glands alive in women as in men." Many politicians have ruined their political careers by cheating on their spouses, sometimes in the most embarrassing ways possible. Former U.S. President Bill Clinton knows this all too well.

In this section of the book we include profiles of three Tragic Heroes who allowed their fame, success, and power to compromise their good judgment. We begin with the aforementioned story of King Oedipus, who ascends to become the monarch of Thebes and makes the tragic assumption that his self-will can overcome an irrevocable prophecy. The more Oedipus attempts to take control of an uncontrollable situation, the more his life unravels. Next we turn to a modern-day example of a Tragic Hero: American golfer Tiger Woods. No human being has ever been better groomed to be a sports hero—and to remain one—than Tiger Woods. Although Tiger was prepared to achieve greatness on the golf course, he was far less prepared to handle success and to live life under the media microscope. The exposure of his marital infidelities, and the media circus that followed, absolutely devastated him. Tiger's career and image on and off the golf course suffered a ravaging blow from which he may never fully recover.

Finally, we examine the life and tragedy of former U.S. President Richard Nixon. As president, Nixon engineered some notable achievements. He was the first president to establish formal relations with China, and he ended America's long involvement in the Vietnam War. But his eternal legacy will always be his terrible mishandling of a break-in at the Watergate hotel by members of his re-election committee. Nixon's decision to cover up the incident led to a tragic downward spiral that culminated in his resignation in disgrace. The unfortunate tales of Oedipus, Woods, and Nixon underscore the hidden dangers of assuming the power and fame associated with great leadership. It appears that to be human is to be prone to intoxication by success, which is a sure recipe for tragedy.

Oedipus the King: The Classic Tragic Hero

Human beings have long pondered whether their outcomes in life are determined by free will or by forces beyond their control. More than 2,500 years ago the ancient Greek playwright Sophocles brilliantly placed this issue in the context of heroism: To what extent is heroism chosen versus destined? And when heroes fall, how much are they responsible?

The play, *Oedipus the King*, tells the story of the mythical king of Thebes whose parents (Laius and Jocasta) are warned by an oracle that any son born to them would kill his father and marry his mother. After Jocasta bears a son, Laius instructs a servant to kill the young infant, but the servant takes pity on the boy and gives him to a shepherd, who takes him to Corinth. The King and Queen of Corinth, who are without children, adopt the young child and call him Oedipus. As a young man, Oedipus learns of the prophecy that he is to murder his father and marry his mother. To avoid fulfilling this fate, Oedipus flees Corinth and travels to Thebes.

During his journey, Oedipus encounters his true father, Laius, at a crossing of roads and the two men have a road-rage incident. Oedipus kills Laius, unwittingly fulfilling the first part of the prophecy. Before arriving at Thebes, Oedipus correctly answers the riddle of the Sphinx, who kills herself, thus freeing Thebes from her harsh rule. Oedipus arrives at Thebes a hero, is crowned King, and is awarded the widowed Jocasta's hand in marriage, thus fulfilling the second part of the prophecy. The remainder of the play describes Oedipus' gradual recognition of how he and others have tragically fulfilled the prophecy. Irony abounds—a blind prophet allows Oedipus to "see" what he has done, and when Oedipus gains full awareness, he gouges out his eyes. Throughout the play, the more that characters try to avoid their fate, the more they take actions that inadvertently guarantee its fruition.

Oedipus possesses the traits of many great heroes, most especially intelligence and courage. These traits allow him to answer the Sphinx's riddle, despite knowing the fate of those who had failed to solve the riddle before him. But as with all tragic heroes, Oedipus' faults are his ultimate undoing. His impulsive temper at the crossroads precipitates his deadly attack on Laius, and his thirst for ambition leads him to become the monarch of Thebes. Pride is the primary instrument of Oedipus' demise, and the Chorus in the play underscores this idea: "Pride breeds the tyrant violent pride, gorging, crammed to bursting with all that is overripe and rich with ruin. . . . Can such a man, so desperate, still boast he can save his life from the flashing bolts of god?" (Sophocles, 2001; 429 BCE, p. 83).

Earlier in this book we noted that heroic leadership requires great vision. One of the lessons of Oedipus is that true greatness in leadership requires vision combined with favorable circumstances. Oedipus' circumstances spelled doom from the start, and thus Oedipus' vision for greatness is equally doomed. After gouging his eyes, he notes, "What good were eyes to me? Nothing I could see could bring me joy" (p. 117).

Tiger Woods: The Ebb and Flow of Fame and Fortune

"Hello world." With these words, the heroic journey of a golf legend was launched. The statement was uttered at a press conference in August of 1996 by a skinny 20-year-old phenom named Tiger Woods, who had just finished shattering every meaningful amateur golf record in sight. Tiger was now announcing to the world that he was turning professional. Soon after the statement, Tiger began winning tournaments and seizing the public's attention. He showed an unprecedented mental toughness and physics-defying shot-making ability. No doubt, during the fall of 1996, Tiger Woods was a hero in the making.

At the 1997 Masters Tournament, Tiger's first major golf championship as a pro, he crushed the competition by a record 12 strokes. From 1997 to 2008, Tiger made the transition from a hero-on-the-rise to arguably the greatest golfer the world has ever seen. He appeared invincible. Opponents crumbled when they played with Tiger. The intimidation was palpable.

People once said of golfing great Jack Nicklaus that "Jack knew he was going to beat you. You knew Jack was going to beat you. And Jack knew that you knew that he was going to beat you." The same principle applied to Tiger Woods. For 12 years he was on top of the golf world, a hero to millions, and one of the most recognized celebrities on the planet.

But in 2009, Tiger's world crumbled. An auto accident outside his home was revealed to stem from a domestic dispute with his wife about Tiger's extramarital affairs. His wife and children left him, precipitating a four-month hiatus from golf and participation in a treatment program. Since his return to golf in 2010, Tiger's game has not been the same. He no longer wins tournaments as often, nor does he scare opponents. As of this writing (early 2013), polls have continued to show that the majority of golf fans view him unfavorably. For the past several years, and despite showing flashes of his former self on the golf course, Tiger has been a hero in decline.

But Tiger's story may be far from over. Our research on heroes suggests that people show forgiveness to fallen sports heroes to the extent that these heroes can return to their former levels of professional success. Football quarterback Michael Vick was vilified for being convicted for dog-fighting, yet he was cheered once he began winning games for the Philadelphia Eagles. Similarly, Pittsburgh Steelers fans forgave Ben Roethlisberger for any wrongdoings once he began performing well on the field. The same is true for Kobe Bryant of the Lakers, Ray Lewis of the Ravens, and other sports stars.

The hero's journey is rarely characterized by a linear trend upward in achievement and popularity. Heroes suffer setbacks, and in the case of young privileged millionaire athletes, the public often reacts with unsympathetic venom. This pattern is seen especially in the sporting world, but it also shows up in the political arena. Richard Nixon, Eliot Spitzer, and John Edwards are all examples of politicians whose careers ended when they were caught behaving badly. Successful people, it seems, often forget the old adage that with great power comes great responsibility.

But our thirst for heroes is so great that we are often open to the idea of redemption and a return to former heroic status. For Tiger Woods, the door is open to redemption, but it would seem that he must do something that once came easy to him—dominate the professional golf tour. There are forces working against Tiger, such as his age, his numerous leg injuries, and improved competition on the professional golf tour. We're not sure if there will be a next phase to his heroic journey, but if there is, we'll enjoy witnessing it.

Coming to Terms with Richard Nixon

Our images of heroes and villains are so powerful that it is often difficult to change them, or even to make them a little more complicated. One fascinating case is that of Richard Nixon, the 37th President of the United States (1969–1974). Looking at historians' rankings of greatness, we see that he generally falls toward the bottom, landing in either the Failure or Below Average group. His presidency is not seen as a complete disaster, but it's ranked quite low.

Nixon's poor rating doesn't come as much of a surprise. It's all about Watergate. In one of our studies, we asked students to type into a computer the first word or short phrase that came to mind when a name flashed on the screen. When they saw "Richard Nixon," nearly two-thirds typed in "Watergate" or a closely related term. Consistent with research by Dean Keith Simonton at UC Davis, scandal is highly memorable, and highly memorable information dominates impressions. And there may be good reason to grade Nixon low because of Watergate and the cover-ups. But Nixon deserves a more thorough look. The scandals that led to the country's only presidential resignation are just part of the story. Our image of Nixon, or what psychologists call our "schema," needs to be more complex.

First, there were certainly times during Nixon's career when he took what we would call the high road. For example, during the 1960 debates with John F. Kennedy, he was remarkably considerate and respectful, perhaps even too deferential in what he said and how he said it. And those debates sunk his candidacy. Also, he refused to dispute the 1960 election, which was decided by very close and perhaps questionable returns from Illinois and Texas. Second, and more important, Nixon was a foreign policy visionary. His strategic thinking was inspired, and he exercised strong leadership in opening relations with China and achieving a fragile but real détente with the Soviet Union. These moves changed geopolitics, much to the benefit of the United States and, quite arguably, the whole world.

While Nixon's breakthroughs in foreign policy are well known, though sometimes overlooked, his initiatives in domestic matters are not at all well known. Although Nixon had his share of ethnic prejudices, he worked consistently, though quietly, toward advancing school desegregation in the South. And he also followed the lead of Daniel Patrick Moynihan in forging policies to help poor children.

The Nixon story is really a tragic one. There has been a great deal written about the childhood origins of his insecurities and hostilities. Some scholars ask whether he should be considered "paranoid." Whatever the causes, Nixon was interpersonally awkward and socially uncomfortable. He was not well liked. And in return, for the most part, Nixon didn't really like other people. These feelings created interpersonal distance which allowed Nixon's dark side too much free rein.

We don't argue that Nixon was a hero. Some of his accomplishments could well be considered heroic but, like many real people, he was an individual of great complexity. For those who care, the good and the bad are both easy to see. Taking Nixon as a starting point, we hope that readers will move toward understanding significant public figures in at least three dimensions, and acknowledge that heroes and heroism are marked by mystery and complexity.

Chapter 6

Transposed Heroes
The Fine Line Between Heroism and Villainy

Transposed Heroes are individuals who undergo a complete reversal in status, either from hero to villain or from villain to hero. This status reversal is nicely illustrated in the story of basketball star LeBron James. For the first seven years of his career, James enjoyed heroic status playing in his hometown of Cleveland, Ohio, where fans adored him and statues and murals of his likeness adorned the city. James was rich, famous, successful, and beloved. Just before his eighth year as a professional, he had the option of either playing the remainder of his career in his hometown or moving elsewhere, which would earn him even more tens of millions of dollars. In July of 2010, in what is now infamously known as *The Decision*, James arranged a one-hour nationally televised show to serve as the platform for making his announcement whether to stay in Cleveland or leave for greener pastures. The show was widely viewed as ostentatious and self-aggrandizing. At the end of the hour, when James announced that he was leaving Cleveland to play for the Miami Heat, the negative fallout was intense. His fans were outraged. Murals in his image were desecrated, then removed. The owner of the Cleveland team publicly denounced James as traitorous, shameful, and cowardly.

Somehow, the reaction caught LeBron James off-guard. Adapting to his new role was difficult:

> During my first seven years in the NBA, I was always the liked one. To be
> on the other side, they call it the dark side, or the villain, whatever they call

Joe Paterno: A Transposed Hero

it.... It was definitely challenging for myself. It was a situation I had never been in before. I took a long time to adjust to it. It didn't feel good.... It basically turned me into somebody I wasn't. When you start to hear "the villain," now you have to be the villain. And I started to buy into it. I started to play the game of basketball at a level or in a mind state that I had never played at before. I mean angry. That's mentally, and that's not the way I play the game of basketball.

(Weir, 2012, p. 1).

The second type of Transposed Hero is the individual who changes from villain to hero. A notable example occurs in the movie, *3:10 to Yuma*. The character of Ben Wade, played by Russell Crowe in the 2007 remake, is a notorious train robber. After one particularly lucrative hold-up, Wade kidnaps a father and a son from the train and notices a rift in their relationship. Revealing his tender side, Wade goes to great lengths to stage a situation in which the father is seen as a hero to the son, bringing the two close together. As the audience, we begin to see other noble traits in Wade and are led to believe that he has transposed permanently to heroism. The ending of the movie throws us another surprise. Wade is placed in a situation where his character is tested, and when he chooses to rob yet another train, we see that he has transposed back to villain status. The movie reinforces a lesson about human nature. Although transposed heroism usually refers to two types of individuals, those who transpose from good to bad and those who transpose from bad to good, these transpositions can also occur within the same individual. Most of us are, at different times in our lives, both heroes and villains.

Transposed Heroism is quite common in fictional accounts of heroes, particularly in the superhero and horror genres. The story of Dr. Jekyll and Mr. Hyde is a perfect example. Ingesting a potion instantly turns the benign Dr. Jekyll into the evil Mr. Hyde. Fictional heroes not only undergo quick reversals of moral codes; they also often experience fast, dramatic changes in power and strength. Popeye merely has to eat spinach to acquire super strength. Sinbad Jr. tightens his belt to acquire super powers. The Incredible Hulk is unleashed any time Bruce Banner gets angry. Writers of fiction know that people are transfixed by stories involving sudden displays of magic and supernatural power. When these powers are unleashed, heroes are either born or undergo instant transformations. The Grimms' fairy tale *The Frog Prince* features a frog who turns into a prince. In *Jack and the Beanstalk*, it takes only one night for the beans that Jack plants to grow into the towering beanstalk needed for his heroism to take place. The prince in *Beauty and the Beast* experiences two magical transformations, from prince to beast and then back again to prince. Obviously, the transpositions that occur in fictional literature do not occur in the real world, yet somehow they fascinate us. We are emotionally drawn to instantaneous shifts in morality and how these shifts play a role in creating or destroying heroes.

In this section, we profile four Transposed Heroes: Two-Face from the Batman comic book and movie franchise; former U.S. Senator John Edwards; professional golfer Jack Nicklaus; and college football coach Joe Paterno. Two-Face's true name is Harvey Dent, the handsome and heroic district attorney of Gotham City. After sustaining a hideous facial injury, Dent loses his sanity and becomes a villain. We then turn our attention to former U.S. Senator John Edwards, an admirable public servant who sinks to villainy when he unfathomably makes a long series of morally questionable decisions. Next we profile golf legend Jack Nicklaus, who began his career as professional golf's villain and ended it as one of the most endearing and heroic golfers in history. Finally, we end with an examination of the unfortunate ending to the career, and the life, of Joe Paterno. Paterno's forced resignation from his coaching duties in 2011 fueled plenty of controversy and acrimony. The suddenness of Paterno's shift from hero to villain after a long, distinguished career makes him one of the most sad and intriguing Transposed Heroes of the early twenty-first century.

Harvey Dent as Two-Face: The Hero Turned Villain in *Batman*

One of the more interesting findings in our study of heroes is the tendency for fictional heroes (and villains) to be more extremely good (and extremely bad) than their non-fictional counterparts (Allison and Goethals, 2011). We suspect that creators of fiction draw from classic prototypes of good and evil when constructing their characters. While elements of these prototypes can surely be found in real-world heroes and villains, fictional prototypes are more cleanly drawn with their essential features accentuated. In this way readers of literature will be especially likely to resonate to fictional portrayals of good and evil.

The character of Two-Face in the Batman franchise represents a double-dose of this tendency toward fictional exaggeration. Two-Face starts out as a hero named Harvey Dent, the clean-cut district attorney of Gotham City and a friend of Batman. At the age of 26, Dent is remarkably young to hold such a high position in law enforcement, but his unwavering commitment to the city's well-being and great success as a crime-fighter have earned him such a high rank. In fact, Dent is nicknamed "Apollo" for his perfect, virtuous image and behavior. As district attorney, he fearlessly prosecutes organized crime bosses and becomes the public face of law, order, and everything that is good in Gotham City.

Then Dent's life is forever altered by tragedy. He aggressively attempts to prosecute Sal Maroni, one of the toughest gangsters in Gotham City. But while in a physical altercation with Maroni, the gangster throws sulfuric acid at Dent, hideously scarring the left side of his face. As the audience, we are then witness not only to the physical transformation of the once-handsome Dent; we are also witness to his psychological unraveling. It is harrowing—the disfigured Dent develops multiple personality disorder and becomes a brutal crime boss himself.

Now known as *Two-Face*, Dent becomes obsessed with duality and the number 2. He begins to rob buildings with the number 2 in the address, commits crimes at 10:22 p.m. (22:22 in military time), and uses .22 semiautomatics and double-barreled shotguns. Two-Face becomes especially known for his terrifying method for deciding his victims' fate: He flips a coin to determine whether to kill them or not. We learn that Two-Face got his trademark coin flip routine from his abusive father, who would employ the coin flip "game" with Dent prior to physically battering him.

Why are we drawn to the tragic 180-degree transformation of Harvey Dent? Perhaps the character of Two-Face reminds us how malleable goodness and heroism can be. The research of Phil Zimbardo (2012) on the *Lucifer Effect* tells us that any human being is capable of both exquisite good and horrific evil. Harvey Dent is one moment a strong, untarnished champion of justice, and in the next moment he is forever transposed into a sinister monster. Witnessing Dent's reversal of morals may illustrate the fine line between good and evil, and may be a chilling reminder of how circumstances beyond our control may send any of us down a dark path at any time.

John Edwards: The Modular-Minded Transposed Hero

During the first decade of the twenty-first century, John Edwards appeared to have everything going for him. For six years he served the state of North Carolina effectively as a U.S. Senator. In 2004 he was the Democratic Party's Vice Presidential nominee, and he was considered one of the front-runners for the Democratic Party's nomination for President in 2008. Edwards was smart, accomplished, wealthy, handsome, and charismatic. His future looked exceedingly bright.

But beneath the polished surface, there were cracks. In 2011, Edwards was indicted on six felony charges of violating multiple federal campaign contribution laws to cover up an extramarital affair during his 2008 presidential campaign. He was accused of using nearly $1 million in secret payments from two wealthy campaign donors to hide his mistress from the press and public during his run for the presidency.

As bad as these allegations sounded, Edwards' story got worse. Not only did he have an affair while running for President, but he fathered a child with his mistress and then repeatedly denied that the child was his. In addition, Edwards asked his aide, Andrew Young, to claim paternity of the child, convincing Young to arrange for the woman to live secretly in Young's home to shield the entire affair from the public. Worst of all, these events played out while Edwards' wife, Elizabeth, was battling breast cancer that would eventually take her life.

Psychologist Mark Leary (2012) recently proposed an explanation for Edwards' stunning descent from hero to villain. Drawing from Robert Kurzban's 2010 book, *Why Everyone (Else) is a Hypocrite*, Leary notes that the human mind consists of many individual mental processes similar to cell phone applications or software subroutines. Each of these modules is designed to handle a specific type of task.

For example, we have modules that calculate risks, manage our sexual urges, make moral judgments, respond to situations in which we are treated unfairly, and so on.

The key to understanding Edwards' self-destructive behavior lies in two facts about these mental modules. First, people are not consciously aware of most of the processes that occur in these modules. We do many things without really knowing why because we simply do not have conscious access to the workings of our compartmentalized mind. Second, because the human mind is composed of many separate modules, many of which operate independently, people show great inconsistency in their behavior. For example, in Edwards' case, the module that maintained his ethical principles may have directed him toward one set of behaviors, while the module that managed his reactions to sexual temptations may have been guided by quite different principles with little or no input from the ethics module. The result, in Kurzban's words, is that Edwards was no different from most people in being "consistently inconsistent."

This mental module theory doesn't excuse Edwards' actions. But Leary argues that it "does help us understand that inconsistency—between ethical beliefs and behavior, between what one says and what one does, and between different actions at different times—is to be expected." There also remains the fact that most people must have some executive system that oversees the coordination of the modules so that inconsistencies are kept to a minimum and so that the goals of the more important modules (e.g., managing ethical behavior) supersede the goals of lesser modules (e.g., fulfilling sexual urges). Any hero who manages his or her modules poorly would seem to be destined to follow John Edwards' footsteps in becoming a Transposed Hero.

Jack Nicklaus: The Villain Who Became a Hero

There are times when our first impressions of a person are wrong. We may form a negative opinion of people before we truly get to know them and, worse, we may become entrenched in this view because it's cognitively easy to do so or because there are other people around whom we prefer to view favorably. This rigid and wrong-headed tendency of people to stick to their first negative impression describes the public's evaluations of one of the sports world's most dominating athletes of all time, Jack Nicklaus.

When Nicklaus arrived on the professional golf scene in the early 1960s, the undisputed king of golf was Arnold Palmer. No golfer in the history of the sport has been as loved and venerated by fans as Arnold Palmer. Unlike most golf pros, Palmer played the game with reckless abandon. He had a swashbuckling style of golf that brought him glorious successes as well as agonizing defeats. Also unlike most golf pros, Palmer connected with the crowds. He was handsome, dashing, wore a contagious smile, and bantered good-naturedly with golf galleries. He never refused an autograph request. His charisma was off the charts. Legions of fans, known as *Arnie's Army*, followed him around the golf course and cheered his every move. Men wanted to be like him, and women wanted to be with him.

When Jack Nicklaus joined the golf tour, he was ten years younger than Palmer and immensely talented. Most conspicuously, the two players differed in their style of golf, in their physical appearance, and in the way they carried themselves. While Palmer was charismatic, Nicklaus was robotic. Whereas Palmer took risks in his golf game, Nicklaus played conservatively. While Palmer was handsome and trim, Nicklaus was overweight and grim. Whereas Palmer reached out to fans and connected with them, Nicklaus was all business on the golf course and concentrated solely on his game.

Playing in his first U.S. Open as a professional in 1962, Nicklaus defeated Palmer. During the tournament golf fans openly rooted for the popular Palmer and against the dour newcomer Nicklaus. They resented Nicklaus's threat to the Palmer dynasty. For a number of years, while Nicklaus made a habit of defeating Palmer in major golf championships, fans rudely shouted insults at Nicklaus during tournaments. In golf, fans behave themselves better than in most other sports, but Nicklaus's success bred a resentment toward him that prompted some fans to shout "fat boy" at him. There was no doubt in the golf world that Palmer was the hero and Nicklaus was the villain.

Over time, however, perceptions of Nicklaus changed for the better. Two things happened to bring about this change. First, as the years passed by, Nicklaus kept winning golf tournaments. In fact, Nicklaus began accumulating a record of achievement in golf that has not been matched by anyone, not even Tiger Woods. Second, around 1970, Nicklaus made a few minor changes to his appearance. He lost some weight, altered his haircut, and began to wear more fashionable clothing on the golf course. Suddenly, the dumpy and frumpy man who threatened a legend was now an attractive legendary figure himself. Without changing the way he conducted himself at all, Jack Nicklaus went from being golf's villain to golf's hero.

Joe Paterno: Discerning the Legacy of a Transposed Hero

When Joe Paterno died on Sunday, January 22, 2012, his passing set in motion a process that is a quite natural one for human beings when contemplating another's demise: The forming of a final impression of the person and his significance. Such a cognitive task would ordinarily be a no-brainer. Death often catapults an ordinary person to heroic status, and an already established hero who dies becomes an even greater hero (Allison et al., 2009). But the case of Joe Paterno was far from ordinary. His story certainly contained many elements of the familiar tale of The Man Who Fell From Grace, but people seeking to understand its meaning were confronted with a confusing story of scandal, emotional pain, and controversy.

Coaching college football was Paterno's life, occupying about 60 of his 85 years. As recently as 2011, Paterno was larger than life, a true legend. He won more games than any other coach and led his Penn State teams with distinction for half a century. Paterno seemed eternal, a welcome fixture in a sports world filled with so much greed and corruption. Everyone knew that Paterno's ethics were above reproach; his motto was "success with honor." Paterno was a hero in the truest sense of the word.

Then in late 2011 some horrible news emerged from State College, Pennsylvania. A former assistant coach at Penn State, Jerry Sandusky, was arrested for sexually molesting young boys. Many of the molestations took place at Penn State's football complex, where Sandusky hosted charity events for under-privileged boys. In 2002 someone witnessed Sandusky assaulting a boy and reported it to Paterno, who in turn reported the incident to his superiors at Penn State.

Those administrators, it turns out, covered up the incident in an apparent attempt to protect the school's reputation. Sandusky continued to sexually abuse boys for another nine years until his arrest nine years later. Paterno's knowledge of Sandusky's crime in 2002 came back to haunt him. People had many questions. Why didn't Paterno do more to protect those boys? After contacting his superiors, why didn't he also contact law enforcement? Paterno's lawyer, Wick Sollers, argued that Paterno fully reported what he knew to the people responsible for campus investigations. "He did what he thought was right with the information he had at the time," Sollers said.

Paterno himself expressed regret at not taking further action. No one believed that Paterno's wrongdoing was at nearly the same level of heinousness as Sandusky's alleged crimes. But we hold heroes to the highest of standards when it comes to personal conduct. People may have a great need for heroes, but people also believe that heroes must never show anything less than the best moral behavior possible.

Did Joe Paterno deserve to be forced to resign? Reasonable people disagreed. Those who supported the decision to dismiss Paterno believed that he failed to do the right thing to the fullest extent possible, and that additional children may have been molested after 2002 because of this failure. Those who opposed the decision believed that Paterno was a convenient scapegoat for the irresponsible conduct of higher-level administrators at Penn State who engineered the cover-up.

Paterno's legendary career came to a sudden, shocking, and ignominious end. Days after his dismissal, statues of Paterno's likeness were taken down, awards named after him were renamed, and his reputation was forever sullied. Almost overnight he went from hero to villain. These traumatic events had certainly to take their toll on Paterno's mental and physical well-being, and likely hastened his demise. A person's death can elevate his or her status in society, and we've noticed that Paterno's death has done more to rehabilitate his image than anything he could have done in life. Only time will tell if Paterno will ever transpose completely back to the status of hero.

Chapter 7

Transparent Heroes
The Unsung Heroes Among Us

A common complaint about television and online newscasts is that they seem to have a single-minded preoccupation with reporting bad news. Villainous behavior dominates the headlines, and it's been this way since the advent of media news coverage. An observer from another planet might conclude, based on our news reporting, that villains far outnumber heroes in our society. Our hypothesis about the cause of the negative news bias is based on our observation that heroic behavior occurs all around us, but that it is both invisible and unexciting. These heroic actions are performed by the parents who nurture us, the teachers who educate us, the coaches who mentor us, the healthcare workers who mend us, the police and firefighters who protect us, and the soldiers who defend us. We call these pervasive and unappreciated individuals *Transparent Heroes*.

Why is good behavior so invisible, dreary, and unworthy of news reporting? Psychologists have identified an important cognitive bias called the *negativity bias* (Baumeister, Bratslavsky, Finkenauer, and Vohs, 2001). This bias refers to the human tendency to show greater sensitivity to negative information about people than to positive information. The bias manifests itself in many ways. If you are given both good and bad information about someone, you're more likely to pay attention to the bad and to remember the bad. Moreover, the bad information will carry more weight in your impression of that person. Negative experiences in our lives have more impact on us than positive ones. If you have a good and a bad experience close together in time, you'll be more likely to feel worse than if you have two neutral experiences.

To the extent that we show the negativity bias in our perceptions of the world, good behavior will always be drowned out by bad behavior even if there is a much

Edith Wilson: A Transparent
Hero or Villain?

greater preponderance of good behavior. For this reason, Transparent Heroes will go about doing their heroic work unnoticed and unsung. Fortunately, Transparent Heroes aren't motivated by fame and fortune. They do their jobs of healing, nurturing, and protecting simply because they know it is the right thing to do. If they were motivated by money or fanfare, they would most certainly pursue an alternative form of heroism. There has been very little previous research on Transparent Heroism, although some scholars have studied the related phenomenon of invisible heroism (e.g., Sorenson and Hickman, 2002).

In this section, we profile nine Transparent Heroes. Because they are transparent, you may not have heard of many of them, but you'll discover just how important their contributions were behind the scenes. We begin with an examination of Montgomery Meigs, whose exemplary efforts in supplying the Union army with food and munitions during the U.S. Civil War made him indispensable to the Union cause. Next we profile the life of basketball coach John Wooden, who won more college championships than any other coach, but that's not why he's in this book. Wooden believed that it was far more important to build character and integrity in his players than it was to win games. We then describe the hidden contributions of Marion Keisker, whose one simple action kickstarted Elvis Presley's legendary career. Without Keisker, the rock 'n' roll music revolution would have been delayed, or it would have unfolded differently, or both.

We then profile an unheralded group of heroes who rarely receive any attention: The prehistoric humans who first used fire to usher in the modernization of civilization. Our good friend and colleague Jesse Schultz contributed this fascinating piece on the makers of fire. Next we explore an indispensable aid to all heroes: their sidekicks. Then we offer a tribute to mothers and fathers who heroically sacrifice so much for their children. In our research, we've found that one-third of all the heroes that people list are family members and that most of these family heroes are parents. We then profile the curious case of U.S. President Woodrow Wilson's wife Edith Wilson, who may have run the country for an extended period of time while her husband lay ill recovering from a stroke. Bayard Rustin is our next hero. His name is largely unknown, but as Martin Luther King, Jr.'s sidekick his influence on the civil rights movement loomed large. Finally, we end with the remarkable story of Rick Rescorla, whose heroic planning and preparation is credited with saving the lives of thousands of people on September 11, 2001.

Montgomery Meigs: A Transparent Hero of the Civil War

Very often, heroes gain their status by either achieving or sacrificing, or both, in highly dramatic fashion. But many important heroes make their marks much more quietly. On the one hand, Martin Luther King's dramatic speeches and his tragic assassination are prototypes of the hero narrative. Similarly, George Washington crossing the Delaware, Willie Mays making "the catch" in the 1954 World Series, or Joan of Arc defiant while burning at the stake exemplify the unforgettable images that we associate with heroes. But as Washington well knew, there's more to winning battles than courage in combat. Napoleon is often quoted as saying "An army moves on its stomach." Whether he really said that is debatable. But there is no doubting that supplying an army is an indispensable if overlooked term in the formula for military success.

From this perspective it's no surprise that George Washington had his best general, Nathanael Greene, overseeing supplies, and that Ulysses S. Grant developed his military genius serving as quartermaster in the Mexican War. And this viewpoint gives us greater appreciation for one of the Civil War's Transparent Heroes, Quartermaster General Montgomery Meigs. Meigs' job was to keep Union armies supplied with muskets, gunpowder, shoes, leather, saddles, horses, wagons, uniforms, canteens, bullets, blankets, and beef. Among other things. The armies he provisioned were scattered across a huge section of the North American continent, from Missouri to Florida, and from Virginia to Texas. It was a daunting challenge and Meigs approached it masterfully. He successfully mobilized one of the world's largest economies in a focused effort to win the war. Meigs was honest, hard-driving, and determined. He ran the logistical operations of numerous campaigns with vision, creativity, and efficiency. One contemporary politician claimed that Meigs handled as much as "fifteen hundred million dollars" during the war and that he "accurately vouched and accounted for it to the last cent" (McPherson, 1988).

Meigs was born in Georgia and worked closely with Robert E. Lee before the Civil War. He might have been expected to join the South. But he had sworn an oath to the Union when he entered West Point and he regarded Lee and others as traitors. He hated the Confederacy and all it stood for. In 1864, when he was seeking a suitable burial ground for Union soldiers killed in battle, he insisted that Arlington, the grounds and mansion across the Potomac River from Washington, D.C., owned by Robert E. Lee's wife, would be a good spot. He went so far as to order that remains be buried in Mrs. Lee's rose garden. Thus was born Arlington National Cemetery. A few months later one of Meigs' sons was buried there, a combat casualty of a Virginia battle.

Near the end of the war, Meigs' importance was recognized when he was included in the honor guard of Abraham Lincoln's funeral. After the conflict he served as architect of government buildings in Washington and became an early member of the National Academy of Sciences. Appropriately he was buried at Arlington.

Meigs' role isn't mentioned in most accounts of the Civil War. There is little glamour in behind-the-scenes work. But the show can't go on without it. Meigs served his country in an indispensable position with uncommon capacity. The praises of this Transparent Hero should be sung more often.

John Wooden: Heroic Teacher and Mentor

When we ask people to list their heroes, nearly half of the lists contain the names of teachers and coaches (Allison and Goethals, 2011). The late, great John Wooden identified himself, first and foremost, as a teacher. A college basketball coach, Wooden called the gymnasium his classroom. Wooden's primary goal never wavered: His job was to teach his students how to succeed, not just in basketball, but in life. To him, the definition of success was simple, unique, and refreshing: "Success comes from knowing that you did your best to become the best that you are capable of becoming," he said.

Always a humble man, Wooden would recoil at any mention of his extraordinary accomplishments as a coach. But it would be criminal of us not to point out that his UCLA Bruins won more basketball championships than any other NCAA Division I team in history. Stunningly, his teams won seven championships in a row from 1967 to 1973. Under Wooden's leadership, UCLA enjoyed four perfect 30–0 seasons, including an eye-popping winning streak of 88 consecutive games. In 2009, *The Sporting News* named him the Greatest Coach of All Time. President George Bush also awarded him the Presidential Medal of Freedom, the nation's highest civilian honor.

Wooden had only a few team rules, and they were strictly enforced. Never be late. Be neat and clean. No profanity. And never criticize a teammate. He developed a seven-point creed by which to live one's life, and he followed it to the letter:

1. Be true to yourself.
2. Make each day your masterpiece.
3. Help others.
4. Drink deeply from good books, especially the Bible.
5. Make friendship a fine art.
6. Build a shelter against a rainy day.
7. Pray for guidance and give thanks for your blessings every day.

Wooden told his players to "never cease trying to be the best you could be, because that's under your control. If you get too concerned with things over which you have no control, it will adversely affect the things over which you have control."

For Wooden, success was never about winning games. Success was reaching one's full potential, and so he taught his players that the final score of a game doesn't matter. He said:

> You can lose when you outscore somebody in a game; and you can win when you're outscored. If you make an effort to do the best you can, the results will be what they should be. The score is the byproduct of doing your best and is not the end itself. The journey is better than the end. Our practices were the journey, and the game was the end. I wanted to help players attain the self-satisfaction of knowing they made the effort to be the best that they were capable of being.

With great satisfaction, Wooden recalled one player who was a mediocre shooter but whose shooting percentage was extremely high because he took intelligent shots. Another player was poor at jumping but became an excellent rebounder because he tirelessly practiced the art of positioning himself perfectly for rebounds. But Wooden's greatest pride was witnessing dozens of his players become doctors, dentists, attorneys, and teachers. "I taught them that they were there to get an education," he said. "Basketball was second."

When Wooden passed away in June of 2010 at the age of 99, his former players and colleagues were effusive in their praise for the man they all called "Coach." Kareem Abdul-Jabbar recalled that Wooden "really wanted us to get our degrees and learn what it meant to be a good citizen, good parents and husbands, and responsible human beings." Dick Enberg noted that "Wooden's philosophy of teaching players lessons of life will serve as his ultimate gift." According to Keith Erickson, Wooden "was the best role model that a young man could possibly ever have." John Wooden was proof that coaches and teachers are heroes who strive to make us all better people.

Accidental Sidekicks: Marion Keisker's Moment to Help Elvis

Each August 16, the anniversary of Elvis Presley's death in 1977 is observed. Or at least most people believe he died then. But there are some who believe that Elvis is still alive. And some of those individuals assert that it is no mere coincidence that the word ELVIS and the word LIVES have the same letters. Several years ago Elvis was compared to Dionysus on a National Public Radio classical music show, and it was argued that in order to understand America, one had to understand Elvis. He was or is a hero for many, both for his music and for his overall impact on American and even world culture. On the 1999 ABC series called *The Century*, narrator Peter Jennings argued that when Elvis burst onto the scene in the Fifties, he paved the way for the Sixties.

Our work on heroes has considered the role of sidekicks, such as Dr. Watson in the Sherlock Holmes stories, or Sancho Panza in the two Don Quixote volumes. In Elvis' case there is a person who played a very small role in his rise to fame, but a crucial and necessary one. This woman, unknown even to many of his most devoted fans, underlines a more general point—that chance and circumstance can change the course of history, and make or break potential heroes.

We are talking about Marion Keisker, a woman who worked at Sam Phillips' Sun Recording Studio in Memphis, Tennessee in the mid-1950s. Peter Guralnick relates the story in his classic 1994 Elvis biography, *Last Train to Memphis*. Phillips, who also played a crucial and much larger role in the rise of Elvis, had started Sun several years before, and had launched the career of a number of artists, including Howling Wolf and Ike Turner. Not long after he graduated from high school, Elvis came by the Sun studio and paid to make a record. He claimed it was for his mother's birthday, but his mother's birthday was many months away. It was clear that he wanted to be noticed. Marion Keisker was at the studio that day and handled the recording. She noted on a 3 x 5 card that Elvis was a good ballad singer. Elvis came around several more times, asking whether anyone was looking for a vocalist for any recordings. He was on the make.

In early July, 1954, when Elvis was 19, a year out of high school, the pivotal moment arrived. Two young musicians, guitarist Scotty Moore and bass player Bill Black were at the studio working with Sam Phillips on some songs they wanted to record. They needed someone to sing. At that point, Marion Keisker asked, "How about the kid with the sideburns?" Elvis lived nearby, but didn't have a telephone. Someone went to his apartment in a nearby housing project, and left a message. Very soon a sweaty Elvis arrived at the studio, having run all the way over.

That night, after some desultory efforts, Elvis began strumming his rhythm guitar and singing the blues number, *That's All Right, Mama*. Sam Phillips said that that was the sound he'd been looking for and recorded it. *That's All Right, Mama* was a black R&B song, and Phillips wanted a country and western (C&W) "B-side" that would have more appeal to white audiences. Pretty soon, Elvis, Scotty, and Bill recorded a bouncy version of Bill Monroe's bluegrass classic, *Blue Moon of Kentucky*. Shortly, both sides were being played on Memphis radio stations. It wasn't long before Elvis became The King of Rock 'n' Roll, and a hero to millions.

Those Whom We Forgot: The Makers of Fire

There are some things in life that have become so commonplace, so normal, that we often take them for granted. One of these things is fire. The origins of the use and making of fire has been lost to history. The earliest evidence for the use of fire dates back some 1.6 million years and is often attributed to *Homo erectus*, though some believe later species of *Homo* were responsible. Whether the users of this fire had actually made it or simply made use of a naturally occurring fire is not known. Or even if it was a product of one lone genius or a group through trial and error. But at some point in history fire was made and that changed history. Humanity suddenly had a means to see in the darkness, repel predators, keep warm, and preserve and tenderize food. With it humanity spread across the globe, becoming far more cosmopolitan than any other species of primate.

We owe much of our civilization and modern world to the knowledge of combustion. Signal fires and smoke signals enabled near-instant communications over distances. The famous cave art at Lascaux was done by firelight. Fire-stick farming, where portions of the land are purposely set on fire to create grasslands, has changed vast portions of the globe. Many European explorers seeing lands like the Americas or Australia for the first time thought that they were unspoiled wildernesses, wholly unaware that much of what they were seeing had already been altered by people.

Because of fire. Because of the people who tamed it.

Smelting gave us metals, steam engines gave us greater mobility, coal-fired power plants gave us electricity, internal combustion engines drive our industry and trade, pasteurization protects us from disease, and the burning fuel of rockets pushes us out to space and realms the early fire-makers couldn't have even imagined. All of this would be difficult or impossible without combustion. In an era of the written word we can now remember the names of those who gave us electricity, or plastics, the automobile, or the first airplane. The names Edison, or Ford, or Wright will go down through history.

But they owe it all to people whose names we'll never know. People who lived in a world totally alien to us and were almost certainly not even members of our own species. And often modern peoples do not understand the difficulty of actually starting a fire without modern aids. Set loose in the wilderness many of us would be helpless without lighters or some other convenience. Yet ages ago a people whom many would denigrate as "primitive" did so regularly armed with nothing but rock, wood, and their own ingenuity. And the heroic thing about it is that those who first tended and created those early fires had to overcome their own instinctual fear. Previous contact with fire, often in the form of a wildfire, usually meant death and destruction. The taming of fire took courage, imagination, and foresight. Although their names have been lost to time, their legacy lives on with us and will so as long as society persists. And perhaps that's all the recognition they need.

The Supporting Cast in Heroes' Narratives: Sidekicks and Others

Our profile of the fictional hero Sherlock Holmes notes that Sir Arthur Conan Doyle's famous detective is revealed to us through the words of his long-suffering friend, Dr. John Watson. The Holmes/Watson team is unique in many ways, but in other ways it is typical of both fictional partners and real-life teams. In fiction, there are many other examples of what we call "hero/sidekick" pairs, starting with the memorable Cervantes characters, Don Quixote and Sancho Panza. Quixote is the elderly would-be knight errant, who rides across the Spanish countryside on the broken-down Rocinante, so that he can right wrongs in honor of his imagined lady, Dulcinea. He is the unrealistic, totally serious idealist, who literally tilts at windmills, thinking that they are evil giants. Sancho tries to impart some realism to Quixote's vision of the world, and in his bumbling attempts adds some humor to the story.

In the Holmes canon, Watson also adds some humor, by deflating some of Sherlock's most self-centered and arrogant remarks. But his central role, beyond that of narrator, is to accompany Holmes on most of his adventures, and occasionally to help him by bringing along his "revolver" on dangerous missions. Besides Watson, the Holmes stories actually have other supporting players. A familiar one for many such narratives is the villain. In this case it is Professor Moriarty, the "Napoleon of Crime." But there is an additional character in many of the Holmes stories, the Scotland Yard detective Inspector Lestrade. Holmes claims that Lestrade is the best of the lot at Scotland Yard, but even so he is portrayed as plodding and conventional. He sees himself as a practical man, in contrast to the theoretical Holmes. But he does acknowledge that Holmes' "methods" are sometimes useful. Interestingly, for the most part the two both disdain and depend on each other. In their different ways, Watson, Moriarty, and Lestrade are foils for Holmes, and allow different facets of his personality to be explored.

The sidekick role was central to a number of the radio and television Westerns of the 1940s and 1950s. The Lone Ranger had his "faithful Indian companion, Tonto" and the Cisco Kid had his partner Pancho. In the Elizabeth George Inspector Lynley mysteries, Lynley's sidekick is a woman, Detective Sergeant Barbara Havers. Like Watson and Sancho Panza, one of Havers' roles is to pinprick Lynley's inflated, upper-class sense of himself. In the more recent television series, *The Closer*, a woman, Deputy Chief Brenda Leigh Johnson, is the hero, and her most frequent sidekick is a man, Sergeant Gabriel. Like other sidekicks, Gabriel tries to compensate for the hero's shortcomings, in this case Johnson's inability to navigate her way around Los Angeles.

Real-life sidekicks exist too, but their roles are more easily portrayed in fiction. We think that former heavyweight boxer Muhammad Ali's close friend Bundini Brown played a role very much like the sidekicks from novels, television, and the movies. He supported and relaxed the Champ, but also provided some realistic grounding. Speech writer and adviser Theodore Sorensen was often described as President John F. Kennedy's "alter ego." Clearly, Sorensen was someone JFK depended on for advice in many domains. And of course Kennedy had another important sidekick, his brother, Attorney General Robert F. Kennedy. In general, sidekicks seem to support and humanize the heroes they team up with, and allow their idiosyncrasies to be seen in bold relief.

Why Our Parents are Our Heroes

A few years ago we conducted a study that underscored the importance of family members as heroes (Allison and Goethals, 2011). In the study, people of all ages and from all walks of life were asked to list their heroes. We were surprised, yet pleased, to see that family members were listed about a third of the time. Most importantly, one-fourth of all people listed their mother as their hero. Mothers were mentioned more than any other person, including fathers.

Mother's Day became a nationally recognized holiday in 1914 because of the efforts of Anna Jarvis, a West Virginian who campaigned to honor mothers after her own beloved mother passed away in 1905. Ironically, by the 1920s Jarvis had become disenchanted with the commercialization of Mother's Day and began campaigning against the holiday. Still, we believe her initial sentiment was on target and we applaud the opportunity to recognize the heroic qualities of mothers everywhere.

Many highly accomplished individuals are quick to attribute their success to their mothers. American presidents are especially likely to do so. Abraham Lincoln once noted that "all that I am, or can be, I owe to my angel mother." George

Washington also observed that "all I am I owe to my mother. I attribute all my success in life to the moral, intellectual and physical education I received from her." Andrew Jackson claimed that "there never was a woman like my mother. She was as gentle as a dove and as brave as a lioness."

When the participants in our study were asked why their mothers were heroic, they generated three main reasons: generosity with time, money, and love. There are many ways that mothers gave their time to us. According to survey respondents, mothers tended to us when we were sick, accompanied us to school and soccer practice, made us dinner, and read stories to us. Our mothers made financial sacrifices, too. They wore old clothes so that we could wear new clothes; they took on part-time jobs to buy us gifts; they saved money for us to attend college; they gave us our weekly allowance; and they made sure we had food on the table. But the most important quality that distinguishes mothers from other heroes, including fathers (according to our respondents), is the free offering of love that mothers give us. Mothers were there for us when we needed emotional support. Mothers hugged us. They comforted us and let us sit on their laps. They kissed us on our cheeks before school and at bedtime at night.

Although mothers are listed as heroes more frequently than fathers, we should emphasize that fathers are a close second. The origin of Father's Day is not entirely clear, but there are several fascinating possibilities. Babylonian scholars have discovered a message carved in clay by a young man named Elmesu roughly 4,000 years ago. In the message, Elmesu wishes his father good health and a long life. Some believe this ancient message represents evidence of an established tradition of honoring fathers, but there is little evidence to support a specially designated Father's Day until modern times.

There is some debate about the origin of the Father's Day that we celebrate today. Some claim that a West Virginian named Grace Golden Clayton deserves the credit. In 1907, Clayton was grieving the loss of her own father when a tragic mine explosion in Monongah killed 361 men, 250 of whom were fathers. Clayton requested that her church establish a day to honor these lost fathers and to help the children of the affected families heal emotionally. The date she suggested was July 8, the anniversary of her own father's death.

Still others believe that the first Father's Day was held on June 19, 1910 through the efforts of Sonora Smart Dodd of Spokane, Washington. Inspired by the newly recognized Mother's Day, Dodd felt strongly that fatherhood needed recognition as well. Her own father, William Smart, was a Civil War veteran who was left to raise his family alone when his wife died giving birth to their sixth child. Dodd was the only daughter, and she helped her father raise her younger brothers, including her new infant brother Marshall.

Whereas Mother's Day was met with instant enthusiasm, Father's Day was initially met with scorn and derision. Few people believed that fathers wanted, or needed, any acknowledgement. It wasn't until 1972 that President Richard Nixon made Father's Day an official holiday. Today the holiday is widely celebrated in the month of June by more than 52 countries.

Why are fathers heroes? The respondents in our survey listed two main reasons. First, fathers are given credit for being great teachers and mentors. They teach us how to fix a flat tire, shoot a basketball, and write a resumé. Fathers tend to be less emotional than mothers, but they lead by example and devote time demonstrating life skills to us. Former Governor of New York, Mario Cuomo, once said, "I talk and talk and talk, and I haven't taught people in 50 years what my father taught by example in one week."

Second, fathers are great providers and protectors. Our respondents told us that their fathers were heroes in their commitment to provide for their families, often at great sacrifice. Many fathers work at two or more jobs outside the home to ensure that their families have adequate food and shelter. Fathers also provide us with a sense of safety and protection. Sigmund Freud once wrote, "I cannot think of any need in childhood as strong as the need for a father's protection."

Perhaps we shouldn't have been so surprised that parents were listed as heroes by so many of our survey respondents. Developmental psychologists tell us that the relationship we have with our parents is the first significant relationship of our lives. It is a relationship that indelibly shapes our values, our aspirations, and our future behavior. Thus when we experience successes in our careers and in our personal lives, it is not surprising that we attribute those triumphs, at least in part, to our parents.

Edith Wilson: An Unsung Hero or Villain?

In August of 1914, the same month that witnessed the world wade into what became known as the Great War, or World War I, the First Lady of the United States, Ellen Axson Wilson passed away. President Woodrow Wilson was devastated as he tried to calm fears of U.S. involvement in the war between Germany and Great Britain, France, and Russia. Ellen had been Wilson's closest companion for nearly 30 years.

Within a few months, Wilson became involved with a Washington, D.C. widow, Edith Bolling Galt. The two were married in December 1915. Edith became a close and trusted adviser as well as an intimate companion. Despite Wilson's best efforts, and despite running for re-election in 1916 on the slogan "He kept us out of war," the President asked for a declaration of war against Germany in April, 1917. It was clear to all parties that if the United States could mobilize quickly enough, the Allies, now including the United States., could defeat Germany. But the Germans hoped that they could defeat their European enemies before the Americans could arrive in time to tip the balance. In the end,

American "doughboys" got to France quickly enough for the Allies to win, but it was close.

An armistice took effect at 11:00 a.m. on November 11, 1918, the eleventh hour of the eleventh day of the eleventh month. President Wilson traveled to Europe to participate in the peace negotiations which culminated in the Treaty of Versailles in 1919. On his return from Paris, Wilson campaigned vigorously for ratification of the treaty, including American entry into the League of Nations. The president believed that the League might be able to prevent future wars. However, opposition in the Congress to the League was intense. Opponents worried that the League would never work, and that it would compromise American sovereignty. Wilson went to the people on a nationwide speech-making tour, arguing eloquently for treaty ratification. Already in poor health, the President had to suspend the tour. Shortly afterwards, in the fall of 1919 he suffered a stroke and was severely disabled—mentally, emotionally, and physically—for the remaining year-and-a-half of his administration.

No other president had been as disabled as Wilson. At the time, many people believed that he should resign. Some historians hold that view today. But Edith Galt Wilson rose to defend her husband and to rigorously control access to him. Ambiguous and overly optimistic reports on the President's condition were released, and only a few close advisers and leading congressional leaders were allowed to see him. It appears that Edith made some decisions without consulting the president. She became, in effect, acting president.

Did Edith Wilson do the right thing? Did she assume more power and responsibility than she should have? It seems clear that she protected Wilson's health. She needed to save him from himself as much as from others. The President wanted to engage in national affairs much more than he was able to. Edith saw that he was not overwhelmed, and that he was given the time, and the freedom from stressful demands, that he needed to regain some measure of health.

But it can be argued that Edith usurped power in a dangerous manner. It is clear that she was navigating in uncharted waters. She was a confident woman who unhesitatingly decided that she would protect Woodrow Wilson's health and his presidency. She believed that doing so was in the interests of the United States. Many students of history disagree. They think that Edith Wilson was not at all heroic. Others believe that she served the country well in a time of crisis and uncertainty. As much as anyone, Edith Wilson illustrates our belief that heroism is in the eye of the beholder.

Bayard Rustin: Peaceful Advocate of Human Rights

A number of heroes can be considered *polymaths*; these are individuals who excel in a number of different areas of life. Bayard Rustin was one such multi-talented person. Rustin was an accomplished tenor vocalist, a renowned scholar, and a versatile athlete. But Rustin's most important contribution to the world may have been his life-long devotion to defending the rights of oppressed groups of people across the globe, especially in America during the civil rights movement of the mid-twentieth century.

As a young man in the 1940s, Rustin helped convince President Franklin Roosevelt to eliminate racial discrimination in defense industries and in federal agencies. He traveled to California to protect the property of Japanese-Americans who had been wrongly imprisoned in internment camps. In the Deep South, Rustin was arrested for violating segregated seating laws on buses, a crime for which he served 22 days on a chain gang. Between 1947 and 1952, Rustin made frequent trips to India and Africa to meet with practitioners of Gandhi's teachings about non-violent protest philosophies. His subsequent influence on Martin Luther King, Jr. was unmistakable. When Rosa Parks was arrested for bravely defying Jim Crow laws in Montgomery, Alabama, Rustin was there to advise King in practicing non-violent forms of protest, such as organizing the Montgomery Bus Boycott.

But Rustin was limited in the help that he could offer King. A gay man, Rustin lived in an era when homosexuality was unacceptable to the vast majority of Americans. During the Montgomery boycott, a reporter threatened to undermine King's cause by exposing Rustin's sexual orientation. King and Rustin agreed that their civil rights crusade would be best served if Rustin distanced himself from King. Rustin was so careful not to undermine King's work that he fled Montgomery at night in the trunk of a car. Still, Rustin continued to advise King and influence the civil rights movement in significant ways from a safe distance.

It was not just the public and the media who felt threatened by Rustin's sexuality. Many African-American ministers involved in civil rights would also have nothing to do with Rustin, and some spread rumors that King was gay because of his close friendship with Rustin. Said Rustin,

> Martin Luther King, with whom I worked very closely, became very distressed when a number of the ministers working for him wanted him to dismiss me from his staff because of my homosexuality. Martin set up a committee to discover what he should do. They said that, despite the fact that I had contributed tremendously to the organization, they thought I should separate myself from Dr. King.
>
> (Monroe, 2012)

As the dream of racial equality made significant headway during the 1970s and 80s, Rustin was painfully aware of the lack of social progress in the area of gay rights. In 1986, he gave a speech entitled *The New Niggers Are Gays*, in which he asserted that:

Blacks are no longer the litmus paper or the barometer of social change. Blacks are in every segment of society and there are laws that help to protect them from racial discrimination. The new "niggers" are gays. It is in this sense that gay people are the new barometer for social change. The question of social change should be framed with the most vulnerable group in mind: gay people.

Rustin devoted his entire life to promoting human rights, not only in North America but in other nations such as Haiti, Poland, and Zimbabwe. When asked to summarize his philosophy, he said, "The principal factors which influenced my life are nonviolent tactics; constitutional means; democratic procedures; respect for human personality; and a belief that all people are one." As with many heroes, Bayard Rustin showed a courageous willingness to sacrifice his own well-being for the noble principle of equality. Throughout his entire life he remained a fierce advocate of civil rights for all people. "When an individual is protesting society's refusal to acknowledge his dignity as a human being, his very act of protest confers dignity on him," he said.

Rick Rescorla: The Hero Who Saved 2,700 Lives on 9/11

Some heroes perform their heroic acts in the public spotlight and are lauded immediately after displaying their courageous and selfless behavior. Other heroes perform their heroic work invisibly, outside the public view, and rarely receive the attention they deserve. Earlier we described these invisible heroes and their invaluable impact as educators, firefighters, law enforcement officers, healthcare workers, and military personnel.

We now turn our attention to one invisible hero in particular, a man named Rick Rescorla, whose behind-the-scenes work before and during the terrorist attacks of September 11, 2001 saved nearly 2,700 lives at the World Trade Center.

Rescorla was the Director of Security for Morgan Stanley, a large investment company headquartered at the twin towers in New York City. Rescorla was one of the few people who anticipated the possibility that terrorists might fly aircraft into the twin towers. As early as 1992, Rescorla warned the owners of the World Trade Center that a truck bomb could attack the pillars of the basement parking garage. Sure enough, in 1993 terrorists used this method, and Rescorla played a major role in evacuating the building. He was also the last man out.

Throughout the 1990s, Rescorla continued to warn authorities that the World Trade Center was a prime target for terrorists flying airplanes, and he recommended to his superiors at Morgan Stanley that the company leave Manhattan. Morgan Stanley declined to leave, as their lease at the World Trade Center did not terminate until 2006. Rescorla received permission to ensure that all employees practice emergency evacuations every three months.

On the morning of September 11, 2001, Rescorla awoke as he normally did, kissed his wife goodbye, and took the 6:10 train to Manhattan. He was at his desk on the 44th floor of the World Trade Center's South Tower by 7:30 a.m. When the first hijacked plane crashed into the North Tower, Rescorla ignored officials' requests to stay put. He grabbed a bullhorn and led the company's 2,700 employees down the stairwell two-by-two, singing patriotic songs such as *God Bless America* to keep them calm.

By the time the second airliner hit the south tower, most of the company's employees were out of danger. When one of his colleagues told him that he, too, needed to evacuate the World Trade Center, Rescorla replied, "As soon as I make sure everyone else is out." Rescorla and two assistants went back to look for them, never to return. He was last seen on the tenth floor of the burning tower. His remains have never been found. As a result of Rescorla's actions, all but 13 of Morgan Stanley's 2,700 employees survived.

It's important to note that Rick Rescorla was already a hero *before* his life-saving work on 9/11. He was a highly decorated Vietnam veteran whose heroic feats in battle earned him the Silver Star, the Bronze Star with Oak Leaf Cluster, a Purple Heart, and the Vietnamese Cross of Gallantry. While serving in Vietnam, Rescorla's leadership, courage, and compassion for his troops were legendary.

Rescorla's wife, Susan, has honored her husband's legacy by creating The Richard Rescorla Memorial Foundation, with the goal of "keeping present the magnitude of Rick's life and to promote the virtues Rick lived by—duty, honor and courage." She authored a book entitled *Touched By A Hero*, which details the sacrifices Rick made to safely evacuate nearly 2,700 people from the World Trade Center on 9/11. "I am so very proud to have had him in my life," she said. "I want to have his legacy live on."

Chapter 8

Traditional Heroes
The Classic Hero's Journey

A *Traditional Hero* is the prototypical hero. By "prototype", we mean the kind of person whom we usually think of when we are asked to think of a hero. The Traditional Hero is the individual who follows the classic hero journey as described by Campbell (1949) in his hero monomyth. The journey contains many stages, but the main ones involve the hero being cast out of his or her ordinary world and into a dangerous new world; the hero receiving assistance from strange and unlikely sources; the hero encountering potentially destructive temptations and father figures; the hero overcoming formidable obstacles; the hero becoming transformed in some way; and finally, the hero returning to the ordinary world with a boon that transforms it. Campbell acknowledged that not all hero stories contain every component of the monomythic journey, and that the details of the journey can vary significantly from story to story. Still, all Traditional Hero stories more or less follow the basic monomyth structure.

In our survey of 450 respondents, reported in Allison and Goethals (2011), we found that people generate the names of more Traditional Heroes than any other category. This fact explains why this section of our book contains more hero profiles than any of the others, and it also raises some chicken-and-egg questions. Do people list so many Traditional Heroes because, as Campbell (1949) claims, this category of heroism taps into the Jungian hero archetype that is so deeply imbedded in our psyche? Or does the abundance of Traditional Hero stories found in books and movies make this hero category more deeply imbedded in us? Put differently, the abundance of Traditional Heroes in our cultural narratives may either reflect, or be the cause of, the powerful schema we have for this category of hero.

George Washington Carver: A Traditional Hero

There is a fascinating contradiction with regard to our judgments about the prevalence of heroes that we would like to address. As we've mentioned, when people are asked to generate examples of specific heroes, Traditional Heroes come most easily to mind compared to the other hero categories in our taxonomy. Yet we've also noted in the Introduction to this book that Transparent Heroes are judged by people to be the most abundant type of heroes in society. How do we explain this discrepancy? There are at least two possibilities. One explanation is that although Transparent Heroes may be judged as most abundant, their contributions are less exciting or dramatic than those of the Traditional Hero. Vivid instances of heroes who undertake daring and dangerous quests may be more available in memory than instances of heroes who teach history at the local high school.

Another possibility is that Transparent Heroes and Traditional Heroes are both viewed as abundant but tap into different mental hierarchies of heroes. For example, when we ask people to "list your heroes," we get different lists of heroes as compared to when we ask people to "list people who are heroes". For the former instruction, we obtain many family members, mentors, and coaches—in short, Transparent Heroes. For the latter instruction, we obtain the names of many Traditional Heroes such as Harry Potter, Mother Teresa, and Oprah Winfrey. We suggest, therefore, that when we ask people to "list your heroes," we are tapping into their vast reservoir of *personal heroes*, most of whom are transparent. But when we ask people to "list people who are heroes," we are tapping into their large mental storehouse of *cultural heroes*, most of whom are traditional.

The Traditional Heroes whom we profile in this chapter are categorized into three subtypes: *moral, competent*, and *complete*. This carving up of heroes is based on our research showing that people are judged to be heroes to the extent that they make great moral contributions, great ability-based contributions, or great contributions that require both great morality *and* great ability. Our profiles of Traditional-Moral Heroes include the Dalai Lama, Pat Tillman, Irena Sendler, George Bailey, Confucius, Mother Teresa, Lois Wilson, Nathan Hale, Dana Reeve, Phil Connors, Israel Spira, Rosa Parks, and Corrie ten Boom. Our profiles of Traditional-Competent Heroes include Marie Curie, Tina Fey, Ellen DeGeneres, John Nash, Althea Gibson, Monica Seles, Dan Anderson, Humphrey Bogart, Edgar Allen Poe, Secretariat, Clint Eastwood, and Lucille Ball. Finally, our profiles of Traditional-Complete Heroes who show both great morality and great competence include Terry Fox, George Marshall, Florence Nightingale, Oprah Winfrey, Winston Churchill, Roberto Clemente, George Washington Carver, Warren Spahn, George Washington, Mikhail Gorbachev, and Henry Fonda's character in the classic film *Twelve Angry Men*. We thank our good friend Jeff Green at Virginia Commonwealth University for supplying a terrific profile of Winston Churchill.

TRADITIONAL-MORAL HEROES

The Dalai Lama: "My Religion is Kindness"

Although scholars have long debated whether leaders and heroes are born or made, there is no doubt a strong belief among lay-people that some great heroes are born into their roles. The story of Jesus of Nazareth is the most powerful story of the "born hero" in the western world. But what about the eastern world? We would say that the greatest born hero in the east is the Dalai Lama, the head of state of Tibet and the spiritual leader of Tibetan Buddhism. The current Dalai Lama, Tenzin Gyatso, is believed to be the latest reincarnation of a series of spiritual leaders who have chosen to be reborn so as to enlighten others. There have been 14 Dalai Lamas since the year 1391.

After the 13th Dalai Lama died in December of 1933, Buddhist monks prayed for guidance to find the new Dalai Lama. They consulted oracles and meditated for signs that would lead them to him. Within a few years they received a vision that the new Dalai Lama would be found in the northeast part of Tibet, and that he would be living in a house with turquoise roof tiles near a monastery. Many monks journeyed to this region of Tibet to search for this house, ultimately discovering one that fit the description in the village of Taktser. Living in the home were two-year-old Tenzin Gyatso and his parents.

The monks presented young Tenzin with a number of objects that were owned by the previous Dalai Lama, and these objects were mixed with other imitation objects. When Tenzin correctly identified the items belonging to the 13th Dalai Lama, the monks knew they had found the reincarnation of their leader. The boy and his family traveled to the city of Lhasa, where he was taken to the Drepung Monastery to study the Buddhist sutra in preparation for his role as the spiritual leader of Tibet.

The Dalai Lama's central purpose is to help people achieve enlightenment from Buddhist spiritual practices. Buddhism provides insight into the true nature of life, and Buddhists use meditation and other practices to develop the qualities of awareness, kindness, and wisdom. The Dalai Lama's job is made somewhat difficult by the fact that neighboring China has never recognized Tibet as an independent political country. When China annexed Tibet in 1959, the Dalai Lama and thousands of his supporters fled into exile. He has lived in Dharamsala, India, since 1960, and heads the Tibetan government from afar.

One of the most respected spiritual leaders in the world, the Dalai Lama embraces religious diversity. "I always believe that it is much better to have a variety of religions, a variety of philosophies, rather than one single religion or philosophy," he said "This is necessary because of the different mental dispositions of each human being. Each religion has certain unique ideas or techniques, and learning about them can only enrich one's own faith." The Dalai Lama also embraces the union of science and spirituality. Recently, he collaborated with MIT to study what role Buddhist meditation plays in human emotion and cognition. He said, "If science proves facts that conflict with Buddhist understanding, Buddhism must change accordingly. We should always adopt a view that accords with the facts."

Born heroes such as the Dalai Lama and Jesus are not revered because of their special lineage or conception. They are revered because they combine their inborn gifts with a lifetime of practicing good deeds and helping others do the same. The Dalai Lama's message is quite simply one of love. "If you want others to be happy, practice compassion. If you want to be happy, practice compassion," he said. "My religion is very simple. My religion is kindness."

Pat Tillman: The Consummate War Hero

Each Memorial Day and Veterans Day in the United States, people are encouraged to pause and remember the roughly 1.3 million Americans who have died while serving their country since 1776. Think about that number: 1.3 million. That's more people than the population of San Diego, California, or Amsterdam in The Netherlands. It's a staggering level of human sacrifice.

While every casualty is deserving of our reverence, the loss of Corporal Patrick Daniel Tillman, a U.S. Army Ranger, is especially noteworthy. Pat Tillman didn't start out with dreams of serving in the U.S. military. Playing football was his passion. He was a star defensive safety for Arizona State University from 1994 to 1997, and during his time at ASU he earned a grade point average of 3.84. Believed to be too small to compete in the NFL, Tillman nevertheless made it to the Arizona Cardinals and began making headlines for his ferocious style of play. He made *Sports Illustrated*'s 2000 NFL All-Pro team. He married his high-school sweetheart Marie. His future was bright indeed.

Then the September 11, 2001 attacks happened, and they forever altered Tillman's priorities. Shortly after the attacks, Tillman said, "We are such a free society, and you don't realize how great a life we have over here. In times like this you stop and think about just how good we have it and what kind of a system we live under, what freedoms we're allowed. And that wasn't built overnight."

Once the 2001 NFL season concluded, Tillman turned down a multi-million-dollar contract offer from the Arizona Cardinals. Instead of playing football, he decided to enlist in the U.S. Army. He simply could not forget the sacrifice that others before him had made, nor could he ignore his own calling to serve. "My great-grandfather was at Pearl Harbor and a lot of my family has fought in wars," he said. "I really haven't done a damn thing as far as laying myself on the line like that. So I have a great deal of respect for those who have, and for what the flag stands for."

Tillman served his country with distinction until a tragic day in April of 2004, when he was killed in Afghanistan, 25 miles from the Pakistan border. At first, the U.S. military reported that Tillman had been killed by hostile forces. He received the *Silver Star*, the *Purple Heart*, and other accolades. Every effort was made to create a powerful story of a hero gunned down by the enemy. But within weeks of his death, the true story of what happened to Pat Tillman was leaked to the press. It turns out that he had been inadvertently killed by friendly fire from his own allied forces. To this day many details about Tillman's death are not clearly understood because of the military's apparent desire to protect its image.

Human beings go to great lengths to remember their heroes. After his death, Pat Tillman's family established the Pat Tillman Foundation to promote Tillman's legacy of changing the world for the better. A major bridge spanning the Colorado River bears Tillman's name. A law school in San Jose established the Pat Tillman Scholarship. The Cardinals and Sun Devils retired the number he wore with those teams. The Cardinals have named the plaza surrounding their stadium the Pat Tillman Freedom Plaza. In 2006 a bronze statue was erected in his honor. Tillman's high school renamed its football field after him. The first USO center in Afghanistan was named after him.

We tell the story of Pat Tillman, not to rebuke the military's questionable conduct surrounding his death, but to underscore the rare nobility of character that motivated Tillman's life choices. Millions of dollars and a life of luxury were less important to him than finding Osama bin Laden and other terrorists who brought down the World Trade Center on September 11. He was willing to die fighting for a just cause. His life, and his death, are well worth pausing to remember.

Irena Sendler: The Hero Who Stood Up to Evil

As we note in several of our hero profiles, the worst of human nature often brings out the best in human nature. The atrocities committed by the Nazis during World War II created fertile ground for heroes to emerge. Among the heroes of that terrible war were Anne Frank, George Wahlen, Israel Spira, George Marshall, Corrie ten Boom, and Winston Churchill. To this list we add the name of a Polish woman who refused to allow innocent children to die in the Warsaw Jewish Ghetto in 1942. Her name was Irena Sendler.

Our first heroes book describes many of the details of Sendler's heroism (Allison and Goethals, 2011). Here are the highlights: Using many creative means, and at great risk to her own well-being, Sendler was able to sneak 2,500 children out of the heavily guarded Warsaw Ghetto, where Jews were housed in terrible conditions before being sent to their deaths in Nazi concentration camps. Sendler was eventually caught by the Nazis, subjected to terrible torture, and sentenced to death. Miraculously, she escaped death, and after the war she attempted to reunite the children she saved with their families.

Sendler's heroic story remained largely unknown to the public until 1999, when an inspired group of high-school students in Kansas learned of her heroism and later wrote a school play in her honor. The play was called *Life in a Jar*, a reference to the jar in which Sendler secretly kept the names of the thousands of children whom she saved. This play has since been performed hundreds of times all around the globe. The students and their teacher deserve great credit for bringing Sendler's amazing tale into the world's consciousness. The students were Elizabeth Cambers, Megan Stewart, Jessica Shelton, and Sabrina Coons; their teacher was Norm Conard.

Irena Sendler displayed the willingness and courage to take action rather than stand passively by while atrocities were committed against other human beings. As Edmund Burke is reputed to have said, "All that is necessary for the triumph of evil is for good men to do nothing." Most non-Jewish Polish citizens in 1942 meekly accepted the Nazis' brutality. Heroes such as Sendler do not cower from evil; they confront it, even at great peril to their own well-being.

The New York subway hero, Wesley Autrey, once said, "I did what anyone could do, and what anyone ought to do." Irena Sendler showed the same humility. She wrote, "Heroes do extraordinary things. What I did was not an extraordinary thing. It was normal." Autrey and Sendler are typical of many heroes who don't believe that their actions are exceptional, but many psychological studies point to the rareness with which average people show a willingness to risk life and limb for others. Most situations that beg for heroes feature strong social pressures that inhibit the heroic response. Heroes are somehow able to overcome these pressures and do the right thing, however difficult and dangerous it may be.

Throughout her life, Irena Sendler never claimed any credit for her actions. "I could have done more," she said. "This regret will follow me to my death." Sendler lived long enough to personally meet those four extraordinary Kansas students who told her story to the world. She passed away in 2008 at the age of 98.

George Bailey: A Hero's Wonderful Life

Sometimes great movies and great movie heroes aren't perceived as great right away. Years may go by before audiences begin to appreciate the artistic and heroic significance of the movie and its characters. A stirring example is the 1946 film *It's a Wonderful Life*, starring James Stewart and directed by Frank Capra. The lead character, George Bailey, emerges as one of the most saintly and selfless characters in movie history. As a child he saves his brother's life and stops the local pharmacist from accidentally poisoning a customer. As a young adult, he sacrifices his own life plans to save the town of Bedford Falls from falling into the hands of Mr. Potter, a greedy slumlord who is as evil as Bailey is good.

But it isn't George Bailey's heroic battle with Mr. Potter that makes him such an unforgettable hero. What moves us most about Bailey's character is the fallout from a mistake made by Bailey's uncle, who misplaces a sizeable amount of cash that Bailey owes the bank. The cash inadvertently falls into the hands of Mr. Potter, who issues a warrant for Bailey's arrest rather than return the cash.

The prospect of prison time prompts Bailey to consider suicide, but a guardian angel appears and shows Bailey what the world would be like had Bailey not existed. Bailey is stunned to learn that without him the world is a dark, grim place with thousands of lives lost or ruined. In this alternative timeline, Bailey is devastated to discover that his many friends are either dead or unrecognizably scarred, and that even his family does not exist.

The guardian angel then returns the distraught Bailey to the original timeline. Recognizing that he's had a wonderful life, Bailey rushes home a happy man, despite being informed by authorities that he is under arrest for misappropriating funds. The prospect of imprisonment means far less to him than seeing his family again. At this moment, dozens of Bailey's friends and neighbors arrive to help him. Hearing that he is in financial trouble, they happily give him money of their own while joyously recounting the many times Bailey has saved them. The amount of cash given Bailey is many times the amount he owes, and so the warrant for his arrest is dismissed. In an ironic reversal of the usual hero storyline, the hero Bailey has been saved by the town's citizens.

Why does this final scene in the film pack such an emotional punch? One reason is that it very powerfully portrays a community's spontaneous and selfless celebration of Bailey's heroism. In a collective act of supreme goodwill, Bailey's unsung and life-long devotion to helping others is finally recognized and rewarded. The movie reminds us that although we need heroes, there are times when heroes need us, and that average people can—and do—perform great heroic acts of collective gratitude to deserving Samaritans among us.

Director and producer Frank Capra lived long enough to witness the burgeoning popularity of *It's a Wonderful Life* beginning in the 1970s. "It's the damnedest thing I've ever seen," Capra said in 1984.

> The film has a life of its own now and I can look at it like I had nothing to do with it. I'm like a parent whose kid grows up to be president. I'm proud, but it's the kid who did the work.

Confucius: The Master Hero of Virtue

There are some heroes whose wisdom is so timeless and profound that they are able to shape the moral philosophy of an entire society for millennia. Confucius was such a hero. Born in 551 BCE in the province of Shantung in northeast China, Confucius lived in an era when China was being carved into feudal states by warlords who engaged in vicious battles, oppressed slave laborers, and heavily taxed citizens. Despite this domestic turmoil, or perhaps because of it, Confucius fashioned a philosophy of virtuous living that is embraced today by hundreds of millions of Chinese, Japanese, Koreans, and Vietnamese.

Most Confucian wisdom is contained in the *Analects of Confucius*, which was compiled by his students after his death. In the *Analects*, Confucius modestly presents himself as a "transmitter who invented nothing". He places strong emphasis on the importance of *study*; in fact, the Chinese character for *study* opens the text. For this reason, Chinese people view Confucius as the greatest of all masters. In Confucianism, people are teachable, improvable, and capable of great morality. Throughout the *Analects*, Confucius preaches honesty, hard work, and learning by example. He communicates his wisdom through conversation, by asking questions, and by imploring students to find their own answers.

Confucianism also encourages the development of a humble attitude. One of his better-known aphorisms is "Real knowledge is to know the extent of one's ignorance"—a sentiment that would be expressed by another philosopher, Socrates, more than a century later in ancient Greece. Foremost, in the *Analects* it is clear that Confucius prepares his students for public service, to develop compassion, and to respect others. His philosophy emphasizes justice, sincerity, and morality in one's personal life and in government. In the chaotic political environment of his times, he looks with a nostalgic eye to earlier times in Chinese history, when leaders treated citizens with wisdom and compassion.

Confucianism exhorts all people to strive for the ideal of the "perfect person." An apt description of perfection is combining "the qualities of saint, scholar, and gentleman." Perfect people display morality, piety, and loyalty. They cultivate humanity or benevolence. They champion strong familial loyalty, ancestor worship, and respect of elders by their children. According to Confucius, strong family values and relationships are the key to a stable society. Mutual respect and devotion to family are central to his teachings.

Although Confucianism is often followed in a religious manner by the Chinese, it is not necessarily clear whether his teachings represent a religion per se. There are certainly a number of aphorisms that bear a resemblance to religious tenets. For example, he expressed one of the earliest versions of the Golden Rule when he wrote, "Do not do to others what you do not want done to yourself." The position adopted by most people is that Confucianism is more of a moral science or philosophy than it is a religion.

There truly is no western counterpart to Confucius. His contributions to philosophy, morality, and education have been profound and enduring. For more than 2,500 years he has remained an integral part of the Chinese cultural identity. In the People's Republic of China, Confucius is honored on October 1, the anniversary of his death. In Taiwan, he is honored on his birthday, September 28. A legal holiday in Taiwan, September 28 is referred to as *Teacher's Day*, honoring the greatest teacher in Chinese history.

Mother Teresa and the Call to Love

Earlier we described the "Great Eight" traits of heroes—*smart, strong, selfless, caring, charismatic, resilient, reliable*, and *inspiring*. Which of these eight attributes is most central to heroism? Recently we asked a group of our students to rank the "Great Eight" list of traits in their order of importance. The results showed that one trait emerged as the most important: *selflessness*. Heroes, it seems, are characterized by their service to others, consistently placing the welfare of other people ahead of their own well-being.

Perhaps no other individual is more strongly associated with the trait of selflessness than Mother Teresa. As a young woman, Mother Teresa felt the call to serve God. At the age of 18 she left her home in Macedonia and joined the Sisters of Loreto, a community of nuns with missions in India. In 1931 she took her vows as a nun and joined a convent in Calcutta. At that time she experienced what she later described as *the call within the call*. "I was to leave the convent and help the poor while living among them," she said. "It was an order. To fail would have been to break the faith."

Mother Teresa obtained permission to leave the convent and work among the poorest of the poor in the slums of Calcutta. Her first year in the slums was painful and challenging. She had no source of income and had to beg for food and supplies. Troubled by doubt and fear, Mother Teresa was strongly tempted to return to the comfort of convent life.

But she persevered, and slowly she began to inspire a group of followers and supporters. In 1950 she founded the Missionaries of Charity to care for—in her own words—"the hungry, the naked, the homeless, the crippled, the blind, the lepers, all those people who feel unwanted, unloved, uncared for throughout society, people that have become a burden to the society and are shunned by everyone." The Missionaries of Charity began with 13 members and today has 5,000 nuns running orphanages, AIDS hospices, and charity centers that care for refugees, the blind, disabled, aged, alcoholics, the poor and homeless, and victims of floods, epidemics, and famine.

During her lifetime, Mother Teresa became an international symbol of love and service to others. She appeared 18 times in Gallup's annual poll of the most admired men and women in the world, finishing first several times in the 1980s and 1990s. A Gallup poll of Americans in 1999 ranked her first among the "Most Widely Admired People of the 20th Century." Much of Mother Teresa's appeal stems from her love for all people regardless of religion or ethnicity. "It is important that everyone is seen as equal before God," she observed. "I've always said we should help a Hindu become a better Hindu, a Muslim become a better Muslim, a Catholic become a better Catholic."

Although Mother Teresa championed the cause of helping the poor in India, she was deeply concerned with the emotional and spiritual well-being of people residing in the more affluent Western world. "I found the poverty of the West so much more difficult to remove," she said.

> The poverty in the West is a different kind of poverty—it is not only a poverty of loneliness but also of spirituality. There's a hunger for love, as there is a hunger for God. The hunger for love is much more difficult to remove than the hunger for bread.

Before her death in 1997, Mother Teresa was widely known as a "living saint." Since her death, she has progressed rapidly toward attaining actual sainthood, an honor the church will bestow upon her in a few short years. The overarching theme of her life was simply loving others. "Not all of us can do great things," she said. "But we can do small things with great love. Love is a fruit in season at all times, and within reach of every hand."

Lois Wilson: The Hero Who Helped Families of Alcoholics

Heroes of great causes don't necessarily start out as exceptional people. In fact, it's not unusual for heroes to be everyday people who experience a life-changing calamity that transforms them into champions of a social movement. Examples include John Walsh, who established the TV program *America's Most Wanted* after his five-year-old son was murdered; and Candace Lightner, who founded Mothers Against Drunk Driving after her 13-year-old daughter was killed by a hit-and-run driver. To this list we add Lois Wilson, who created the Al-Anon Family Groups after experiencing many years of emotional heartache and financial ruin while living with her alcoholic husband, Bill. Lois was among the first to recognize that alcoholism is a family disease that has adverse emotional effects on every member of the alcoholic's family.

The story of Lois and Bill is quite poignant. After marrying Bill in 1918, Lois witnessed him and their marriage spiral downhill due to the ravages of the disease of alcoholism. During the 1920s and 30s, Bill's drinking problem destroyed his career, his relationships, and his health. Lois tried, but there was nothing she could do to stop him from drinking. Desperate for children, they were turned down by adoption agencies when they discovered Bill's problem. They lost their home. Bill checked in and out of alcoholic sanitariums as he neared the point of either insanity or death.

Miraculously, in 1934 Bill had a spiritual awakening, stopped drinking, and co-founded Alcoholics Anonymous. While her husband attended AA meetings, Lois would socialize with family members of other alcoholics and became aware of the devastating effects of the disease on spouses and children. In 1951 she established the Al-Anon Family Groups, a program of recovery for families and friends of alcoholics. Today there are over 29,000 Al-Anon groups worldwide, with a membership close to 400,000.

What are the core tenets of Al-Anon? First, it is promoting the idea that no one but the alcoholic can stop the drinking. In Al-Anon, family members beaten down by the disease learn that they can be as sick as the alcoholic, even if they don't drink. Al-Anon members focus on two main goals: enriching their own moral and spiritual lives, and not contributing further to the alcoholic's disease. During the early years of Al-Anon, Lois spoke to many groups, sharing her wisdom and inspiring tens of thousands of people. She was instrumental in helping develop Al-Anon books, pamphlets, manuals, and guidelines. The program grew and became a healthy, widely respected organization.

As with many heroes, Lois had parents who taught her generosity and service to others. She always gave Bill unconditional love, even during the worst moments of their marriage. Lois exuded a positive attitude, which has its imprint all over Al-Anon's principles of recovery. "The world seems to me excruciatingly, almost painfully beautiful at times," she said, adding that "the goodness and kindness of people often exceed that which even I expect."

Nathan Hale and the Powerful Heroic Script

Heroes are often known through a particular image or association. When we hear their names, something specific springs to mind. While most schoolchildren know almost nothing about early American hero Nathan Hale, they are likely to know what he supposedly said when he was hung for spying: "I only regret that I have but one life to give for my country." But this quote actually sheds light on a deeper aspect of the way people think about heroes and heroism.

Nathan Hale was a young Revolutionary War soldier from Connecticut. A Yale graduate and a teacher, in 1776 he undertook a dangerous assignment during the battle for New York. He would go undercover and pretend to be a loyalist to the British crown. His mission was to collect information about General William Howe's deployment of British and Hessian troops in and around the city. Before long, Hale was recognized and captured. There was no doubt that he was guilty of spying. Hanging was a certainty. But Hale was offered the chance to speak before his sentence of death was carried out. He gave what many witnesses said was an eloquent speech, with the most memorable passage expressing his regret at not being able to give more than one life.

What is most interesting about that statement is that it was almost surely based on lines from fiction that Hale, like most educated citizens of the time, knew well. They come from a climactic scene in Joseph Addison's famous 1712 play, *Cato,* where the hero, facing death like Hale, proclaims "How beautiful is death, when earn'd by virtue? Who would not be that youth? What pity is it that we can die but once to serve our country."

What is the significance of Hale basing his own last words on those of a fictional hero? Fictional heroes are molded to reflect popular conceptions, or images, of courageous and altruistic behavior. But they not only reflect those popular conceptions, they also shape them. The playwright wants to do more than create characters and scenes that are familiar to the public. More important is putting an original stamp or interpretation on ideals such as heroism. In *Cato*, Addison certainly did that. He created a powerful script for heroic young men facing death.

Nathan Hale wanted to leave behind an eloquent and moving statement, both to claim honor for himself and to provide inspiration for others. The war would be long and difficult, and fashioning a heroic model might contribute as much or more than detailing the movements of enemy combatants. Surely the example of a brave young soldier willingly dying for the cause would provide a needed morale boost to General Washington's weary army. Hale crafted carefully a powerful expression of his unwavering commitment to the cause. Joseph Addison's words helped him create one that Americans remember many, many years later.

Dana Reeve: The Unsung Selfless Hero

It is not unusual for heroes to emerge from crisis. We call these crisis situations *heroic moments*. At these times, the hero truly separates herself from others by rising to the occasion, displaying uncommon selflessness, courage, and grace. In 1995, when her husband Christopher Reeve was paralyzed from the neck down after a horse-riding accident, Dana Reeve seized the heroic moment and became one of the most selfless and inspiring individuals that we've heard about in many years.

Prior to the accident, Dana and Christopher Reeve led a charmed life. They were talented, attractive, successful, and happy. He was an accomplished actor known especially for his film role as Superman during the 1970s and 80s. Dana herself was a successful actress and singer. She graduated cum laude from Middlebury College in 1984, met Christopher in 1987, and married him in 1992. They soon had a son. Life was good.

Then came the horrific accident that shattered Christopher's uppermost vertebrae. At first, things looked bleak and hopeless. But Dana was the source of support and love that fueled his determination to survive and live a life that would become an inspiration to millions. A pivotal moment came just days after the accident. After assessing his dire situation, Christopher considered suicide. He mouthed the words to Dana, "Maybe we should let me go." In tears, she replied,

I am only going to say this once: I will support whatever you want to do, because this is your life, and your decision. But I want you to know that I'll be with you for the long haul, no matter what. You're still you. And I love you.

Hearing these words, he never considered ending his life again.

Christopher insisted that Dana resume her singing and acting career. She remained busy but rarely left Christopher's side. She bristled at the media label of her as *Saint Dana* and *Superwoman*:

I felt very uncomfortable with that. There was nothing superhuman about standing by Chris. That compliment always felt a little false. What's so saintly about that? Lucky me. I'm with him! Really, my job here is to be the voice for the many, many spouses who are caregivers, who don't have the advantage of the world patting them on the back every day.

When Christopher died in 2004, Dana felt compelled to continue her efforts to seek better treatments for paralysis. For her, there was no choice. "I have to carry on his mission," she said. She was unanimously elected as head of the Christopher Reeve Foundation, which eventually changed its name to the Christopher and Dana Reeve Foundation.

Sadly, within a year of Christopher's death, Dana was diagnosed with lung cancer. "Now, more than ever, I feel Chris with me as I face this challenge," she announced. "As always, I look to him as the ultimate example of defying the odds with strength, courage, and hope in the face of life's adversities." Dana underwent aggressive treatments but lost her battle with cancer on March 6, 2006. Her good friend, actor Robin Williams, best summed up the loss: "The brightest light has gone out."

We can learn several things from the Dana Reeve story. First, it is that tragic circumstances often beget heroes who seize the heroic moment. The worst of times can bring out the best in people. A second lesson is that heroes need social support. The heroic journey of Christopher Reeve might not have happened at all without the continuous loving support of Dana. Throughout Christopher's recovery, she remained a beacon of hope. "We have become accustomed to living our life with joy amidst pain and challenges," she said, while telling Christopher that "I still you love you; I will continue to love you. We will get through this together, and I promise to keep you challenged and not to pity you."

Groundhog Day's Phil Connors and the Heroic Theme of Redemption

One of the most compelling actions that a hero can perform is an act of redemption. A redeeming act is any behavior that corrects a previous misstep or wrongdoing. Redemptive acts are common occurrences in athletic competitions, as when a football placekicker boots the winning field goal after botching a kick the previous week. Especially powerful instances of redemption are great acts of morality that follow prior moral transgressions. This type of moral redemption is portrayed in a most poignant way in *Groundhog Day*, a movie released in 1993 starring Bill Murray and produced by Harold Ramis.

In *Groundhog Day*, the lead character, Phil Connors, is a television weatherman who is arrogant, nasty, and utterly self-absorbed. Connors spends February 2 covering the Groundhog Day festivities in Punxsutawney, Pennsylvania, a place he despises. But when he wakes up the following morning, he discovers that it is February 2 in Punxsutawney all over again. To his horror, this day continues to repeat itself, and Connors is trapped in Punxsutawney in a seemingly endless time loop.

At first, Connors uses the repetition of the day to steal money and to manipulate women to sleep with him. Yet the one woman he grows to love, his producer Rita, won't succumb to his advances. Connors grows depressed when he realizes that his methods will never allow him to achieve real intimacy with Rita. He becomes suicidal, believing he is stuck, alone forever, in a dull town on an endlessly cold winter day.

Connors' road to redemption begins when he honestly confides to Rita what is happening to him. She shows him great empathy, suggests that his plight may actually be a gift, and for the first time spends the entire day with him. When Connors awakes to repeat yet another February 2, he is a new man. He takes piano and ice-sculpting lessons. He helps a poor homeless man. He saves a boy from a bad fall, performs the Heimlich maneuver on a choking victim, and fixes an old woman's flat tire.

Rita witnesses the change in Connors and falls in love with him. The arrogance and selfishness that once characterized him have been replaced by kindness, enlightenment, and a drive to make the best out of one's circumstances. At the end of the day, they fall asleep, in love and in his bed. And when Connors awakes, she is still there, it is finally February 3, and the cycle has been broken. Connors' long redemptive journey has been completed.

Over the years, *Groundhog Day* has received high acclaim from both critics and audiences. The movie has found its way onto Roger Ebert's "Great Movies" series. In 2009, the American literary theorist and legal scholar Stanley Fish named the film one of America's all-time greatest movies. In 2006, the film was added to the United States National Film Registry for being "culturally, historically, and aesthetically significant."

Groundhog Day's story of redemption moves many people deeply, a reaction that caught director and producer Harold Ramis by surprise. He said:

> This movie spoke to people on a lot of levels. The spiritual community responded to this film in an unprecedented way. Hasidic Jews held up signs outside of theaters asking, "Are you living the same day over and over again?" Then I started getting letters from the Zen Buddhist community, the Yoga community, the Christian fundamentalist community, the psychoanalytic community, and everyone claiming that this was their philosophy and that I must be one of them for having made this movie.

The story of a hero's redemptive journey has universal appeal and touches something powerful inside the human psyche. To legions of people, there is great spiritual significance in Bill Murray's unforgettable portrayal of the hero Phil Connors. *Groundhog Day* suggests that all of us, whatever our flaws or circumstances, can redeem ourselves.

Rabbi Israel Spira: A Hero of the Holocaust

Sometimes unimaginably terrible circumstances produce the most inspirational stories of human heroism. The Nazi concentration camps of World War II housed Jews, gypsies, gays, the disabled, and other groups deemed "undesirable" by the Nazis. Conditions at the camps were nightmarish. Prisoners were subjected to starvation diets, forced into slave labor, and routinely beaten. Millions died in the gas chambers, or from firing squads, starvation, overcrowding, disease, or exposure to cold.

In 1982, Yaffa Eliach authored an important book called *Hasidic Tales of the Holocaust*, in which Jewish survivors of the concentration camps told their harrowing stories of survival. One of the most moving tales was that of Israel Spira, a rabbi who suffered horribly in the camps, yet survived to become one of the great spiritual leaders of the Jewish community in Brooklyn, New York after the war. His wife and children were not so fortunate; all of them were murdered by the Nazis.

Spira recalled one particular incident that took place during his imprisonment in the Janowska concentration camp in Poland. On a cold winter night, a German voice over the loudspeaker barked out the following order: "You are all to evacuate the barracks immediately and report to the vacant lot. Anyone remaining inside will be shot on the spot!" Exhausted and emaciated, the prisoners stumbled to the vacant field and saw before them a large open pit. The voice commanded, "Each of you dogs who values his miserable life must jump over the pit and land on the other side. Those who miss will get what they rightfully deserve—ra-ta-ta-ta-ta." The voice imitated the sound of a machine gun.

According to Spira, jumping over the pit would have been nearly impossible even under the best of circumstances. The prisoners were "skeletons", feverish from disease, and physically exhausted from their daily labors. Spira himself suffered from bruised and swollen feet. Awaiting their turn to jump, he and a close friend watched prisoners die in a hail of bullets with each unsuccessful attempt. The bodies began to pile up in the pit. Spira's friend recommended that they should not bother trying and simply accept death, but Spira encouraged him to jump.

They leapt into the darkness and found themselves alive on the other side of the pit. Incredulous at their success, Spira's friend asked him how he did it. "I was holding on to my ancestral merit," said Spira. "I was holding on to the coattails of my father, and my grandfather and my great-grandfather, of blessed memory."

Spira then asked his friend how he reached the other side of the pit. "I was holding on to you," he said.

Spira miraculously survived several years in the camps. During that time, he buoyed the spirits of his fellow Jews by secretly performing important Jewish rituals and ceremonies, such as lighting the menorah, saying blessings, and obtaining matzah. To acquire materials for these observances, Spira would establish a rapport with the camp commandant or guards. When asked why he bothered to recite the Hanukkah blessing amidst such suffering and death, Spira noted that he saw "faith" and "devotion" in the faces of the prisoners all around him. "If, indeed, I was blessed to see such a people with faith and fervor, then I am under special obligation to recite the blessing," he said.

Heroes help people even under the most grim of circumstances. Spira witnessed the horrors of the Holocaust unfolding right before him, but it didn't deter him from doing everything he could to lift the spirits and faith of those around him. Six million people perished in the camps, but Spira lived to become a highly revered religious figure for many years before passing away peacefully in 1989. He once said, "There are events of such overbearing magnitude that one ought not to remember them all the time, but one must not forget them either. Such an event is the Holocaust."

Rosa Parks' Transforming Act of Civil Disobedience

Heroism can take a lot of time to achieve, or it can happen in a split second. In this book we profile many heroes who devote their entire lives to doing heroic deeds, accumulating an impressive body of work over many decades. Examples of this type of heroism achieved across the lifespan include Mahatma Gandhi, Nelson Mandela, and Martin Luther King, Jr. But we also give ample coverage to heroes who perform a single bold action that instantly catapults them to heroic status. New York subway hero Wesley Autrey is a vivid example of this type of instantaneous heroism.

Perhaps once in a generation we are witness to a rare and extraordinary individual who assumes the characteristics of both kinds of heroes. Rosa Parks was one such person. Her single act of civil disobedience on December 1, 1955 forever transformed the American racial and political landscape. And her life-long commitment to promoting racial equality paved the way for sweeping changes in American culture and helped bring about the Civil Rights Act of 1964.

Before 1964, Jim Crow laws enacted during the post-Civil War Reconstruction required racial separation in buses, restaurants, and public transportation. Those laws also legally sanctioned racial discrimination that prevented blacks from pursuing many careers and from residing in certain neighborhoods. Rosa Parks lived and worked under such conditions. One rainy day in 1943, a bus driver demanded that she give up her seat for a white passenger. While changing seats she dropped her purse, and to retrieve her spilled belongings she had to take a moment to use a seat reserved for white riders. The bus driver became enraged and barely let her step off the bus before speeding off.

Years of this kind of subjugation eventually took their toll on Parks. On December 1, 1955, after working a long day, she headed to the bus to make her way home. On this day she once again complied with the rules, which required black passengers to enter the front of the bus to pay the fare then exit and re-enter the back of the bus where blacks were required to sit. When the bus became full, Parks was asked by the driver to give up her seat for a white passenger. This time she refused. Later she recalled that although she was tired from working a long day, more importantly she was "tired of giving in."

Police arrested her, and four days later Parks was convicted of disorderly conduct. A 26-year-old Baptist minister, the Rev. Martin Luther King, Jr., heard of her arrest and organized a boycott of Montgomery buses. Tens of thousands of blacks were galvanized by Parks' simple act of defiance. She had single-handedly triggered an unstoppable flood of protest and legislative work geared toward bringing about long overdue social change. A year after Parks' arrest, the Supreme Court ruled that Alabama's laws requiring segregation on buses were illegal, and eight years later the landmark 1964 Civil Rights Act was signed into law by President Lyndon B. Johnson.

Some heroes are ordinary human beings who perform a single heroic act in response to a situation that requires immediate action. These heroes are everyday people who encounter a *heroic moment*, and they rise to the occasion by doing the right thing in that moment. Rosa Parks is remembered as a quiet woman whose simple act on a bus helped spark what was arguably the greatest social movement in American history.

Parks was voted by *Time* magazine as one of the 100 most influential people of the twentieth century. Long after that fateful day on the bus, Parks remained a quiet crusader for equal rights for all human beings. "I would like to be known as a person who is concerned about freedom and equality and justice and prosperity for all people," she said.

Corrie ten Boom: The Holocaust Hero with a Hiding Place

People are moved by powerful tales of heroism in defiance of Nazi Germany's eradication of Jews during World War II. For this reason, we earlier described the life of Rabbi Israel Spira, and now we focus on another remarkable story of selflessness and courage during this tragic period of human history. The hero to whom we now turn is Corrie ten Boom of the Netherlands.

Ten Boom was one of the leaders of the Dutch resistance during the Nazi occupation of the Netherlands. It is estimated that Corrie ten Boom helped 800 Jews avoid being shipped to Nazi concentration camps during the war. Ten Boom's father, Casper ten Boom, played a critical role in shaping her values and worldview. The ten Booms were devout Christians who lent a helping hand to people of all faiths. When Casper was asked if he knew he could die if he were caught helping Jews, he replied, "It would be an honor to give my life for God's chosen people."

To hide Jews in their home, the ten Booms built a secret room in Corrie's bedroom, located on the top floor of the building. The hidden room was behind a false wall that the ten Booms secretly constructed. The room was tiny, about the size of a medium-sized closet. To enter the room, people had to crawl on their hands and knees through a small panel in a lower cupboard. An electronic buzzer was installed to give the home's residents warning of a raid. When the Nazis raided the ten Boom house in 1944, six people used the hidden room to avoid detection.

Eventually, though, an informant reported the ten Booms' activities to the authorities and the entire ten Boom family was shipped to concentration camps. Corrie and her sister Betsie were sent to the Vught concentration camp and later to the notorious Ravensbrück camp in Germany. It was here that Betsie died on December 16, 1944. Before she died, Betsie reassured Corrie that God and love would triumph over the evil that surrounded them. "There is no pit so deep that God's love is not deeper still," Betsie told her.

To her surprise, Corrie was released from Ravensbrück camp on New Year's Eve of December 1944. She later learned that her discharge was due to a clerical error. She also learned that one week after her release all the women her age were sent to the gas chamber. After the war, in 1947, Corrie was approached one day by one of the cruelest former Ravensbrück camp guards. "Will you forgive me?" he asked, and held out his hand. Ten Boom recalled the moment:

> I stood there and could not. Betsie had died in that place. Could he erase her slow terrible death simply for the asking? It could not have been many seconds that he stood there, hand held out, but to me it seemed hours as I wrestled with the most difficult thing I had ever had to do. We then grasped each other's hands, the former guard and the former prisoner. I had never known God's love so intensely as I did then.

Heroes rarely choose the easy path in life. It would have been easy, and safe, for Corrie ten Boom and her family to turn away Jews who asked for sanctuary from Nazi oppression. But the ten Booms recognized that they would be accomplices to evil if they had condoned Hitler's genocidal Final Solution at work in their community. The ten Booms put their lives in danger, and some of them did ultimately lose their lives, trying to protect the innocent. There are no better heroes among us.

TRADITIONAL-COMPETENT HEROES

Marie Curie: Trailblazing Scientist Who Paid the Ultimate Price

In one of the other profiles in this book, we describe the heroism displayed by technicians working to repair Japan's damaged nuclear power plants. This remarkable sacrifice gives us pause to look back at the history of nuclear energy and our evaluations of the people who first harnessed it. Robert Oppenheimer, for example, served as the scientific director of the Manhattan Project that developed the first nuclear weapons during World War II. Oppenheimer's work was made possible by the innovative discoveries of many scientists before him, most notably the person who first discovered radioactivity, Marie Curie.

People are judged to be heroic to the extent that they overcome formidable obstacles to achieve great things. Albert Einstein once said that Marie Curie faced "the most unheard-of difficulties which have seldom been encountered in the history of experimental science." She lived in an era when women were denied opportunities to pursue professional careers. Curie's scientific brilliance and steadfast determination propelled her to success. She was also fortunate to have progressive parents who supported her educational pursuits, and a husband, Pierre, also a scientist, who valued her as an intellectual equal.

Marie and Pierre Curie were the first to recognize the special properties of pitch-blende waste left over from uranium mining operations in Austria. The dangers of radiation were unknown at that time, and while extracting this residue the Curies unknowingly exposed themselves to radioactive fumes. For years they carried out much of their work without proper safety measures in place. Curie herself often carried test tubes containing radioactive isotopes in her pocket and stored them in her desk drawer, noting the attractive blue-green light that the substances emitted in the dark. These exposures to the hidden toxicity of radiation samples were likely responsible for the leukemia that killed her in 1934.

Curie's career accomplishments as a scientist were substantial and enduring. She was the first person to coin the term *radiation* and to develop a theory of radiation. Curie was also the first female professor at the University of Paris, and the first recipient of two Nobel Prizes, one in physics and one in chemistry. She developed important techniques for isolating radioactive isotopes and was responsible for identifying two new elements, *polonium* and *radium*. When she died, she became the first woman to be buried under the famous dome of the Pantheon in Paris in recognition of her own accomplishments rather than being the wife of a famous man.

"We must believe that we are gifted for something," Curie once said, "and that this thing, at whatever cost, must be attained." She most certainly lived and died by those words. Although Curie's contributions to science were remarkable, she and others who helped usher in the nuclear age have been criticized by some for making weapons of mass destruction possible. We argue that these criticisms are misplaced. Curie opened up an entire new frontier of science that has benefited the human race much more than it has harmed it. We applaud her courage in overcoming the gender biases of her day to become one of the greatest scientists in human history.

Tina Fey: An Uncommon Celebrity Hero

A recent study by Gregory Baer suggests that celebrities are more likely than the general public to experience turbulence in their personal lives. Entertainment stars suffer from much higher rates of food, drug, and sex addiction, and they are more prone to divorce compared to the general population. Explanations for these data focus on the unique stresses and strains of the show-business lifestyle. Celebrities often endure long work hours, frequent travel from home, exposure to sycophants, and the stress of living under the media microscope.

With this backdrop, the life of Tina Fey is a refreshing exception to the rule. An accomplished writer, comedienne, actress, and producer, Fey began her career at the University of Virginia, where she studied drama. Unlike many students, Fey didn't abuse alcohol or drugs. "I want to be on record saying this, so that my daughter can see it one day in the future," she once said. "I have never done any drugs. I am extremely square and obedient in nature!"

After graduating from Virginia in 1992, Fey began performing improvisational comedy with Chicago's famed group The Second City. She met her future husband, Jeff Richmond, who was the first and only man with whom she has been intimate. Fey has said that she didn't lose her virginity until she was 24 years old. Always humble, Fey has joked that she "couldn't give it away," even though she was named one of the 50 most beautiful people in the world by *People* magazine.

In 1997 she became a writer for *Saturday Night Live*, and within two years she became the first ever female head writer for the show. Fey also enjoyed great popularity in a performing role as the co-host of *Weekend Update* with Jimmy Fallon. In 2004 she wrote and starred in the feature film *Mean Girls*, which attracted both critical and box-office success. Two years later Fey was given the opportunity to create, write, and star in her own TV series, *30 Rock*, a behind-the-scenes comedy about the production of a show similar to *Saturday Night Live*.

In its first three years on the air, *30 Rock* earned five Emmy Awards, and Fey herself has won Emmy, Golden Globe, People's Choice, and Screen Actors Guild awards for her role in the show. In 2008 the Associated Press awarded her their AP Entertainer of the Year award, naming her the performer who had the greatest impact on culture and entertainment.

We should add that Tina Fey's strong commitment to noble causes also makes her a hero. She has actively supported Autism Speaks, which helps families with autistic children, and Mercy Corps, a group devoted to ending world hunger. Fey also supports the Love Our Children USA organization, which fights violence against children, and Light The Night Walk, which benefits the Leukemia and Lymphoma Society.

Psychologists view self-control as a muscle. Keeping our self-control muscle in shape enhances our ability to make good on our life-defining commitments. Because doing the right thing is harder than knowing what that right thing is, our self-control muscle needs our regular attention. Tina Fey has somehow eluded all the self-destructive tendencies that often grip people in the entertainment industry. Our analysis of her life suggests that she has shown a commitment to exercise her self-control muscle, in both small and large ways, throughout her career. "I know my limits," she admits.

Ellen DeGeneres: Heroic Comedienne and Underdog Advocate

People not only love an underdog who prevails; they also revere the supportive people who help underdogs prevail. Ellen DeGeneres is a vivid example of an individual who has used her celebrity status to advocate for members of society who traditionally have not had a voice. After establishing herself as one of America's best comic talents, DeGeneres has dedicated her life to improving the lives of disadvantaged children, animals, and cancer survivors.

Raised in Louisiana, DeGeneres started her career as a stand-up comic at small local clubs. Audiences loved her and she soon began touring nationally. Her big break came when she appeared on the Johnny Carson show in 1986. In 1997, during an episode of her highly acclaimed television sitcom *Ellen*, DeGeneres made her homosexuality public. Since that time she has become a tireless advocate of gay rights. As host of her Emmy Award-winning *Ellen DeGeneres Show*, she has strongly condemned the recent trend of teenage boys committing suicide after being bullied about their sexual orientation. "Something must be done," said DeGeneres. "This needs to be a wake-up call to everyone that teenage bullying and teasing is an epidemic in this country, and the death rate is climbing. We have an obligation to change this."

DeGeneres has also been heavily involved in causes that protect animal rights. She recently teamed up with the U.S. Postal Service to promote a campaign aimed at increasing animal adoption from local shelters. "This is a subject I am extremely passionate about," DeGeneres said. "By working together, we can find good homes for millions of adoptable, homeless and abandoned pets." DeGeneres was named PETA's 2009 Woman of the Year for her effective role in promoting the welfare of animals.

As befits a hero, the list of charities that DeGeneres supports with her time and money is lengthy. She helped launch the Small Change Campaign to support and benefit the organization Feeding America, which distributes food to hungry Americans. DeGeneres has been a strong promoter of Breast Cancer Awareness Month on her show, and she has also supported the Children's Health Fund, the Society for Animal Protective Legislation, St. Jude Children's Research Hospital, the American Wild Horse Preservation Campaign, and the Humane Society. DeGeneres has contributed significantly to the Hurricane Katrina Relief Fund through the American Red Cross. In 2009 she received the Tulane University President's Medal. Tulane President Scott Cowen said, "She never forgot New Orleans, especially after Katrina."

Our research on heroes reveals that people view heroes as either extremely competent, extremely moral, or both. Ellen DeGeneres falls into this last category. Her comic genius has been compared to that of Jerry Seinfeld, Woody Allen, and Steve Martin, and her television shows have earned dozens of Emmy Awards. Most impressively, she has used her stature in the entertainment industry to fight for the rights of disadvantaged people and animals. In the eyes of millions, her advocacy of numerous underdog causes has elevated Ellen DeGeneres to the status of a heroic leader.

John Nash: A Hero's Brilliant Triumph Over Mental Illness

Our studies of heroes reveal that people are quick to assign heroic status to those who successfully overcome daunting obstacles. Sometimes these obstacles are external and physically imposing, as when Sir Edmund Hillary and Tenzing Norgay reached the summit of Mount Everest in 1953. But sometimes these obstacles are internal and psychologically formidable. John Forbes Nash, the groundbreaking mathematician, is a striking example of a person who courageously battled, and overcame, the demon of severe mental illness that gripped him through much of his life.

From a very young age, Nash displayed a natural genius for mathematics. The only signs of the paranoid schizophrenia that would debilitate him later in life were his tendencies toward acerbic isolation and aloofness. Because of his mathematical brilliance, people overlooked his quirkiness. Nash was admitted to Princeton University's doctoral program at the tender age of 20, and he was offered a faculty position at MIT at the astonishingly young age of 23.

Throughout his twenties, Nash made landmark contributions to the fields of economics and mathematics. In his 27-page doctoral dissertation, written at the age of 21, he formulated his now-famous solution, called the *Nash equilibrium*, to vexing two-person non-cooperative games. Nash also enhanced our understanding of differential geometry and partial differential equations. His contributions have had a significant and enduring impact on evolutionary biology, artificial intelligence, military strategy, and market economics.

But by the age of 30, Nash began having auditory hallucinations that completely incapacitated him. He believed that an organization composed of men wearing red ties was placing him in danger, and he began inventing individual characters, some of them extraterrestrials, whom he believed were after him. Nash left his tenured position at MIT, was admitted to a series of mental hospitals in America and in Europe, and received numerous therapies, including drug and insulin shock therapies.

None of these treatments provided long-term relief, and for years Nash led a disgraced and solitary life as an outcast of society. But miraculously, by the age of 60 Nash's symptoms had abated and he slowly regained his sanity. His friends were contacted by Stockholm's Nobel Prize committee, who wanted to know if Nash was lucid enough to receive the award. They assured the committee that he was now fine. And so, in 1994, Nash received the highest acclaim that a scientist can receive, the Nobel Prize for his groundbreaking contributions to economics. Shortly afterward, an Academy Award-winning movie was made about his life, called *A Beautiful Mind*, starring Russell Crowe as Nash.

Someone once asked Nash, "How could you, a mathematician, believe that extraterrestrials were sending you messages?" Nash replied, "Because the ideas I had about supernatural beings came to me the same way my mathematical ideas did. So I took them seriously." Scientists who study paranoid schizophrenia claim that it is virtually impossible for a person to overcome the illness without treatment. That Nash was able to conquer his inner demons on his own may have been every bit as remarkable as any mathematical discoveries he made.

Althea Gibson: Barrier Breaker and Way Paver

African-Americans have had to break numerous barriers in U.S. society. For a brief period after the Civil War, blacks in the country seemed on the verge of genuine political equality, and an uneasy but real social equality. However, with the end of Reconstruction in 1877, African-American advances were stopped cold. Conditions became worse and worse during the early 1900s Jim Crow era. When Al Smith received the nomination for president at the Democratic Party convention in Houston, Texas in 1928, African-Americans were separated from whites in the convention hall by chicken wire.

During the administrations of Franklin Roosevelt (1933–1945) some forward progress was achieved but racial segregation in the South and other parts of the United States was firmly implanted, and Southern blacks were almost completely disenfranchised. The late 1940s saw two major breakthroughs. In 1947 Jackie Robinson broke the color line in Major League Baseball with the Brooklyn Dodgers, and in 1948 President Harry Truman desegregated the armed forces of the United States by executive order. But individual African-Americans had to put themselves on the line to chip away at one obstacle after another. One such person was the tennis player Althea Gibson.

Gibson was born in South Carolina and brought up in Harlem. She won table tennis tournaments in the Police Athletic Leagues and attracted the attention of people who thought she could excel in the game of tennis. One of her sponsors was Dr. Walter Johnson from Lynchburg, Virginia, who later assisted Arthur Ashe to develop his tennis career. With the help of Johnson and other patrons, Gibson finally was able to graduate from college and break into a highly segregated tennis circuit.

Finally in 1950, after white tennis player Alice Marble wrote in a magazine article that only "bigotry" prevented Gibson from playing in major tournaments, Gibson became the first African-American, male or female, to play at Forest Hills in New York, home of the U.S. Open tennis championships. The next year she became the first black person to play in the prestigious Wimbledon tournament in England.

Her performances improved steadily, and in 1956 she won the French Open. In 1957 she won both the singles and doubles championships at Wimbledon. That year and the next she triumphed in the U.S. Open. The Associated Press named her Female Athlete of the Year in 1957. Turning professional, she won the women's singles title in 1960.

Later, Gibson took a turn at a professional golfing career but had only modest success. She returned to tennis and eventually became a valued instructor. In 1975, she was named Commissioner of Athletics in New Jersey and stayed in that position for ten years. Later Gibson suffered a stroke and endured multiple health and financial problems. She went on welfare and contemplated suicide. Tennis great Billie Jean King, among others, helped her through some of the most difficult times. However, her health continued to decline. She died in 2003 at the age of 76.

Gibson was helped by many people throughout her life—before, during, and after her career. At the same time, as the "Jackie Robinson of tennis" she blazed the trail for others, including Arthur Ashe. Gibson was one of the individuals who both gave and received aid in helping African-Americans advance in one significant sector of American society. To many, that qualifies her as a genuine if largely unrecognized hero.

Monica Seles: Tennis Hero and Tragedienne

Athletic heroism rarely occurs without years of preparation, hard work, and sacrifice. Achieving great success as an athlete requires arduous training to perfect skills and to attain world-class conditioning. A young hero-to-be starts out as a fresh upstart, an underdog who slowly begins building a resumé of successes. He or she is said to be *trending* toward heroism (see Chapter 1). Eventually the young phenom overtakes the older established stars and achieves the status of hero.

Monica Seles is an example of an individual who was not just trending toward heroism; she was trending toward being the greatest female tennis player of all time. Born and raised in Yugoslavia, Seles began winning professional tennis tournaments as a young teen. At the age of 16, she won her first Grand Slam singles title at the 1990 French Open, defeating World No. 1 Steffi Graf in the final match.

Seles absolutely dominated the women's tennis scene in 1991 and 1992. During those two years she replaced Graf as the world's best player by winning 22 titles and reaching 33 finals out of the 34 tournaments in which she played. Virtually unstoppable, Seles compiled a 159–12 win–loss record, which included winning 55 of 56 matches in Grand Slam tournaments. At the tender age of 19 she was on top of the tennis world and seemed destined to obliterate all of tennis's records.

Then tragedy struck. On April 3, 1993 during a quarter-final match at the Citizen Cup tournament in Hamburg, Germany, a man named Günter Parche ran onto the tennis court and stabbed Seles with a boning knife between her shoulder blades. Parche later said that he did it because he wanted Steffi Graf to become the number one ranked player again. Seles' stab wound was serious but took only a few weeks to heal. The incident, however, shattered her emotionally.

Parche was charged following the incident but was given only a two-year suspended sentence. Seles was devastated at the news and vowed never to play tennis in Germany again. "What people seem to be forgetting is that this man stabbed me intentionally and he did not serve any sort of punishment for it. I would not feel comfortable going back. I don't foresee that happening."

Although Seles was fit to play tennis throughout much of 1993 and 1994, she became clinically depressed in the aftermath of both the stabbing incident and her father's cancer diagnosis. Seles soon developed a food addiction and put on weight. Although she returned to tennis in 1995, she was never again the dominant player that she had been previously. In 2009, Seles released a book entitled *Getting A Grip: On My Body, My Mind, My Self* which chronicled her bout with depression and food addiction, her journey back to the game, and her new life beyond tennis.

When Seles retired in 2008, she was adored by fans who sympathized with her tragic story and admired her courage in overcoming many obstacles. Today Seles says that despite everything that she's been through, she is happy with her life. "The 'what ifs,' they are there. But I think the difficult years made me who I am today," she said. "And I think I'm a much happier person than I used to be."

The heroic journey can be unpredictable. Just as no one could have predicted Tiger Woods' fall from grace in 2009, no one anticipated Monica Seles' tragic encounter with a deranged man with a knife. Yet somehow, the knife attack allowed Seles to become an unsurpassed hero of a different type. *Sports Illustrated's* Jon Wertheim summed it up best:

> Transformed from champion to tragedienne, Seles became far more popular than she was while winning all those titles. It became impossible to root against her. At first, out of sympathy. Then because she revealed herself to be so thoroughly thoughtful, graceful, dignified. When she quietly announced her retirement last week at age 34, she exited as perhaps the most adored figure in the sport's history. As happy endings go, one could do worse.

Daniel Anderson: The Hero Who Redefined Alcoholism

One significant contribution of heroes is their ability to change the way we think about the world. Heroes challenge conventional thinking or traditional ways of conceiving everyday phenomena, and they do so in a way that improves the quality of people's lives. Daniel Anderson is a striking example of a hero who completely defied the conventional wisdom about the causes and treatment of alcoholism.

In the early 1950s, while working as a psychologist at Willmar State Hospital in Minnesota, Anderson began to question the prevailing view that alcoholism was caused by poor willpower and a weakness of character. At that time alcoholism carried with it a severe social stigma, with alcoholics receiving the same degree of disdain as common thieves and pedophiles. But Anderson hypothesized that drug and alcohol addiction wasn't caused by poor character or corrupt morals. He proposed that chemical addiction was a complex disease characterized by psychological, physical, social, and spiritual deficits.

With the goal of improving treatment for alcoholics, Anderson developed what is now known all around the world as the *Minnesota Model*. The central elements of the Minnesota Model are:

1. the recognition that addiction is an illness with multiple components;
2. the idea that improved mental and physical health is achieved through total abstinence;
3. the notion that education about the nature of chemical dependency helps people maintain sobriety;
4. the importance of having a trained interdisciplinary staff to aid addicts in recovery;
5. the recognition that the duration of treatment is highly individualized;
6. the importance of living in a therapeutic community that includes attending lectures, participating in support groups, and receiving individual therapy;
7. an emphasis on preparing and credentialing the recovered alcoholic to work in the field and become an important part of the multi-disciplinary treatment team; and
8. the idea that recovering addicts should be treated with dignity and respect by a caring, concerned staff.

Anderson's Minnesota Model represented a radical departure from previous treatment programs. Most significant was the model's emphasis on removing the stigma associated with alcoholism. "Anderson's most heroic quality was what he gave the struggling alcoholic: The gift of respect," said Marcia J. Lawton, founder of Virginia Commonwealth University's Alcohol and Drug Education and Rehabilitation program in the Department of Rehab Counseling. "He believed strongly that treatment should involve preserving the dignity of recovering alcoholics and giving them unconditional love."

Anderson was instrumental in creating the Hazelden Foundation treatment center in Minnesota, which has served as a model for alcohol and drug treatment facilities around the world. Throughout his career, Anderson was applauded for his selflessness. Shortly after establishing Hazelden, he became a highly sought-after consultant as other treatment programs grew in number. Anderson "always had the bests interests of patients at heart in his work," said John Schwarzlose, president of the Betty Ford Center in Rancho Mirage, California. "Some in Dan's position would have seen the Betty Ford Center as a potential threat to Hazelden's preeminence. Dan's reaction, however, was not only to graciously agree to help, but to encourage our center to improve on what Hazelden had done."

Our research on heroic work has shown how heroes have developed new ways of looking at old situations. In sixteenth-century Europe, Copernicus challenged the medieval view of the earth being the center of the universe. In ancient China, Confucius challenged the moral philosophies of Taoism and Legalism. In more modern times, the Dalai Lama, Martin Luther King, Jr., Gandhi, and other spiritual leaders have all challenged conventional thinking by advocating peaceful solutions to difficult conflicts. We argue that Dan Anderson's revolutionary contributions to our understanding of alcoholism and addiction have been no less significant. Tens of thousands of recovered individuals owe a tremendous debt of gratitude—and perhaps even their lives—to Anderson for his wisdom, compassion, and heroism.

Tough Without a Gun: Heroic Portrayals by Humphrey Bogart

It is somewhat ironic that the title of Stefan Kanfer's recent biography of Humphrey Bogart borrows Raymond Chandler's comment that "Bogart can be tough without a gun." Bogart uses a gun in some of his most iconic roles, including in the climactic scene in *Casablanca*, where he shoots the Nazi Major Strasser (but only after Strasser shoots first).

But there is a special brand of unarmed toughness to Bogart in many of his films. That quality has come to define a certain kind of male hero: powerful, self-contained, and independent, but ultimately kind, decisive, and moral.

One distinctive characteristic of powerful people is their self-control, their ability to direct their own behavior rather than let others manipulate them or "push their buttons." They know how to be patient, and how to wait out others so that they can take their own course of action. Ralph Waldo Emerson is often quoted as saying "A man is a hero not because he is braver than anyone else, but because he is brave for ten minutes longer." Abraham Lincoln, as an example, is credited with incredible patience, and an ability to keep his temper and his poise. He could not be rushed into action, but when he sensed the time was right he acted forcefully and without hesitation.

Perhaps Bogart illustrates this kind of controlled heroism most powerfully in the climactic scene of the 1948 film *Key Largo*. His character appears at a hotel on the Florida Keys run by the father and widow of a slain war buddy. He has come to pay respects to both. While he is there, the hotel has to endure not only a hurricane, but also a group of ruthless gangsters. Their leader is the notorious outlaw Johnny Rocco, played tensely by Edward G. Robinson. Initially the gangsters push Bogart around, along with the others. The audience hopes that he is simply biding his time, but it begins to look like he doesn't have the courage to confront them. Perhaps he is waiting for the right moment, but maybe he'll just let the thugs run over him.

Eventually the gang forces Bogart to pilot a motor boat to Cuba. There are four of them, but they don't know that Bogart has a gun. Underway at sea, Bogart causes one of the outlaws to fall overboard and then shoots two more. Finally, only Bogart and Johnny Rocco remain. Bogart is lying over the hatch overseeing the passageway to below decks. He waits for Rocco to come out. Rocco repeatedly calls out "Soldier!" in an attempt to get Bogart to reveal where he is. He offers Bogart a share of the money his gang has stolen. He gets increasingly angry and anxious as nothing he says or does draws a response from Bogart.

Finally, Rocco pretends that he is unarmed, and slowly comes into view, with a hidden gun. Of course, Bogart prevails in the shootout and returns to Key Largo as a hero. He was tough with his gun, but even tougher before he had to shoot. His patience and composure directed the action. He was brave for a few minutes longer.

Edgar Allan Poe: American Literary Giant

Heroes are often indirect leaders who influence through what they have done, how they have acted, what they have produced, or what they have fashioned. Heroes who are admired because of their artistic or literary works, or musical or theatrical performances, probably appeal to fewer people than transforming heroes such as Nelson Mandela or Martin Luther King, Jr. Still, their contributions have enriched the lives and cultures of many. One such hero is the writer Edgar Allan Poe.

A number of elements have made Poe's writings so influential and moving. First, his stories of death and the supernatural have thrilled many. A chilling example is one of Poe's briefest stories, *The Tell-Tale Heart*. It has been said that Poe often tried to establish the mood of a story in the first sentence. *The Tell-Tale Heart* offers a perfect illustration: "True! Nervous, very, very dreadfully nervous I had been and am; but why *will* you say that I am mad?" The narrator's madness becomes more apparent from there. He murders an old man, buries his heart under the floorboards, and imagines that its beating can be heard by the police. In a fit of nervous agony, he confesses to the crime that none suspected.

Second, Poe's wrenching poems about lost women are heart-breaking, from "the beautiful Annabel Lee" to "the lost Lenore." It is not clear whether such poems were inspired by his dead mother, his dead wife, or some unattainable woman Poe had encountered. Third, Poe's work is widely credited with the invention of the detective story, through the character C. Auguste Dupin. Dupin appears in three of Poe's most famous tales. Sir Arthur Conan Doyle paid tribute to Poe's character, who undoubtedly shaped Doyle's own literary hero, Sherlock Holmes.

Edgar Poe was born in Boston in 1809, the same year as Abraham Lincoln. His father abandoned him the next year, and his mother died soon after. Poe was taken in by a couple called John and Frances Allan of Richmond, Virginia. He was educated as a young boy in Scotland and England, but returned to America and attended the University of Virginia. He left the university after a short time, possibly because of financial constraints. By that time he was completely alienated from his foster parents, the Allans. Poe then joined the army, and eventually won an appointment to West Point. He didn't last long there, either.

When he was 26, Poe married his 13-year-old first cousin, Virginia Clemm. By that time his literary career was well underway. The couple moved between New York, Philadelphia, and Baltimore, as Poe tried to find a steady position as editor or literary critic. In the meantime, he continued his prolific writing, and in 1845 published his best-known poem, "The Raven." In this classic piece he ends up asking the mysterious bird, standing "on the pallid bust of Pallas just above my chamber door," whether in the afterlife he will find "a rare and radiant maiden, whom the angels named Lenore?" The unforgettable reply: "Quoth the raven, 'Nevermore.'"

Secretariat: The Hero Who Obliterated Triple Crown Records

The current cinema often reveals either the creation or the reworking of hero narratives. Drama in the movies emerges from the struggles that make heroes so engaging, especially underdog heroes. But it's not always the underdog that becomes the hero. One great example is a non-human hero lauded every spring during the Triple Crown racing season, and celebrated in the 2010 film that bears his name: the thoroughbred racehorse Secretariat.

Secretariat burst onto the national consciousness in 1973. It had been 25 years since the great Citation had won the Kentucky Derby, the Preakness, and the Belmont Stakes. After Secretariat won the first two races, millions of people rooted for him to win the Belmont, the final trial. As race day approached, he was the favorite, not the underdog. But in some ways the challenge of winning the elusive Triple Crown itself made him an underdog and the sentimental as well as the betting favorite.

Secretariat was born in Caroline County, Virginia in 1970. As a two-year-old he enjoyed spectacular success and was voted horse of the year, a rarity for so young a colt. A very large chestnut horse with distinctive white markings, he was nicknamed "Big Red." His fame slowly spread outside of the racing world. His great strength and grace inspired many.

Going into his third year of racing Secretariat was highly touted. Even though he finished a disappointing third in the race just before the Kentucky Derby, he was the betting favorite. Secretariat didn't disappoint. He not only won the Derby, but also set a record that still stands. In the second Triple Crown race, the Preakness, Secretariat won handily, but didn't break the record. Or did he? There is controversy about the exact time, as there were problems with the official clock. The *Daily Racing Form* claimed that Secretariat actually did break the record. Since then three other Preakness winners have tied the *Racing Form*'s alleged time for Secretariat. But none has beaten it.

There's absolutely no controversy about the Belmont record. Secretariat won that race by 31 lengths, and it is estimated that he would have beaten the previous record holder by 11 lengths. The Belmont is one-and-a-half miles, the longest of the Triple Crown. During the race his trainer thought that jockey Ron Turcotte would cause Secretariat to have a heart attack. He was going too fast in the early going. But the horse wanted to run that day, and he turned in one of the most legendary performances in all of racing's history.

There are numerous stories about Secretariat's greatness. One notes that Secretariat was a large horse with a big rear end. It often took him a while to get up to full speed. Amazingly, during his Kentucky Derby win, he ran each of the five quarter miles faster than the previous one. He kept accelerating for the entire race.

There were two other Triple Crown winners in the 1970s, Seattle Slew in 1977 and Affirmed the next year. But neither was regarded as quite the hero that Secretariat was. His performances weren't equaled then, and they haven't been since. He raced for a short time after his Triple Crown victories in 1973, but was limited to stud duties once his racing career was over. He died in 1989.

Go Ahead, Make My Day: Clint Eastwood as Contemporary Hero

Actor and director Clint Eastwood is now over 80 years old. Arguably, he did his best professional work in the years after he qualified for Social Security and Medicare. In the first decade of this century, between 2000 and 2009, he directed or starred in at least seven important films. Eastwood's work makes him a hero to many, both insiders in the film-making industry and the general public. But during his career he has also had many harsh critics, among reviewers and, again, in the general public.

Eastwood's early career took off in the late 1950s with his role in the so-called "adult western" television series, *Rawhide*. There he played a young cowhand named Rowdy Yates. While the part paid the rent, Eastwood felt confined by having to play a younger man without much depth. He jumped at the chance to portray the "Man With No Name" in Sergio Leone's *A Fistful of Dollars*, the first of the "spaghetti westerns" Eastwood starred in during the 1960s. In the late 1960s Eastwood starred as a rogue New York City policeman in the film *Coogan's Bluff*. It made good money, but was criticized, as were many of his films, for glorifying both violence and macho law enforcement that exceeded legal boundaries. More important, it provided the template for Eastwood's *Dirty Harry* films, a series of four that spanned the 1970s and early 1980s. The last of those films, *Sudden Impact*, contained the iconic line, "Go ahead, make my day," which Harry says to a bad guy threatening to shoot a hostage. President Ronald Reagan used the phrase in 1985 when he threatened to veto a tax increase.

Although the "Man With No Name" and "Dirty Harry" characters defined Eastwood's persona for much of the 1980s and 90s, he also starred in several other genres and began a directing career with the film *Play Misty For Me*. Slowly he gained recognition from the critics, and in 1992 his film *Unforgiven*, a western, won Eastwood Academy Awards for Best Director and Best Picture. He was also nominated for Best Actor. Eastwood felt the acclaim was overdue.

As impressive as these accomplishments were, Eastwood's work of the last decade has gained him respect bordering on awe, and qualifies him as a hero to many. In 2003 he directed *Mystic River*, a tense police drama set in Boston. It won Academy Awards for Best Actor, Sean Penn, and Best Supporting Actor, Tim Robbins, as well as Best Picture and Best Director nominations for Eastwood. In 2004, *Million Dollar Baby* won Academy Awards for Best Director and Best Picture, and a nomination for Eastwood as Best Actor. It also won Best Actress and Best Supporting Actor awards for Hillary Swank and Morgan Freeman. In the next few years Eastwood directed two films about the World War II battle of Iwo Jima, *Flags of Our Fathers* and *Letters from Iwo Jima*. The latter was nominated for Best Picture and Best Director.

Since then, Eastwood has directed *Changeling* with Angelina Jolie, *Gran Torino*, in which he also acted, and *Invictus*, an inspiring film starring Morgan Freeman and Matt Damon about Nelson Mandela and South Africa's victory in the 1995 World Cup rugby championship.

Only a director of Eastwood's stature would have won support from a major studio to produce the Iwo Jima films, and only one so skilled would have been chosen by Freeman, who had obtained the film rights to *Invictus*, to direct that film. The seven films starting with *Mystic River* were all released when Eastwood was in his 70s. It will be fun to see whether his achievements are as remarkable in his 80s. He is off to a good start with the 2011 film, *J. Edgar*.

Lucille Ball: A Heroic Comic Genius

Very few of us possess exceptional talent in one area of life, and still fewer have talent in multiple areas. Throughout her career, Lucille Ball proved herself to be the most gifted comedian of her generation as well as a pioneering businesswoman who reshaped the Hollywood studio landscape. Her wildly popular television shows broke new artistic ground and provided raucous entertainment to millions of her adoring fans each week.

Surprisingly, as a young woman Lucille Ball struggled to break into show business. At age 16, she enrolled in the John Murray Anderson School for the Dramatic Arts in New York City. She was sent home a few weeks later after her drama coaches told her that she "had no future at all as a performer." As a young aspiring actress, Ball was hired to play a role in the Broadway show *Vanities*, but was quickly fired. Later, she was briefly hired for, then let go from, the production of *Stepping Stones*.

Undeterred, Ball was able to play many small movie roles in the 1930s as a contract player for RKO Radio Pictures. She soon acquired the ignominious reputation as Hollywood's "Queen of the Bs." But a life-changing event occurred in 1940, when Ball met and fell in love with Cuban-born bandleader Desi Arnaz. They married, but their relationship was strained by the fact that each had a hectic performing schedule that often kept them apart. When CBS wanted Lucy to star in a television series, she insisted that Desi play her husband, believing that working together with him would help their marriage. But the network executives balked, arguing that the public would never accept an All-American redhead and a Cuban as a couple.

Eventually, CBS agreed to produce the show on Lucy's terms, and the *I Love Lucy* show was born. The series was the beginning of television's first dynasty, and it broke new ground in several areas. Ball was among the first women to star in her own show, and the first to be shown pregnant with her and Desi's baby. *I Love Lucy* pioneered a number of methods still in use in television production today. Shooting long shots, medium shots, and close-ups before a live audience, using multiple cameras, required discipline, technique, and skilled choreography. Ball eventually became the first woman in television to become head of a production company, which she and Desi named Desilu.

Airing from 1951 to 1960, *I Love Lucy* was the perfect forum for Lucille Ball to showcase her comic genius. She perfected the art of physical comedy while also demonstrating impeccable comedic timing. Audiences roared at her wide range of facial and vocal expressions in response to the many outlandish situations scripted for her. The on-screen chemistry between her and Desi was palpable, and there were consistent comic sparks between them and their loving yet insufferable neighbors, Fred and Ethel Mertz. *I Love Lucy* dominated the weekly TV ratings in the United States for most of its run. The series garnered more than 200 awards, including five Emmys. After the show ended, Ball starred in two other successful sitcoms, *The Lucy Show* and *Here's Lucy*.

Lucille Ball's professional triumphs, unique comedic gifts, and uncommon business acumen made her a true hero. The U.S. Postal Service honored her with a commemorative postage stamp. She appeared on the cover of *TV Guide* more than any other person and was voted as the Greatest TV Star of All Time. *TV Guide* also named *I Love Lucy* the second best television program in American history, after *Seinfeld*. Lucille Ball was chosen as the second out of the 50 Greatest TV Icons, after Johnny Carson. In a public poll, however, she was chosen as the greatest TV icon ever. We certainly agree with the public on this one.

TRADITIONAL-COMPLETE HEROES

Terry Fox: The Audacious Modern-Day Pheidippides

The ancient Greek story of Pheidippides is familiar to many people. You may recall that Pheidippides was the Athenian messenger who ran 26 miles from the town of Marathon to the city of Athens to announce the Greek victory over Persia in the Battle of Marathon. He died from exhaustion immediately after delivering his message, and his story inspired the creation of today's 26-mile marathon race.

Recently, Canadian entertainer Sook-Yin Lee made a convincing argument that a heroic young man named Terry Fox is our modern-day Pheidippides. In 1979, Terry Fox was just an average Canadian college student working toward a degree at Simon Fraser University. He went to see a doctor after experiencing a lingering pain in his right knee. To his shock the doctor diagnosed him with osteosarcoma, a rare form of bone cancer. As Fox underwent painful treatments, including a leg amputation, he was disheartened to learn how little money was dedicated to cancer research. After Fox was fitted with a prosthetic leg, he decided to do something extraordinary to raise awareness and money for research. He would run across Canada, a distance of 5,000 miles.

Fox vowed to do everything in his power to complete his run, even if he had to "crawl every last mile." When Fox informed his mother of his plans to run across Canada, she asked him why he couldn't just run through British Columbia with a start at the Alberta border. Fox answered, "Because not only do people in B.C. get cancer, people all across the country do, too, and that's why I've got to run across the country." Fox recognized the magnitude of the challenge. Very few people with two good legs have been able to run 5,000 miles.

Fox, with only one natural leg, was undeterred. "I was determined to take myself to the limit for this cause," he said.

On the morning that he began his run on the coast of Newfoundland, only a tiny crowd of well-wishers were there to support him. During the first few weeks of his run, he received scant attention from the media. On more than one occasion, annoyed drivers almost ran him off the road. But Fox, a fine natural athlete, ran with remarkable determination. Stunningly, he averaged 26 miles per day, the equivalent of a daily marathon. The physical demands took their toll on Fox's body. He suffered shin splints, an inflamed knee, cysts on his stump, and dizzy spells.

It soon became clear that Fox was accomplishing his goal. As the weeks went by, his incredible run began to capture Canadians' attention. Large crowds were now greeting him at each town, and generous donations to his cause began pouring in. People were awed by Fox's courage, audacity, and gritty tolerance of pain to achieve his dream of finding a cure for cancer. As Fox passed the halfway point across Canada, it appeared that nothing would stop him from making it to British Columbia.

Unfortunately, the spread of cancer in Fox's body did stop him. Fox had run for 143 days and traveled 3,339 miles. But he was simply in too much pain to complete his journey. After conferring with doctors, he held a tearful press conference at which he announced that his cancer had spread to his lungs. He died a few short months later at the age of 22.

By the time of Fox's passing, his extraordinary story had galvanized Canada. Tens of millions of dollars were raised to fight cancer, and the contributions continued to stream in. Shortly after Fox's death, Canadian Prime Minister Pierre Trudeau addressed the nation:

> It occurs very rarely in the life of a nation that the courageous spirit of one person unites all people in the celebration of his life and in the mourning of his death. . . . We do not think of him as one who was defeated by misfortune but as one who inspired us with the example of the triumph of the human spirit over adversity.

Today, Fox's heroic status in Canada is unquestioned. A 1999 national survey named him as the nation's greatest hero. The annual Terry Fox Run, involving millions of participants, raises millions of additional dollars for cancer research. The story of Terry Fox reveals an important lesson about our most courageous heroes: They leave an indelible imprint on us. "He gave, gave and gave until he had nothing more to give but his life," said one fan. Fox's legacy of audacity and perseverance is forever sealed.

George Marshall: The Hero With a Plan

As we've noted earlier, leaders exert their impact either directly, through face-to-face interactions with their followers, or indirectly by exerting impact through the works that they create (Gardner, 1995). George C. Marshall was one of those rare individuals whose exemplary leadership was both direct and indirect. As a U.S. Army General, he inspired his subordinates and fellow officers through direct contact with them. And later, as Harry Truman's post-war Secretary of State, he influenced millions by devising a plan that helped Europe recover from the ravages of war.

Marshall's leadership skills were first tested shortly after he was appointed in 1939 to the nation's highest military rank, the Army Chief of Staff, by President Franklin D. Roosevelt. At that time the U.S. Army consisted of 189,000 poorly trained and ill-equipped men. Anticipating America's involvement in World War II, Marshall coordinated a large-scale expansion and modernization that grew the army to eight million strong by 1942. Marshall proved to be a skilled planner, organizer, and delegator. He was also an inspiration to his fellow officers.

Not surprisingly, Marshall's role in planning the 1944 invasion of Normandy was pivotal. But when D-Day arrived, Roosevelt placed General Dwight D. Eisenhower in command of the operation, telling Marshall, "I didn't feel I could sleep at ease with you out of Washington." Throughout the war, Marshall was the central coordinator of Allied operations in Europe and the Pacific. Winston Churchill later credited Marshall as the "organizer" of the Allied victory.

After the war, as Secretary of State, Marshall was deeply concerned about the condition of war-torn Europe, which was gripped by famine, poverty, and social ruin. He was also very much aware that Soviet Russia stood to benefit from a European collapse. On June 5, 1947 at Harvard University's commencement ceremonies, Marshall gave a speech in which he outlined a plan for the United States to provide massive assistance, in the form of money and materials, to ensure Europe's economic recovery. He referred to this plan as the European Recovery Program but it soon became commonly known as *the Marshall Plan*. For his efforts to bring about world peace, he was awarded the Nobel Peace Prize in 1953.

After leaving office in 1953, Harry Truman was asked which American had made the greatest contribution in the last 30 years. Without hesitating, Truman chose Marshall. "I don't think in this age in which I have lived, that there has been a man who has been a greater administrator; a man with a knowledge of military affairs equal to General Marshall," said Truman. In an interview with Dick Cavett, Orson Welles called Marshall "... the greatest human being who was also a great man ... He was a tremendous gentleman, an old-fashioned institution which isn't with us anymore."

Sir Winston Churchill once offered this tribute to Marshall:

During my long and close association with successive American administrations, there are few men whose qualities of mind and character have impressed me so deeply. He was a great American, wise in war, understanding in council, resolute in action. In peace he was the architect who planned the restoration of the battered European economy. He always fought victoriously against defeatism, discouragement and disillusion. Succeeding generations must not forget his achievements and his example.

Florence Nightingale: The Heroic Lady With the Lamp

Great leaders and heroes are often associated with memorable nicknames. John F. Kennedy was *The King of Camelot*; the Beatles were *The Fab Four*; Babe Ruth was the *Sultan of Swat*; Charles Lindbergh was *The Lone Eagle*; Michael Jordan was *Air Jordan*; Harry Truman was *Give 'Em Hell Harry*. These nicknames or phrases serve several purposes. They evoke a powerful image while capturing the most central defining feature of a hero. They also tend to be enduring expressions of endearment and respect that help preserve the memory of a person's greatness.

Florence Nightingale was nicknamed *The Lady With the Lamp* for her tireless efforts to nurse wounded British soldiers back to health during the Crimean war in the 1850s. The nickname has its origins in an article that appeared during the war in *The Times* of London. According to the article, Nightingale was

> a ministering angel without any exaggeration in these hospitals, and as her slender form glides quietly along each corridor, every poor fellow's face softens with gratitude at the sight of her. When all the medical officers have retired for the night and silence and darkness have settled down upon those miles of prostrate sick, she may be observed alone, with a little lamp in her hand, making her solitary rounds.
>
> (Cook, 2012, p. 236)

Prior to the Crimean war, hospital conditions were nightmarish. Sanitary practices were poor or non-existent, and it was common for patients to be either neglected or mistreated. Nightingale was intent on making sweeping changes to hospitals and to the practice of nursing, particularly during wartime. While assigned to a military hospital during the war, she realized that her first challenge was simply getting the military doctors to accept her and the other nurses. Once this was accomplished, Nightingale restored order to the hospital, improving patient care to the point where the death rate among patients fell by 67 percent.

But Nightingale was far more than an extraordinary leader of the nursing profession. She pioneered the use of new techniques of statistical analysis, developing the polar-area diagram, which mathematically demonstrated the rate of needless deaths as a function of unsanitary conditions. Nightingale was an innovator in developing and using sophisticated data-analytic tools, techniques, and graphical analysis to illuminate the causes and treatments of many social problems, including famine, irrigation, and healthcare.

After the war, Nightingale founded the Nightingale School for the training of nurses at St. Thomas's Hospital in London, England. She began to acquire international fame as the leading expert on military and civilian sanitation and its effects on mortality rates. In 1860, Nightingale wrote *Notes on Nursing*, a landmark book that became required reading for all nursing students at the Nightingale School and other schools of nursing throughout the world.

As with many heroes, Nightingale devoted her life to helping make the world a better place. Her career was extraordinary when one considers the fact that most Victorian women of her era did not attend universities or pursue professional vocations. She established herself as a great leader in a world dominated by men, earning the respect of both male and female subordinates and co-workers. In 1883 Queen Victoria awarded Nightingale the Royal Red Cross for her work. She also became the first woman to receive the Order of Merit from Edward VII in 1907.

Nightingale saw herself as the spiritual mother of all the men of the British army whom she had saved. She once said:

> Nursing is an art, and if it is to be made an art, it requires an exclusive devotion as hard a preparation, as any painter's or sculptor's work; for what is the having to do with dead canvas or dead marble, compared with having to do with the living body, the temple of God's spirit? It is one of the Fine Arts: I had almost said, the finest of Fine Arts.

Oprah Winfrey: The Hero with Talent, Resilience, and Charisma

By the time you've reached this point in our book, you've no doubt noticed a general pattern in the lives of many of our most treasured heroes. Great heroes often grow up in impoverished or tumultuous households (e.g., Bill Cosby, Drew Barrymore, Johnny Cash, John Lennon, etc.). Great heroic leaders confront and overcome daunting obstacles that would defeat most ordinary people (e.g., Israel Spira, Dana Reeve, Winston Churchill, Lois Wilson, and John Nash). And they show extraordinary generosity and selflessness, endowing society with many gifts and boons (e.g., John Wooden, George Bailey, Reed Richards, and Mahatma Gandhi).

Seldom does any one hero show all of these characteristics. But one contemporary hero who comes very close to fitting the ideal mold is none other than television host and philanthropist Oprah Winfrey. Fans of Oprah know her poignant history quite well. She grew up in extreme poverty and was subjected to sexual abuse by family and friends. As a 14-year-old she became pregnant but lost the baby soon after its birth. She never let her race or gender stop her from succeeding in the white male-dominated profession of television broadcasting. And once a success, she became a tireless advocate of many humanitarian causes.

We believe that Oprah possesses one trait of leadership and heroism that has especially helped her on the road to heroism: *charisma*. When we've asked people to name the most important qualities that heroes possess, charisma is one of the most frequently listed traits. The dictionary defines charisma as "a personal quality attributed to those who arouse fervent popular devotion and enthusiasm." For the past 25 years, Oprah's magnetic personality has helped her attract legions of devoted fans. The telltale signs of Oprah's charisma are quite evident. She exudes confidence and intelligence. She is also extremely likeable, humorous, and socially skilled.

Oprah has been credited with revolutionizing the television talk show format. When she interviews guests on her show, they are made to feel so utterly safe and comfortable that Oprah is able to extract highly personal information from them. *The Wall Street Journal* coined the term "Oprahfication" to describe public confession as a form of therapy. During Oprah's annual *Favorite Things* episode, her frenzied audience received prizes while demonstrating the kind of unbridled love for Oprah not seen since the days of Beatlemania in 1964.

As with most charismatic people, Oprah has been able to wield tremendous influence over people. Two University of Maryland economists conducted a study to determine Winfrey's impact on Barack Obama's successful run for president in 2008. The study showed that Oprah's endorsement of Barack Obama was worth one million votes to him in the Democratic primary elections. Sure enough, if Winfrey hadn't endorsed him, Hillary Clinton would have earned the Democratic Party's nomination for President. In short, Oprah Winfrey was responsible for Obama's election victory and thus forever changed the world.

At a more personal level, Oprah's greatest legacy resides in the way she has modeled the trait of resilience during times of adversity. She has inspired millions by teaching them the following life lessons:

> Where there is no struggle, there is no strength.
> The only people who never tumble are those who never mount the high wire. This is your moment—Own it.
> Don't back down just to keep the peace. Standing up for your beliefs builds self-confidence and self-esteem.

The big secret in life is that there is no big secret—whatever your goal, you can get there if you're willing to work.

Winston Churchill: The Resilient Hero

Winston Churchill epitomizes one of the most important of the Great Eight traits of heroes: *resilience*. On the surface, Winston Churchill seems like a poor choice for a hero, particularly a twenty-first-century hero. He was portly, unattractive, had a slight lisp, and constantly smoked cigars. He could be surly and condescending to friends and foes alike. As a privileged member of the British aristocracy, he would seem to be particularly unattractive to Americans, who gravitate to underdog heroes. But Churchill is a hero of ours and gets our vote for being among the most important heroic leaders of the twentieth century.

Churchill possesses several of the Great Eight traits. His strength and charisma while Germany was bombing England in preparation for an invasion helped inspire Great Britain to literally soldier on. (If England had fallen, Hitler arguably might have ruled Europe for decades.) Churchill's incredible speeches energized and inspired the British people. For example, one speech ended with:

> We shall fight on the beaches, we shall fight on the landing grounds, we shall fight in the fields and in the streets, we shall fight in the hills; we shall never surrender.

Churchill possessed a fierce wit, a characteristic of many heroes. When Lady Astor exclaimed, "If you were my husband, I'd poison your tea!" Churchill immediately replied, "If I were your husband, I'd drink it." When another woman confronted him with "Winston, you're drunk," he retorted, "Madam, you are ugly. In the morning I shall be sober." He described a fellow politician as a "modest man who has much to be modest about."

But Churchill's greatest strength may have been his resilience. Without his ability to overcome obstacles, health problems, and political catastrophe, he may have been out of politics when Hitler started conquering Europe. Would anyone else have been prepared to oppose and defeat Hitler?

Churchill's political career had nine lives. He became a celebrity at age 25 after escaping from a P.O.W. camp in South Africa during the second Boer War. He was elected to Parliament the next year. When he was 41 (in 1915), Churchill was named First Lord of the Admiralty and helped plan the Gallipoli campaign in the Dardanelles. It was a bold attempt to hasten the end of the First World War, but it ended in disaster, and Churchill was demoted and marginalized. He eventually was given cabinet positions again, but damaged his political career when he opposed independence for India in the 1930s.

Hours before Germany invaded France, when it was painfully clear that Hitler would not be appeased, Churchill became Prime Minister. The politician who had been mocked and isolated for his obsession with Hitler's rearming of Germany suddenly was the hope of Great Britain and the world.

Whereas his political resilience was necessary to get him to this position, physical and emotional resilience was necessary to successfully prosecute the war. He suffered from depression (which he called his "black dog") throughout his life, but successfully hid it. He also had two mild heart attacks (one while visiting the White House) and pneumonia during the war. But he pressed on relentlessly, buoyed the spirits of the British people, and tirelessly and effectively devised war plans to oppose Germany. He traveled over 100,000 miles during the war years. In the end, he saw Germany and Japan surrender though he was defeated in the 1945 election as the populace quickly turned to domestic concerns.

We respect heroes and admire them for their ability to overcome adversity. The greater the adversity, the greater the heroism required to prevail. But resilience shows us another side of a hero: the ability to triumph despite a past marred with previous failures. Churchill was just such a hero. His lengthy service to his beloved Great Britain was marked by a string of successes, but also missteps that left him relegated to the political sidelines. Washed up. A has-been. Yet when an epic struggle loomed, his nation turned to him as the sole person capable of leading it to victory.

Roberto Clemente and the Night that Happiness Died

What is the recipe for heroism? Because heroism is in the eye of the beholder, there is no set list of ingredients. But our research reveals that especially powerful heroes are believed to possess the following four characteristics:

1. They have an exceptional talent;
2. They have a strong moral compass;
3. They overcome significant adversity; and
4. They die in the process of helping others.

Roberto Clemente was one of those rare and extraordinary individuals who beautifully, and tragically, fit this mold of a great hero. Today, nearly four decades after his untimely death, Clemente's accomplishments, selflessness, and charisma make him an unforgettable hero. Former Major League Baseball commissioner Bowie Kuhn once said of Clemente, "He had about him the touch of royalty." Dozens of schools, hospitals, parks, and baseball fields bear his name today.

We won't delve into many details of Clemente's genius on the baseball field. We will say that, while playing for the Pittsburgh Pirates from 1955 to 1972, he won multiple batting titles, gold glove awards, world championships, and most valuable player awards. He hit for average and he hit for power. He possessed great speed and a rocket of a throwing arm. Los Angeles Dodgers announcer Vin Scully once said, "Clemente could field a ball in New York and throw out a guy in Pennsylvania."

People who knew Clemente argue that as great as he was a player, he was an even better human being. When traveling from city to city as a player, he routinely visited sick children in local hospitals. According to author David Maraniss, Clemente spent significant time in Latin American cities, where he would often walk the streets with a large bag of coins, searching out poor people. Wrote Maraniss: "To the needy strangers he encountered in Managua he asked, 'What's your name? How many in your family?' Then he handed them coins, two or three or four, until his bag was empty." Clemente once said, "Any time you have an opportunity to make things better and you don't, then you are wasting your time on this Earth."

Clemente, a native Puerto Rican, also overcame significant adversity. He grew up in poverty. He faced discrimination, living in an era that tended to be intolerant of non-white, non-English-speaking people. Because baseball at the time was dominated by Willie Mays, Mickey Mantle, and Hank Aaron, Clemente was often overlooked in discussions of great athletes. Clemente was also hampered throughout his career by chronic back and neck problems. Yet he still managed to accumulate an exemplary record of achievement on the field.

To this day, the manner in which Clemente died still brings people to tears. In late December of 1972, he heard that Managua, Nicaragua, had been devastated by a massive earthquake. Clemente immediately began arranging emergency relief flights from Puerto Rico. He soon learned, however, that the aid packages on the first three flights never reached victims of the quake. Apparently, corrupt officials had diverted those flights. Clemente decided to accompany the fourth relief flight to ensure that the relief supplies would be delivered to the survivors. The airplane he chartered for a New Year's Eve flight, a Douglas DC-7, had a history of mechanical problems and was overloaded by 5,000 pounds. Shortly after takeoff, the plane crashed into the ocean off the coast of Puerto Rico, killing the 38-year-old Clemente and three others.

News of Clemente's death spread quickly. In Puerto Rico, New Year's Eve celebrations ground to a halt. "The streets were empty, the radios silent, except for news about Roberto," said long-time friend Rudy Hernandez. "Traffic? Except for the road near Punta Maldonado, forget it. All of us cried. All of us who knew him and even those who didn't wept that week."

Nick Acosta, another friend, summed up the fateful night that Clemente died. "It was the night the happiness died," he said.

George Washington Carver: The Humble and Ingenious Hero

Heroes are sometimes born into dire circumstances. Their very survival while young may be in doubt, and yet somehow they endure and craft a lifetime of great heroic accomplishment. George Carver came into this world in Missouri in 1864, one year before slavery was abolished in that state. While an infant, Carver was stolen by a group of raiders who traded him back to his owners in exchange for a horse. A frail and sickly child, Carver was unable to work in the fields but he did show an aptitude for studying plants. Little did anyone know that Carver was destined to become one of America's greatest botanists, educators, and inventors.

George Carver witnessed firsthand how the American South had been economically ravaged by the Civil War. As Director of the Department of Agriculture at Alabama's Tuskegee Institute, Carver worked with another heroic African-American educator, Booker T. Washington, to improve the quality of black Americans' lives through education, skill acquisition, and economic development. Carver noticed that the farming soil of the South had been depleted by many decades of growing only cotton and tobacco. Carver urged Southern farmers to diversify by planting peanuts, pecans, sweet potatoes, and soybeans—crops that would restore nitrogen to the soil while also adding protein to Southerners' diets. When farmers found little demand for these new crops on the market, Carver began exploring the commercial possibilities of peanuts and sweet potatoes by embarking on an ingenious program of laboratory research.

Carver used his creative gifts to invent hundreds of new uses for peanuts, pecans, and other new crops that he helped introduce. Among the items that Carver developed were adhesives, axle grease, bleach, buttermilk, chili sauce, fuel briquettes, ink, instant coffee, wood stain, talcum powder, synthetic rubber, shoe polish, shaving cream, pavement, plastic, paper, metal polish, meat tenderizer, mayonnaise, and linoleum. These products energized the Southern economy and turned Carver into a national hero.

Carver's creative output was astonishing, as was his selflessness. He did not patent or profit from most of his discoveries; he freely gave his inventions to humankind. In 1940, Carver donated his life savings to the establishment of the Carver Research Foundation at Tuskegee. He is also credited for improving race relations, mentoring children, and composing fine poetry and artwork. He exemplified the virtues of hard work, optimism, humility, and service to others.

A gifted educator, Carver was also devoted to developing character in his students. He compiled a list of eight virtues for his students to embody:

1. Be clean both inside and out.
2. Neither look up to the rich nor down on the poor.

3. Lose, if need be, without squealing.
4. Win without bragging.
5. Always be considerate of women, children, and older people.
6. Be too brave to lie.
7. Be too generous to cheat.
8. Take your share of the world and let others take theirs.

In 1939, Carver received the Theodore Roosevelt medal for restoring Southern agriculture. In 1941, *Time* magazine compared Carver to the Renaissance Italian artist and inventor Leonardo da Vinci. In 1943, U.S. President Franklin Roosevelt honored Carver with a national monument dedicated to his accomplishments. After Carver died, it was only appropriate that he receive this stirring epitaph: *He could have added fortune to fame, but caring for neither, he found happiness and honor in being helpful to the world.*

Warren Spahn: The Greatest Left Hander Ever

In February 2011, President Barack Obama awarded the Medal of Freedom to over a dozen distinguished Americans, most poignantly perhaps one of his predecessors, the 41st President of the United States, George Herbert Walker Bush. Those honored included two distinguished professional athletes, baseball player Stan Musial and Boston Celtics center Bill Russell.

There is nothing wrong with Obama having recognized Musial and Russell. Musial was a true gentleman, when that accolade is hardly ever appropriate today, and he was a baseball superstar, equal to his more visible contemporaries, Joe DiMaggio and Ted Williams. Bill Russell's role in the 1960s civil rights struggles deserved commendation. But other players were perhaps more worthy, including some who were war heroes from America's "greatest generation." One of the most interesting and inspiring for us is Warren Spahn of the Boston then Milwaukee Braves.

Spahn is a particularly interesting sports hero. For one, he holds the record for most career wins for a left-handed pitcher, 363, and most wins by any pitcher since the live-ball era started in the 1920s. He led the major leagues in strikeouts four times, innings pitched four times, wins eight times, and shutouts nine times. These feats are even more remarkable when we consider the trajectory of Spahn's career. He played in the majors briefly as a 21-one-year-old in 1942, but then served in the U.S. Army for the next three years. He didn't win his first game until he was 25 years old, in 1946. If he had been able to pitch during the war years, he probably would have won another 50 games, and would have been one of only three pitchers to win 400 games (the others being Walter Johnson, 417 wins, and Cy Young, 511).

Be that as it may, his war record is of some note. He fought in the Battle of the Bulge and at the Ludendorff Bridge, and he won Purple Heart and Bronze Star medals. Early in his career, manager Casey Stengel thought Spahn didn't have enough courage and aggressiveness to succeed as a major league pitcher. He cited that judgment as one of his biggest gaffes: "I said 'no guts' to a kid who went on to be a war hero and one of the greatest pitchers you ever saw."

For his achievements as a war veteran and as perhaps the most durable and effective pitchers of all time, Spahn is included in our list of heroes. And there is another reason he deserves recognition. He was one of baseball's greatest wits. Baseball buffs know that Willie Mays' first hit was a dramatic home run off Warren Spahn, in 1951. Spahn reminisced about the moment. First, he said "I'll never forgive myself. We might have gotten rid of Willie forever if I'd only struck him out." He added that the pitcher's mound is 60 feet, 6 inches from home plate, and that for 60 feet it looked like "a helluva pitch." (Mays tormented Spahn, hitting 18 home runs off him, a career record for a hitter against a pitcher.) Most notably, during the 1957 World Series, which the Braves won, a sports columnist asked Spahn whether that was the most pressure he'd ever faced. Spahn deadpanned, "Well, there was the Battle of the Bulge."

Warren Spahn, on several counts, was a great American hero.

George Washington: The Indispensable Man

As President's Day approaches each year, Americans honor one of the most important heroes in United States history, the person called the *Indispensable Man* by definitive biographer James Thomas Flexner. Although most Americans know that Washington was the first president, and led the Continental Army to victory in the long Revolutionary War, he is something of a plaster saint. He kept his contemporaries at a distance and maintained a dignified and elevated persona for most of his public life. What was Washington like, and what is *most* but also *least* heroic about him?

The biographical sketch is familiar. Washington became a wealthy land-owner in Virginia in the mid-1700s. As a young man he served bravely but not always brilliantly in the Virginia militia, but well enough to be an obvious choice to lead the first Continental Army starting in 1775, at the age of 43. He won the war mostly by not losing decisively, and by not letting the British destroy his army. Quite remarkably, he resigned from the army after the war, though he easily could have become a military dictator or even king.

The British monarch, George III, asked what Washington would do after the war. When told that he would simply go back to his farms, the king said that if he did that, he would be the greatest man in the world. After just a few years back at Mount Vernon, Washington was convinced to attend the constitutional convention in Philadelphia in 1787, and served as its president. When the executive branch of the new government was created, many of its specific duties were left unclear. Everyone knew that Washington would be the first president, and that he would conduct the office honorably and effectively. He was elected unanimously for two terms, the only man to be so chosen. He left office exhausted two years before his death, but succeeded in establishing firmly the country's system of government.

Washington was highly emotional but very tightly controlled. He was thin-skinned and extremely sensitive to slights. Nevertheless, he could rise above the hurt and anger that went with his responsibilities, and almost always do the right thing.

Perhaps the most interesting and complex aspect of Washington's life, both personally and professionally, is what he did and did not do regarding slavery. When he took command of the armies in 1775, no African-Americans, even those who were free, were allowed to fight. But war challenged national prejudices. Manpower requirements led Washington to recruit blacks, and even to promise freedom to some of those who fought. By the end of the war, perhaps 15 percent of the Continental Army, including the most effective units, was black.

At the same time, Washington developed deepening doubts about the morality of slavery. Some of the young men who influenced him most, including the French general Lafayette, urged Washington to act to move the new nation toward emancipation. They refused to let Washington ignore the glaring contradictions between the lofty republican principles of equality on which the nation was founded, and the institution of slavery. Still, Washington did little to free slaves at Mount Vernon, or to support early abolition proposals from Benjamin Franklin and others. Political and economic considerations, both public and private, led Washington to back away from what he knew clearly was right.

However, in his last act Washington did all that he could to steer the country in the right direction. He freed his own slaves in his will. Unfortunately, few others followed. It would take another great president, Abraham Lincoln, to oversee the end of American slavery.

Mikhail Gorbachev: A Revolutionary Hero in the Kremlin

On Christmas Day 1991, the United States and its allies in what was known as "the free world" received a holiday present that had been "devoutly wished for" for nearly four decades. Mikhail Gorbachev resigned the presidency of the Soviet Union and its government went out of existence. Gorbachev was immediately replaced by Russian President Boris Yeltsin. The Americans had won the Cold War.

Mikhail Gorbachev behaved heroically in taking a series of steps that produced a peaceful revolution, one that changed not only the states within the former Soviet Union, but the whole world. Gorbachev came to power in the Soviet system as a minister of agriculture and, by the early 1980s, was overseer of the Soviet economy. In 1985 he became General Secretary of the Communist Party when his three elderly predecessors—Leonid Brezhnev, Yuri Andropov, and Konstantin Chernenko—died, one after the other, in the course of three years.

Gorbachev was only 54 years old, and sought to breathe new life into a sclerotic system with a repressive government and a floundering economy. His leadership was marked by two departures that would have been unheard of under earlier Soviet rulers: *perestroika*, meaning restructuring, and *glasnost*, meaning openness. Under *perestroika*, Gorbachev tried to open up the governmental structure to make it more adept in keeping up with changes in the global economy. Under *glasnost* he attempted to make more room for divergent political opinion and even press criticism of the Communist Party. Gorbachev went so far as to allow other political parties to field candidates in elections.

On the international front, Gorbachev cultivated improved relations with the west and managed to build constructive bridges to both the United States and the United Kingdom, even though they were both led at the time by outspoken anti-communists, President Ronald Reagan and Prime Minister Margaret Thatcher. Famously, Thatcher once told Reagan that Gorbachev was someone they could do business with.

The most important events in Gorbachev's time in office centered around the decline of Communist dictatorships in the Soviet satellite states of East Germany, Hungary, Czechoslovakia, and Romania. In each case opposition groups within the country began to challenge party orthodoxy and official repression. In each case observers wondered whether the Soviets would intervene and crush liberalization as they had in Hungary in 1956 and Czechoslovakia in 1968. On a critical October night in 1989, Gorbachev made it clear he was not going to send in Russian troops to crush protesters at the Berlin Wall, and in a wave of euphoria citizens crossed from East to West Berlin and back. The wall was literally chipped away in the ensuing days and weeks.

Despite all the reforms, the Soviet economy could not make the progress needed to legitimize Gorbachev's approaches, and he was forced out of office. But by that time the creaking, repressive regime had fallen apart. Soviet republics gained their independence and a promising new era began. Like many such revolutionary movements led by a true hero, many of the achievements were rolled back. But Mikhail Gorbachev was a heroic leader for world peace, and an easing of international tensions. Fittingly, he was awarded the Nobel Peace Prize in 1990.

Twelve Angry Men: A Most Unlikely Hero

In his classic text, *Social Psychology*, Roger Brown argued that the character played by Henry Fonda in the 1957 film *Twelve Angry Men* is a special kind of hero. Fonda's character combines intelligence and virtue, or, as we have framed it in our book *Heroes*, competence and morality. Those personal qualities allow the lead character in the movie based on Reginald Rose's play to achieve something that we know almost never takes place. That is, he convinces a jury of 11 other men who all vote "guilty" to switch their vote to "not guilty." In real life, the majority position, especially an 11–1 majority, almost always wins. How does Henry Fonda pull off this near-miracle, and why does the action of the play make the outcome seem so plausible?

The research on group polarization shows that group decisions generally reflect whatever outcome the majority of information and arguments in a situation actually favors. Therefore, in a trial, the verdict typically reflects the evidence and argument that emerge during the trial. But in the case of *Twelve Angry Men*, Henry Fonda is able to show that much of the trial evidence and testimony that pointed toward a guilty verdict is flawed or misleading. He is even able to discredit the testimony of an eye-witness. While this is quite clever, in a real trial the defense lawyer would have done what Fonda does during the jury deliberation. Roger Brown argues that in this case the jury deliberation is, in effect, a retrial. So Fonda becomes a hero on the basis of his intelligence. He is insightful and well reasoned.

But morality is also built into his character. He is a good guy. He wears a white suit. He is calm and kind. He establishes warm relationships with other apparently good people in the room, and maintains a polite distance from those who are bullying, bigoted, bored, or bombastic. He shows respect for an old man, an immigrant, a young man from the slums, and a meek middle-aged man whom everyone else ignores. As one person after another is persuaded, either by information and argument, or because they identify with Fonda and want to be on his side, we find that the good guys vote "not guilty" and the villains hold out for a conviction. The latter are all revealed to be biased or just plain too preoccupied to care about the defendant's life. There is, Brown argues, a correlation between verdict and virtue in Rose's play.

It is common for fictional heroes to combine morality and competence. Two examples from our earlier book are Randle Patrick McMurphy from the novel *One Flew Over the Cuckoo's Nest* and Rick Blaine, Humphrey Bogart's character in the classic movie *Casablanca*. In their cases, and in many others, the competence is established early, and the question is whether their morality will rise to the top. In Henry Fonda's case, the sequencing goes the other way. His morality, his "good guy-ness," is clear from the outset. The drama of the play and movie centers around whether he will have the ability to persuade others to do the right thing. When he does, however unlikely such an achievement may be in real life, the script makes it seem perfectly plausible. We leave the theater feeling quite satisfied.

Chapter 9

Transfigured Heroes

The Cognitive Construction of Greatness

The Jungian concept of archetype implies that we are motivated to notice objects, events, or people who correspond to our evolutionarily based unconscious latent images. For example, Jung (1969) wrote about the *demon* archetype. Human beings have a readiness to perceive human or animal creatures as demons and to react to them accordingly. They might be repelled by them, or may be held in fascination. Archetypes seem to follow the rules of schematic perception such that when there is enough similarity between an object and an archetype, the object will be seen as an exemplar of the archetype. In accordance with Piaget's (1952) principles of assimilation and accommodation, objects that are reasonably similar to schemas or archetypes will be misperceived or misremembered slightly so that they actually do fit the schema. This is the process of assimilation. Also, perceptions that are assimilated to schemas can, by varying from the schema in small ways, actually change the schema. Piaget referred to this process as accommodation. The schema changes to accommodate the perception of the object.

Some of our favorite examples, described in this chapter, are iconic lines from movies. Often the line is so good and so appropriate, it is recalled exactly. For example, Roy Scheider in the movie *Jaws* famously tells actor Robert Shaw, "You're going to need a bigger boat" after seeing the huge shark that has terrorized the town of Amity. Sometimes, however, the line is altered, or "transfigured," to make it more fitting and expressive. People remember Clint Eastwood in the movie *Dirty Harry* asking the villain, "Do you feel lucky?" as the bad guy thinks about

Betsy Ross: A Transfigured Hero

reaching for his gun. Of course, the actual line is, "You've got to ask yourself a question. Do *I* feel lucky?" Similarly, we think of Kevin Costner in *Field of Dreams* standing in his cornfield hearing a voice saying "If you build it, they will come." People use that phrase frequently to express the idea that people will be drawn to attractions that are constructed for them. If they utter those words, it's another example of misremembering and misquoting. Costner hears "If you build it, *he* will come," referring to Shoeless Joe Jackson. But "if you build it, they will come" is a handier phrase in everyday conversation. Similarly, people combine phrases from the famous Sherlock Holmes stories and recall him saying, "Elementary, my dear Watson." But those exact words never appear in Sir Arthur Conan Doyle's stories or novels. There are variations, but the misremembered line best summarizes our sense of the way Holmes talked to Watson.

Just like quotes from movies or stories, heroes are misperceived and misremembered to make them more heroic. We transform them to make them fit the *hero* archetype or schema more perfectly. Individuals so misperceived fall into the category we called *Transfigured Heroes*. As the profiles below illustrate, transfigured heroes can be created from either real people or fictional ones. For example, we will discuss Marty Robbins' classic country song "Big Iron." Its lyrics relate how the mysterious rider who suddenly appears in town is transformed from a threatening stranger ("...no one dared to ask his business, no one dared to make a slip") to the handsome Arizona Ranger come to capture the outlaw Texas Red, dead or alive. Woody Guthrie's song "Pretty Boy Floyd" transforms a real, fairly ruthless fugitive from the law into a well-meaning folk hero resisting the corrupt establishment.

Another of our sketches profiles Betsy Ross, lionized for sewing the first American flag in Philadelphia to help General George Washington inspire the dispirited Continental Army. It is not at all clear that she did that. But the heroic myth lives on. Our need for inspiring figures who help the noble cause shaped the persona of Betsy Ross until she was converted into a Transfigured Hero.

Some of our research work has emphasized the *death positivity bias* (Allison and Eylon, 2005; Allison and Goethals, 2008; Allison, Eylon, Beggan, and Bachelder, 2009). We often evaluate people who have died more positively after their death. This is especially true when they are young and when they were killed violently. The so-called Kennedy Myth sprang up almost immediately after the charismatic President John F. Kennedy was assassinated in 1963. Kennedy was not only suave and good-looking, he was the youngest man elected to the presidency, at age 43, and the youngest to die, at age 46. His life and death were such that he became an ideal candidate for becoming a Transfigured Hero.

Our other Transfigured Heroes include Merlin, legendary wizard from King Arthur's court. We are grateful to Jesse Shultz for contributing this piece. We also profile the famed aviator Amelia Earhart, the Chilean miners who were rescued after being trapped underground for more than two months in 2010, Saint Patrick, the Navy SEALs who killed Osama bin Laden in 2011, and the legendary Robin Hood, who, we are told, robbed from the rich and gave to the poor. In each case we find the story of a person who demonstrated unquestioned heroism transfigured so that he or she fits the heroschema even better than before.

Robin Hood: The Thief Who Became a Hero

One of the most enduring heroic figures in Western legend is that of Robin Hood. Yet we don't even know whether he was a real person. He might have been a yeoman farmer and an authority-defying outlaw back in thirteenth-century England. But real or not, through court records, ballads, plays and poems, the supposed hero emerged. Not only Robin Hood, but the enemies and allies that make his story so compelling took shape as well. Maid Marion. John Little, or Little John. Friar Tuck. And then there are the villains, the Sheriff of Nottingham and the wicked Prince John, brother to the noble King Richard the Lionheart.

In 2010 Robin Hood was back in the movies, this time portrayed by Russell Crowe. Through what evolving narrative did he get there? Let's work backwards, starting with Crowe, bearded and scowling, returning from war in the Middle East. Nearly 20 years earlier, we encounter Kevin Costner, also returning from war in the Middle East, but this time clean-shaven. Rewinding further back through dozens of appearances in films and television to Errol Flynn's definitive 1938 portrayal, we encounter a mustache and goatee taken directly from the lip and chin of Douglas Fairbanks' 1922 silent film. We can easily push back another 500 years through the aforementioned novels, plays, and poems to Robin's earliest appearances in popular ballads.

Starting with the earliest conceptions, we see a typical evolution of the heroic legend with the times. For example, in the sixteenth century, the folk hero, the yeoman, the bandit, the enemy of the Prince is suddenly granted an Earldom. And soon the narrative has him going along with Richard to fight in the crusades.

How might the story have grown? Robin is a common enough diminutive of Robert, one of medieval England's most popular names. Hood simply signals that he wore a hood, as bandits were commonly supposed to do. Since the earliest appearances of the name are in court records, we are tempted to suppose that the name Robin Hood was simply applied to any unnamed bandit. Then the saga evolved, until various outlaw stories were conflated into the mythical bandit prince we now call Robin Hood.

Over the centuries, Robin Hood will fill many roles. He may have begun as a story told around the camp fire, where his first job was to defy authority, perhaps any authority, but certainly illegitimate authority. He does this admirably. As he looms larger, he is assigned a number of other jobs. As an emerging hero, he must be more than a murderer and a thief. His moral development must happen quickly. He soon learns to rob only from the rich. This strategy may reflect common sense more than ethics, because the rich tend to have more worth stealing. So fairly soon he learns not only to rob from the rich but also to give to the poor.

Robin Hood thus becomes a quite perfect hero. He fights the good fight, for the common good, against the privileged forces of evil. He is wise, competent, and ethical. He is charismatic enough to become a leader of men and dashing enough to be an object of affection for women. And his legend becomes a model for many others, including Jesse James and Pretty Boy Floyd. Russell Crowe put his own gloss on the story, but its basic elements have been present for centuries.

Big Iron: A Western Hero Narrative

Fiction not only provides us with examples of heroes—from Sherlock Holmes to Superman, from Wonder Woman to detective Brenda Leigh Johnson in the television series *The Closer*—it also illustrates familiar hero narratives. One kind of fiction rich in hero narratives is popular songs. In our society, songs about the old West, like comic books, pulp fiction and movies about that time and place, have given us some wonderful poetry depicting hero narratives. One in particular stands out: "Big Iron," by country and western singer Marty Robbins.

The song opens describing a mysterious stranger, who rides into town and may be up to no good. Because of his large gun, the "big iron," he is a potential threat to society. Because he keeps his own counsel ("Hardly spoke to folks around him, didn't have too much to say"), he is clearly scary: "No one dared to ask his business, no one dared to make a slip, for the stranger there amongst them had a big iron on his hip." As long as his silence continues, the belief that he is a bad guy intensifies and spreads: "He's an outlaw loose and running came the whisper from each lip, and he's here to do some business with the big iron on his hip." But as it turns out, there are worse people in town, especially "an outlaw by the name of Texas Red," who had already gunned down 20 men.

Soon the strange rider lets it be known that he is an Arizona Ranger whose sole mission is to eliminate Red, one way or another: "He came here to take an outlaw back alive or maybe dead, he said it didn't matter he was after Texas Red."

As events unfold, Texas Red learns that the ranger is after him, and they meet in the center of town for a gunfight. The song reveals that the scary stranger has now become a good-looking hero, but he is also the clear underdog: "Folks were watching from their windows, everybody held their breath, they knew this handsome ranger was about to meet his death." But of course the stranger (now hero) prevails, in some of the most famous lines from country and western music: "And the swiftness of the ranger is still talked about today. Texas Red had not cleared leather 'fore a bullet fairly ripped, and the ranger's aim was deadly with the big iron on his hip."

The arc of the narrative in this case is typical. Dramatic tension is created by a mysterious and possibly sinister individual who represents a potential threat to a community. But this town already has a villain, and the stranger gets transformed in the locals' minds when they discover that he represents good rather than evil. He becomes the "handsome ranger" with the stunning skills needed to defeat a seemingly unbeatable foe.

Villains should avoid hubris. In the most common narratives, the good guys finally win. In the case of Texas Red, though "vicious and a killer," "he made one fatal slip, when he tried to match the ranger with the big iron on his hip."

Willie Mays' Catch: The Iconic Image of a Hero

James Hirsch's recent biography *Willie Mays: The Life, The Legend* brings back memories of heroic greatness for those old enough to have watched or read about The Say Hey Kid during the 1950s and 1960s. It also creates a new hero for those too young to have followed baseball in those storied decades. One reviewer of this account of Mays' career is moved to ask whether perhaps Mays really was the greatest who ever lived. While not the hitter that Babe Ruth and Ted Williams were, Mays did hit 660 lifetime home runs, trailing only Hank Aaron and Ruth from the pre-steroids era, and posted a career batting average over .300.

But as Hirsch makes clear, Mays the batsman was eclipsed by Mays the fielder and Mays the base runner. And while it's been said that Mays' glove was where triples go to die, his throws overshadowed his catches. In 1951, when Mays was Rookie of the Year, a teammate said that it was dangerous to cut off his throws back to the infield. You might get your head taken off. A ball thrown by Willie Mays from the outfield still had plenty of heat on it when the catcher nabbed it for a putout at the plate.

Heroes are situated in time and place, and Mays was no exception. Jackie Robinson and Larry Doby broke the color lines in the National and American leagues, respectively, in 1947. But they were mature, comparatively well-educated men when they reached the majors. Willie Mays was barely 20 in his first year, and his exuberance, his innocence, and his all-out effort on every play lit up New York and other major league cities as few players ever had. The game had become plodding, as teams waited for one of their sluggers to hit game-winning home runs. Mays charged ground balls that got through the infield and even threw out a casual runner at first base. Only the reckless few tried to take the extra base on Mays' arm.

Not only was Mays lucky to be one of few African-American players to reach the majors as a comparative youngster, he was fortunate to play in one of the oddest-shaped ballparks in the big leagues. New York's Polo Grounds had the deepest center field in baseball, and provided the perfect stage for Mays to demonstrate his glove and his arm.

Heroes are often known through specific images or associations. Most Americans know almost nothing about Nathan Hale, but can recite what they've been taught are his famous last words, "I only regret that I have but one life to give for my country." In Willie Mays' case, there is the "Say Hey" association, but trumping that is a visual image, called simply *The Catch*. In the first game of the 1954 World Series, the heavily favored Cleveland Indians had runners on first and second with no outs in the eighth inning. The score was tied, 2–2. Indians slugger Vic Wertz is said to have "crushed" a pitch that would have been a three-run homer in any other park with any other center fielder. But Mays famously ran it down, and then did what Mays regards as more difficult and important: his throw back to the infield, preventing Larry Doby from scoring from second base.

Most baseball heroes are linked to numbers—60 for Babe Ruth, 755 for Hank Aaron, 56 for Joe DiMaggio. But in Willie Mays' case, the timeless image of his catch and throw lifts him to the highest level of sports heroism.

Sherlock Holmes: An Enduring Fictional Hero

Our research on heroism shows that about one-third of the heroes that people claim to have are fictional. Fiction writers can create characters who are unusually clear and prototypical examples of heroes. These characters exemplify the defining traits of morality and competence with no ambiguity and little nuance. They are ideal types, such as Superman or Wonder Woman.

But many fictional heroes are more real and much more interesting on account of their idiosyncrasies, sometimes endearing, sometimes annoying, sometimes both at the same time. Oftentimes these heroic figures have sidekicks or partners, who function as straight men, by providing a foil for the hero, allowing them to reveal their more human, unique and engaging characteristics.

One example is the detective Sherlock Holmes. Created by Sir Arthur Conan Doyle in 1887, Holmes is presented through the stories told by his partner, Dr. John Watson. Watson first meets Holmes in Doyle's short novel *A Study in Scarlet*. They are both looking for rooms, and decide to move in together at 221B Baker Street. Trying to figure out the kind of work Holmes does, Watson makes a list he labels "Sherlock Holmes—his limits." It starts "Knowledge of Literature—Nil." The same for philosophy, and astronomy. His knowledge of politics is feeble, botany variable, chemistry profound, and sensational literature "immense." "He appears to know the every detail of every horror perpetrated in the century."

Watson soon learns that Holmes is a consulting detective, and quickly becomes an assistant and chronicler of Holmes' adventures. As we learn more about the pair, we come to feel sympathy for Watson, having to live with the eccentric Holmes. Holmes rebukes Watson for not using his head—"You see, but you do not observe." He criticizes Watson's stories for being too dramatic and sensational, while ignoring their important demonstrations of inference and deduction. Furthermore, Holmes can be quite rude to his housekeeper, Mrs. Hudson, and treats the Scotland Yard police, especially Inspector Lestrade, with disdain.

Still, we find Holmes a convincing hero. His acute mental abilities, his irreverent but dashing style, and his independence in judging the perpetrators of crime make him a compelling figure. He doesn't always follow the letter of the law, but he does act justly and humanely. Although he seems perplexed by women, and leaves the "fairer sex" to Watson, we are impressed by his kindness and his admiration for particular women. In fact, the first short story in Doyle's several collections of Holmes mysteries is about the stunning Irene Adler, the character Holmes always referred to as "*the* woman." Holmes admires her character and willingly acknowledges that she outsmarted him.

Several of the Holmes stories—*The Hound of the Baskervilles*, *The Speckled Band*, and *The Red Headed League*—have kept his legend alive for more than a century after they were written. Some of his verbal jousts, such as the one regarding "the curious incident of the dog in the night-time" ("The dog did nothing in the night-time." "That is the curious incident."), have found their way into everyday conversation. The Holmes character is unique enough, yet flexible enough to support stories written by many other authors and portrayals by many different actors, on stage and on screen, the most recent being by Benedict Cumberbatch on the BBC in 2010, and by Jonny Lee Miller on CBS in 2013. Time will tell whether Holmes will keep providing us a compelling hero template. The signs look good that he will. Both film and television sequels are reportedly taking shape.

Amelia Earhart: Bold Achiever of Mystery

Mystery is an important yet often overlooked aspect of heroism and villainy. Mysterious people and circumstances draw our attention, and the way we resolve those mysteries affects our appraisals of good or evil. Consider the classic movie *Casablanca*, where the audience is drawn to the lead character, Rick, because his past allegiances and present intentions are shrouded in mystery. When Rick makes the right choice in the end, we celebrate his great heroism. Another striking example of a powerful, mysterious hero is found in the country and western song "Big Iron," discussed above. The lyrics describe how the citizens of a town become wary of a mysterious stranger who moves into town and keeps a safe distance from the townspeople. Big Iron eventually defeats the town's villain in a gun battle, eliminating the mystery and catapulting Big Iron to the status of hero.

The details surrounding the deaths of many celebrity heroes, such as Marilyn Monroe, John F. Kennedy, and Elvis Presley, are also replete with mystery, and our efforts to make sense of those details only enhance the heroes' reputations. Such is the case in the remarkable story of the famed aviator Amelia Earhart. Audacious and unconventional, Earhart blazed a trail of achievement and adventure during the 1920s and 30s that few people, male or female, have since been able to match.

As a young girl in 1907, just a few years after the Wright Brothers' famed first flight, Earhart got her first glimpse of an airplane at a state fair. She was unimpressed. "It was a thing of rusty wire and wood and looked not at all interesting," she said (Butler, 1999, p. 34). During her late teens Earhart attended a stunt-flying exhibition, during which one of the stunt pilots mischievously nose-dived his plane down toward Earhart and her friends. They dove for cover, but Earhart stood her ground. "I did not understand it at the time," she said, "but I believe that little red airplane said something to me as it swished by" (p. 35). At that moment Earhart knew she was born to fly.

Earhart soon became a pioneer in the field of aviation, at first setting records for speed and distance for women, and later breaking flying records independent of gender. Between 1930 and 1935, Earhart set seven women's speed and distance records in a variety of aircraft. On May 20, 1932, five years to the day after Charles Lindbergh's historic flight, she became the first woman to fly from North America to Europe. Earhart felt that her flight proved that men and women were equal in "jobs requiring intelligence, coordination, speed, coolness and willpower" (p. 77). Later, she became the first person, man or woman, to fly from Hawaii to California, from California to Mexico City, and from Mexico City to New York.

In an era when women were encouraged to accept a passive role in society, Earhart shattered convention in both her professional life and her personal life. She married fellow aviator George Putnam but referred to the arrangement as a "partnership" with "dual control." In a letter written to Putnam and hand delivered to him on the day of the wedding, she wrote, "I want you to understand I shall not hold you to any medieval code of faithfulness to me nor shall I consider myself bound to you similarly." Earhart believed in equal responsibilities for both "breadwinners" and retained her own last name rather than becoming "Mrs. Putnam." Aware of his wife's growing fame, George Putnam understood that many people would refer to him as "Mr. Earhart" (p. 133).

In 1937, she made the fateful decision to become the first woman to fly around the world—a total of 29,000 miles. She and her partner, Fred Noonan, departed from Miami on June 1, and by June 29, when they landed in New Guinea, all but 7,000 miles had been completed. The next leg, to Howland Island, covered more than 2,000 miles of open Pacific waters and was by far the most challenging section of their journey. Shortly after leaving New Guinea they flew into clouds and rain that made it difficult to use the sun and stars to chart their course. Later, dotted clouds over the ocean may have confused Earhart by casting shadows that resembled the myriad of Pacific islands. No one knows for sure why Earhart never made it to Howland Island. To this day the details of her demise remain a mystery. There has been no shortage of sightings, myths, hoaxes, urban legends, and unsupported claims. The aura of mystery has only heightened the appeal and stature of Amelia Earhart.

Merlin: Supporting Hero of Myth

A good heroic tale can often last for centuries or even millennia. The strength of Hercules, the swashbuckling of Sinbad, or the rise and fall of a king. The Arthurian tales from Britain have persisted for centuries, being retold, modified for changing times, and eventually being immortalized in modern literature and film. But behind Arthur's rise to High King, his love for fair Guinevere, and his final death at the hands of his own son, Mordred, there was the wizard Merlin.

While Merlin has often been relegated to myth, the time he lived in was very much real. The withdrawal of the Roman Empire from Britain had left a power vacuum that was soon filled with various strong men and warlords. One of these was Vortigern, who came to power in 426 AD. And this is where history, lore, and myth collide, for it is in the court of Vortigern that a young Welsh boy named Myrddin enters. Vortigern had been told by his court magicians that a mysteriously crumbling tower he sought to build could only be shorn up by a human sacrifice and that sacrifice had to be a boy with no father. Supposedly being born of a mortal woman and an incubus, Myrddin, or Merlin, was exactly what Vortigen needed. Merlin somehow convinced the king that it was a pool of water under the tower that was causing the collapse and that if he drained it he would find two sleeping dragons.

This was where Merlin cast his first prophesy. Once the pool was drained, a red dragon and a white dragon emerged and began to fight. Merlin explained as the red dragon was victorious that this was Vortigern's future. He, as the white dragon, would someday fall to the red dragon. The red dragon represented two brothers, Aurelius Ambrosius and Uther Pendragon. It came to pass as Merlin had described and he came to serve Aurelius, then Uther, and finally Uther's son, Arthur.

Unlike many other tales of heroism, Merlin's lacks almost any form of personal gain. He doesn't become the ruler of a kingdom for his efforts. Nor does he win the hand of a fair maiden, with the possible exception of the fairy Viviane. He nurtured and protected young Arthur, found the sword Excalibur, saw that when Uther fell Arthur was ready to take the throne, and directed the construction of the Round Table. Later tales told of him raising Stonehenge with his magic. In the end he asks nothing for himself and the legend says that he still lives, awaiting a time when he will be needed again.

In a sense there is truth to the legend, for Merlin still lives on. No story of King Arthur and the Knights of the Round Table would be complete without him. He was cast as a villain in Mark Twain's *A Connecticut Yankee in King Arthur's Court*. A forgotten prince in Mary Stewart's excellent series of novels about him. The main character in a miniseries and a TV series bearing his name. He even transcended genre and appeared in the science fiction series *Stargate*, where they persistently mispronounced his Welsh name of Myrddin. And certainly he will appear in further novels and movies, no doubt supporting Arthur or some contemporary hero on their quests. He will be there to help.

Like a true hero.

Heroism in the Darkness: The Anonymous Navy SEALs

Much of America and many parts of the world were transfixed late Sunday night, May 1, 2011, when President Barack Obama told the nation that U.S. forces had caught and killed 9/11 mastermind Osama bin Laden. An American SEALs (SEa,

Air, Land) Group had successfully completed an extremely dangerous mission. It will go down as one of the country's most celebrated moments, and stand in dramatic contrast to the day, nearly ten years before, that introduced most of America for the first time to the name Osama bin Laden. The Navy SEALs were American heroes by anyone's standards.

There are two important dynamics of heroism that should be noted in this case. The more familiar is that dramatic events such as this, especially in times of national insecurity, create ripe opportunities for exaggeration and related distortions. We are reminded of the false heroism of Jessica Lynch, who was reported to have acted with resourceful resolve during the Iraq War in 2003. The story of her heroism was fabricated by her superiors. She justifiably felt used.

Similarly, a false story explaining football and war hero Pat Tillman's death in Afghanistan was manufactured for political public relations purposes. In the case of the SEALs, the psychological dynamics that can lead to such fabrications were on clear display. Originally, we were told that bin Laden had a gun and had shot at American forces. We were also told that he used a woman, possibly his wife, as a human shield. Such a narrative fit our need for a bright line between the good guys and the bad guys, the heroes and the villains, and also between brave, moral behavior on the part of the good guys and craven, desperate behavior on the part of the bad ones.

As more facts came out, the original narrative was quickly corrected. Apparently bin Laden did not have a gun, and he did not use the woman as a shield. In this instance, there appears to be no intent to deceive for the sake of slaking our thirst for an uncomplicated heroic saga that can serve political purposes. But our inclination to make Transfigured Heroes was on full display in the case of the SEALs.

A more unusual aspect of this case is that we don't know, and may never know, the identity of the men who actually brought bin Laden down. Just after the event, President Barack Obama visited them in Kentucky. But we have learned little more about this anonymously celebrated group of American heroes. They are Transparent Heroes as well as Transfigured. We were told that part of the reason for the secrecy was security. These heroes didn't and don't need targets on their backs.

Another more important element in the transparency was that the SEALs are an extremely tight group. Their strongest loyalties are to each other. They win or lose, succeed or fail, as a group. There are many different roles within the team, but their group identity is primary. As a result, there was no need to recognize individuals. This unusual aspect of what happened creates mystery and perhaps the opportunity for more embellishment and distortion. But we should simply be grateful for what these heroes did. There is no need to make more of it. Their actions and the success of those actions speak for themselves.

The Chilean Miner Rescue: Protecting a Heroism Narrative

The world always seems hungry for heroes. That appetite was on display in 2010 when 33 Chilean miners were set free after 69 days being trapped under a half-mile of rock and rubble. At different times, all 33 miners, or their leader, Luis Urzua, or the rescuers, or the Chilean president, or the whole country seemed to be heroes. An undoubtedly great event had taken place, and observers craved to identify the heroes of the historic rescue. The individual who seemed to be the most obvious was Urzua. As the foreman of the crew locked underground, he seemed to have performed magnificently as the group's leader.

Most impressive seemed to be Urzua's ability to get the miners through the first 17 days, before a probe finally reached them. During that time the miners had no way of knowing whether they would ever be rescued. Urzua persuaded the men to stringently ration their food and water. They had enough for 48 hours, but Urzua anticipated that the rescue might take much longer than that. At first the men limited themselves to a few bites of tuna fish, some fruit, and a half-glass of milk each day. But as the days stretched on, the men were issued rations only every 48 hours. Finally, the outside world made contact with the men, and hopes rose that they might in good time be rescued. Initial estimates were four months. But the efficiency of the rescue operation was truly magnificent. In that context, the behavior of the miners as a whole and of Urzua as leader seemed flawless.

But then other information trickled in that suggested that their story was not so simple or so neat. As the men faced starvation, and possible cannibalism, discord and despair descended on the group. While Urzua tried to maintain cohesiveness, subgroups began to form, each with its own agenda. Some planned their own escape. Petty squabbles and even fist fights broke out. Some men refused to get out of bed, seemingly overcome by hopelessness and depression. As food became more limited, and the men had to drink filthy, polluted water, their bodies began to consume themselves. And their minds just waited for death.

Once the miners were contacted, and hopes rose for a rescue, a very pretty picture was painted of Urzua's leadership and the miners' response to it. The narrative included the fact that Urzua was the last person to be rescued. It all seemed very tidy. However, while none of the disturbing information above was included in most accounts, there were signs that all was not well. For example, only 28 of the 33 miners appeared in early videos sent up to the surface. Where were the others, and why were they not seen?

Once the rescue was achieved, it seemed that what happened below ground would stay there. The men involved had no reason to air their fears, failures, and conflicts in the world spotlight. Even more, perhaps, than the miners, the public had little use for dissonant elements that might diminish the heroic story. Human beings need a steady diet of heroism. The thirst for it seems unquenchable. And few want heroic waters to be polluted by the complexities of human interaction under intense stress.

Constructing Heroic Associations: Making a Good Line Better

There are many iconic quotes or lines from books, movies, and television that crystallize an image of a hero, or a heroic moment. Earlier we profiled Traditional Hero Nathan Hale, and his unforgettable last words, "I only regret that I have but one life to give for my country." In Clint Eastwood's *Dirty Harry* movies, the image of Clint saying "Go ahead, make my day," is unforgettable. Such quotes create a clear, sharp and unforgettable image. But some memorable moments are made more so by readers and audiences making a good phrase even better, thus making the words even more heroic and more memorable.

Several examples are notable. We have written before about the fictional detective Sherlock Holmes, and the related importance of sidekicks for many such heroes. For Holmes, that person is his friend and colleague Dr. John Watson. If people know only one specific Holmes quote, it is likely to be this comment to his partner: "Elementary, my dear Watson." That's all well and good, but in the four Conan Doyle novels, and his dozens of stories, Holmes never utters that phrase. He says "elementary" often enough, and he frequently says "my dear Watson," but he never links the two. But the two go so naturally together that they create a better image of Holmes and his relationship with Watson than the many phrases that only come close to the memorable combination.

Speaking of Clint Eastwood, people easily recall one of the last scenes in *Dirty Harry* where the villain is deciding whether to reach for his pistol. He's uncertain whether Harry has any more bullets in his .44 Magnum handgun. Harry snarls, "Do you feel lucky?" It's a popular culture phrase. But there's one problem. Eastwood never says it. Rather, he says, "You've got to ask yourself a question: 'Do I feel lucky?'" But the phrase as remembered is more natural and quotable, and can be used conversationally more easily. And in fact, Dirty Harry follows up his statement above with "Well, do you, punk?"

Another example from film: In the well-loved movie *Field of Dreams* the character played by Kevin Costner hears a voice in his cornfield, "If you build it, they will come." That memorable phrase is often used in conversation. It makes a point about how activity of various kinds can attract others, and it is nicely associated with the characters in the film. Except again, that's not what Costner hears. The voice in the cornfield refers to a single individual, perhaps Shoeless Joe Jackson, or perhaps Costner's father. It says: "If you build it, he will come."

One of television's most iconic series, subsequently made into a number of films and several sequel series, was *Star Trek*. And fans love Captain Kirk's line, "Beam me up, Scotty." This classic phrase underscores the role of one of Kirk's sidekicks, Scotty, who frequently is called upon to transport Kirk safely from danger. But once again, this exact phrase is never uttered.

One final example: Watch the movie *Casablanca* again, and listen carefully. Does Ingrid Bergman, playing Ilsa Lund, ever smile at Dooley Wilson, the piano player, and demand, "Play it again, Sam"? The answer is no. She says variations of that line, but never uses those exact words.

Why does this happen? Human beings have a need to organize experience in coherent ways. We create meaning, and construct memories that make the flow of events we encounter even more meaningful. This is especially true as we shape certain individuals into Transfigured Heroes. Vivid images, such as the Iwo Jima statue in Washington, and pithy quotes, such as "Make my day," stay with us. If we can make them even easier to remember than they are already, our constructive memories will do that for us.

Saint Patrick: The Construction of a Legend

It is a well-known psychological fact that people construct a reality for themselves that suits their needs and motives. Often these constructions reflect a blending of fact and fantasy. And so it is with Saint Patrick, the patron saint of Ireland, whose legacy—real and imagined—is celebrated around the world every March 17.

Not much is known about Patrick, and as befitting a legend there are some misconceptions. For starters, Patrick was not Irish. He was born in England in the year 420 AD. At about the age of 16, Patrick was captured and taken to Ireland as a slave. During his enslavement, the story goes that Patrick dreamed that God wanted him to escape in a getaway ship. Patrick fled Ireland in exactly this way, returned to Britain, and joined a monastery. After 12 years of training, he became a bishop and, legend tells us, he experienced a second revelation—an angel in a dream telling him to return to Ireland as a missionary.

With the Pope's blessing, Patrick returned to Ireland to convert the Gaelic Irish, who were then mostly Pagans, to Christianity. He was quite successful at winning converts, even among the royal families. For 20 years he traveled throughout Ireland, establishing schools, churches, monasteries, and dioceses.

Legend also credits Patrick with teaching the Irish about the concept of the holy trinity by showing people the shamrock, a three-leaf clover. Another tale about Patrick is that he drove the snakes from Ireland. Different versions of the story describe Patrick using a wooden staff to drive the serpents into the sea, banishing them forever from Ireland. The fact that there never have been snakes on Irish soil is immaterial; the truth rarely deters a good legend. Patrick died on

March 17, 493 AD, and for centuries the world has celebrated on that day to honor both Patrick and the Irish culture.

In our studies of why people need heroes, we have found that a common reason focuses on a hero's ability to change the world for the better. One respondent to our survey said that heroes "offer hope for good in humanity," and another wrote that heroes "courageously go on journeys that change the world." There is no doubt that Saint Patrick believed he was on a humanitarian mission to spread the word of Christianity to Ireland. The story of his path from slave to saint is inspiring, and there is little doubt that his work forever transformed the Irish people.

We have also found in our studies of heroes that their accomplishments are often exaggerated and, in some cases, fabricated. At the time of Saint Patrick, the Irish culture had a rich tradition of oral legend and myth. Orally transmitted stories are, of course, more prone to distortion over time than are written stories. Today, with regard to Patrick, it simply isn't possible to discern fact from fiction. But then, that isn't the point of any heroic legend, whether the legend is Davy Crockett, Robin Hood, or Saint Patrick. The point of any heroic story is to be entertained, educated, and inspired. Each March 17, we'll all drink to that.

Hub Fans Bid Kid Adieu: Ted Williams 50 Years Later

Ted Williams is indisputably one of the sports world's great heroes. He played his last game over 50 years ago, on September 28, 1960. It's interesting to note that Williams was 42 when he retired that year, deemed too old for his chosen profession, while at the same time, John F. Kennedy, age 43, was deemed too young for his. Furthermore, it's a fitting part of the mythology of baseball that Williams hit a home run in his last at bat. It was a dreary day at Fenway Park, and only about 10,000 fans showed up to watch the sorry Red Sox. The world has changed. It's hard to think that nowadays the last game of a sports icon wouldn't be a huge, overhyped, sold-out event.

But a hero of a different kind was also at that last game for Ted. And he helped define Williams as a hero, and helped us understand just what made him a hero. That other hero was the writer John Updike, then a 28-year-old fan, who was in Fenway by accident. Apparently Updike had "an adulterous assignation that day" but he was stood up (McGrath, 2010). So, he decided to go the ballpark. And in a few weeks, he wrote his famous *New Yorker* piece, with the title of this profile, "Hub Fans Bid Kid Adieu" (Updike, 1960).

The article was important in understanding heroism because Updike focused on some of the crucial things that were heroic about Williams. As McGrath wrote in the *New York Times*, "Updike identified with the artist in Williams: his focus and perfectionism" and his single-minded dedication to becoming the best in his craft. Williams once said that he wanted people who saw him on the street to say, "There goes the greatest hitter who ever lived." And while many people would argue that Babe Ruth deserves that accolade, Williams holds the all-time record for one of the most important of all baseball statistics. He got on base more frequently than any other player in history, a phenomenal 48.2 percent of the time he went up to bat (Ruth is second). While Williams didn't need Updike to make him a hero, that writer put a human face on Williams' pursuit of excellence. He underscored the importance of dedication and focus for achievement at the highest level.

At the same time, Updike achieved a kind of heroism of his own, albeit to a much smaller group of admirers. He changed the ways baseball, and to a lesser extent, other sports, were written about. For example, he referred to Fenway as a "lyric little bandbox," injecting romanticism and fantasy into accounts of baseball. Red Smith has done that for horse racing. He is often quoted as saying that, to get to the Saratoga Race Course from New York City, you "drive about 175 miles north, turn left on Union Avenue and go back 100 years." In 1960, Updike was one of the first who wrote in that manner for baseball. Of course Updike had good material to work with. Williams is a hero based on his exceptional athletic gifts, and his dedication to making the very most of them. Was he "the greatest hitter who ever lived"? We wonder what you think. As always, we believe that heroes exist in the eyes of the beholders.

Betsy Ross: The Hero Who (May Have) Sewed the First American Flag

On June 14, 1777 the Second Continental Congress of the United States, meeting in Philadelphia, adopted an American flag. The banner chosen was the now-familiar "stars and stripes" that has been saluted and honored ever since. In recognition of Congress' action, June 14 has been observed as Flag Day for nearly a century, since President Woodrow Wilson officially proclaimed the holiday in 1916.

Most Americans know the name Betsy Ross, having been taught that she designed and sewed the first stars and stripes in consultation with none other than George Washington. That account has made her a hero of the American Revolution. But a great deal of uncertainty surrounds the creation of the flag chosen in Philadelphia in 1777.

The idea that Betsy Ross designed that flag took hold in 1870, when Ross's grandson, William Canby, published a paper telling the story of General Washington leading a committee from the Congress to Betsy Ross's house to discuss the making of the new country's flag. Some historians note that 1870 was only five years after the end of the Civil War, and that the American people were eager for any story that celebrated the nation's founding. They were especially receptive by 1876, the country's centennial year. Thus Canby's account fell on fertile soil. But what do we really know?

Betsy Ross was born Elizabeth Griscom in Philadelphia on New Year's Day, 1752. Her first husband, John Ross, was the nephew of a Pennsylvania delegate to the Continental Congress. Betsy and John ran an upholstery business, but their marriage was short-lived. John, a militia man during the war for independence, was killed in action in 1776. Betsy married twice more, but was widowed in both instances. She had two daughters with her second husband, and five with her third. She kept working as an upholsterer until 1827. She died in 1836.

But what role did she have in the creation of the American flag? All that Ross herself ever claimed was that she contributed the five-point star to the flag, replacing the six-point star, because it was easier to make. Ross was one of many women in Philadelphia who sewed flags for the Continental Army, but we really can't know her exact contribution to designing and making the first flag.

Our understanding of heroes emphasizes that heroes and heroism exist in the eye of the beholder. Other writers have offered specific definitions of heroes. In contrast, we have observed who people name as heroes, and what traits they say heroes have. We find that almost a third of the people named as heroes are fictional. In that sense it doesn't really matter whether Betsy Ross even existed (she definitely did!) or just what she contributed to the first flag. A narrative has evolved naming her as a hero, identifying her as making an important contribution to the country's founding. That's good enough for us. Her grandson's story, very likely tweaking the truth, makes her a Transfigured Hero.

Many people call the American flag that has 13 red and white stripes and 13 white stars in a circle on a blue field, the original American flag, "the Betsy Ross." We think that's appropriate. Although we don't know all the facts, we do know that Betsy Ross is one of many women who made important contributions to the American founding. In our eyes, they are all heroes.

Pretty Boy Floyd: An Outlaw Hero

Legal briefs often include quotes from song lyrics, including those written by rock, country, and folk artists. Most often quoted is Bob Dylan, followed by the Beatles and Bruce Springsteen. The top three are not very surprising. Number four is more so: Woody Guthrie. On further thought, we know that Guthrie very much influenced Dylan and Springsteen. So his listing makes more sense.

Some of the most quoted Guthrie lines are from his ballad "Pretty Boy Floyd." The song tells of a young man forced by circumstance to become an outlaw, but an outlaw who helps the less fortunate. He is portrayed as a Robin Hood-like character, or one like Jesse James, who robs from the rich and gives to the poor.

Guthrie wrote, "But a many a starving farmer, the same old story told, how the outlaw paid their mortgage and saved their little homes." Probably the most memorable pair of lines is the one most often seen in legal briefs, for obvious reasons: "Yes, as through this world I've wandered, I've seen lots of funny men; some will rob you with a six-gun, and some with a fountain pen."

Woody Guthrie's heroic portrayal of Pretty Boy Floyd has had wide influence. A rock band calls itself Pretty Boy Floyd and Larry McMurtry wrote a quasi-fictional novel portraying him favorably. John Steinbeck contributed to the heroic construction. In his classic novel, *The Grapes of Wrath*, published in 1939, the same year as Guthrie's song, the character Ma Joad refers to Floyd as someone driven to crime as a result of hardships of the Great Depression. Floyd is featured in movies and comic books as well, generally as an outlaw with a good heart.

The facts about Charles Arthur "Pretty Boy" Floyd do not tell an obviously heroic tale. He took to robbery as a young man, apparently imitating the exploits of the "Cherokee Badman," a.k.a. Henry Starr, nephew of Belle Starr, the leader of an extended family of outlaws. Newspaper pictures and headlines about Starr were compelling to young boys. After Floyd got his own start on a life of crime, he quickly graduated to many varieties of murder and mayhem. He teamed up with the notorious "Public Enemy Number 1," John Dillinger, and rose to the top of FBI Director J. Edgar Hoover's list of wanted criminals. He and a partner killed the husbands of two women they had become involved with.

But there was another side to the story, the side the song told. Floyd gained the reputation of being kind to people in his adopted state of Oklahoma, and in turn they helped him hide from the law. Most interesting about the legend created by Guthrie, Steinbeck, and others is that so many people seem ready to accept it. Are we predisposed, perhaps through the kinds of archetypes discussed by Carl Jung, to be attracted to strong, active, and perhaps handsome people (note the nickname, Pretty Boy, which Floyd hated) who challenge and defy authority? Is that why we are much moved by Guthrie lyrics such as "Well, you say that I'm an outlaw, you say that I'm a thief. Here's a Christmas dinner for the families on relief." We need more research on why narratives like this resonate with so many people.

Jack is Back: The Kennedy Administration, 50 Years Later

In 2010, prominently displayed in Boston, on street lamps and signs, was a poster saying *Jack is Back*. It was not clear from a distance what that meant, or who Jack was or is. But if you were there, and got closer, you would see a picture of John F. Kennedy, and read that he was elected President of the United States 50 years ago. Kennedy served as the nation's leader for less than three years, but was rated as the sixth greatest president in a 2009 survey of historians, and the Kennedy magic is still strong to many Americans. A half-century after his death, he is still a hero across the country and around the world, especially in Boston. What accounts for Kennedy's status as a hero to so many people after such a long time?

John F. Kennedy was the youngest elected president in U.S. history. He won the election of 1960 at the age of 43, narrowly defeating Richard Nixon. Despite the closeness of the election, his approval rating was over 70 percent when he took office. The public was entranced with his charismatic persona, and the sense of action, vigor, and energy that he conveyed. His beautiful wife Jacqueline and young children added a storybook quality to his presidency. Kennedy's popularity continued throughout his term, as he became a champion of public service, and emphasized altruism and sacrifice, possibly more than any other president. Very few passages from presidential inaugural addresses are recalled or even recognized. But, aside perhaps from FDR's "the only thing we have to fear is fear itself," Kennedy's call to service is the most familiar line from any inaugural address: "Ask not what your country can do for you, ask what you can do for your country." Kennedy is positively associated with the Peace Corps, with the successful resolution of the Cuban Missile Crisis—when the world stood on the brink of nuclear war—and the introduction of what became the 1964 Civil Rights Act.

But part of the Kennedy legacy reflects his tragic death, by an assassin's bullet on November 22, 1963, just over 1,000 days into his administration. Research by Dean Keith Simonton (1987) shows that assassinated presidents have higher "greatness ratings" than they might have otherwise. Our own writings discuss the death-positivity effect and how assassinated people are "frozen in time," in a way that keeps their memory fresh and positive (Allison and Goethals, 2008). Also, oftentimes metaphors or apt phrases capture an idea or crystallize a feeling about an individual, or an event, or even a concept. In Kennedy's case, the play *Camelot* was linked to his administration. For many, the lyrics from the final number of that play captured the sense that many Americans had of JFK's time in office: "Don't let it be forgot that once there was a spot, for one brief shining moment, that was known as Camelot."

Kennedy himself would have been unsettled by this sentimental appraisal. At a commencement speech at Yale University in 1962, he asserted that

> in our time we must move on from the reassuring repetition of stale phrases to a new, difficult, but essential confrontation with reality. For the great enemy of truth is very often not the lie—deliberate, contrived and dishonest—but the myth—persistent, persuasive and unrealistic.

We won't judge how realistic is the heroic image of JFK. As always, that is in the eye of beholder. But we can observe that to many John F. Kennedy is one of America's great heroes of the twentieth century.

Chapter 10

Transforming Heroes
Those Who Forever Changed Our World

One of the last century's most important conceptual advances in the leadership literature was James MacGregor Burns' (1978, 2003) development of the idea of "transforming leadership." The basic notion was described in Burns' 1978 book *Leadership* as the kind of leadership that raises both leaders and followers to higher levels of motivation and morality. Built into this idea was the further notion that leaders can change the motives of followers by helping to satisfy their lower order needs and focusing them on more elevating motives, such as distinguished achievement, moral behavior, or fundamental values. Mohandas Gandhi is an excellent example of a transforming leader who worked tirelessly to focus more cautious Indian leaders on the goal of independence from Great Britain. Central to his success was his unwavering focus on non-violence and *satyagraha*, or discovery of and adherence to God's truth through universal brotherhood and the force of love. Gandhi wanted people to satisfy but also simplify their basic material needs so that they could focus on higher motives. His complete embodiment of these principles inspired fellow Indians, and other leaders the world over, most importantly, perhaps, Martin Luther King, Jr. Burns contrasted transforming leadership with *transactional leadership*, in which leaders and followers simply work together for short periods of time to satisfy routine needs.

Bernard Bass (1998) is well-known for empirical studies of what he called *transformational* vs. *transactional* leadership, a distinction very similar to Burns' distinction between transforming and transactional leadership. (Although Burns

Bill Cosby: A Transforming Hero

is often credited with the concept of "transformational leadership," he always used the term "transforming leadership" instead (Burns, personal communication, 2012). For Bass transactional leadership is inspiring and highly motivating leadership that causes people to think carefully and creatively about a group's challenges. Transformational leaders attempt to instill passion and generate commitment, rather than merely rewarding followers for effective performance.

The concepts of transformational and particularly transforming leadership apply well to the exceptional individuals whom we here classify as *Transforming Heroes*. They are people who are admired for initiating some kind of significant change in the world. They may simply be admired from afar for expressing and embodying important values—perhaps new ones, or perhaps enduring ones that have been overshadowed by other seemingly more urgent priorities—or they may actually engage and inspire people to follow their lead. That is, they may change our values or our behavior, or, very often, both. Nelson Mandela is an important example of a Transforming Hero. For some he simply made the values of peace and reconciliation more prominent and powerful. For many others of all colors in South Africa and beyond, he described, modeled, and inspired changes in the ways they thought about and worked with their fellow citizens. He was a transforming leader who became a hero—a transforming one—for the many people who followed his example.

Just as there are many kinds of heroes, within the category of Transforming Heroes we can distinguish two important subtypes. Some Transforming Heroes are leaders and heroes in specific domains. For example, the early rock 'n' roll star Buddy Holly transformed popular music through his style of writing, singing and performing iconic songs such as "That'll Be The Day." Other Transforming Leaders, such as Gandhi and Mandela, transformed the way whole societies were organized. They had a significant impact on people even beyond the borders of their own nations. Some Transforming Heroes originally have an impact only within a specific domain, but their influence spills over to much broader areas of society. For example, in contrast to Buddy Holly, the so-called King of Rock 'n' Roll, Elvis Presley, not only changed popular music. He also became a hero to many young men and women by showing that the social order's rules and customs could be altered. People of all ages could be more expressive and enjoy music of many different forms from many different subcultures within American society. It's been said that Elvis reminded young women that they had a body below the waist, and that they could move it. If true, that is highly transformational. Similarly, former heavyweight champion Muhammad Ali not only transformed the world of boxing, he embodied a whole new way for African-Americans to define themselves and relate to the larger society. In affecting African-American identity, he changed the mores of interracial interaction, and thus white Americans as well as black. Along with Transforming Heroes like Martin Luther King and many other groundbreakers, Ali nudged the United States of America toward a more equitable society, where phrases such as "liberty and justice for all" really meant something.

Our profiles of Transforming Heroes include physicist Albert Einstein, whose theories of relativity transformed modern science; Christopher Columbus, whose transatlantic voyages changed world history; Haitian political activist Myriam Merlet, killed in the 2010 Port-au-Prince earthquake, who fought relentlessly for the rights of women, and against the political use of rape; and Bill Cosby, who transformed family television, and America's understanding of the range and promise of black households. These and other Transforming Heroes represent the pinnacle of heroic influence.

TRANSFORMING-GLOBAL HEROES

Muhammad Ali: The Odyssey of a Heroic Champion

Declaring oneself a hero doesn't ordinarily do the trick. But former heavyweight boxing champion Muhammad Ali is an international hero in the eyes of sports fans and ordinary citizens around the world. Ali began calling himself "The Greatest" early in his career, and clearly alienated many. Now people generally realize that his braggadocio was always part of the act, something that enabled him to perform at his best in the ring, and entertain and inspire millions.

As we describe in *Heroes*, Ali's odyssey to heroism was complicated. But by the time of the 1996 Olympics in Atlanta, Georgia, there was no question as to which former American medal winner would light the torch at that year's Games. Two years later, it was only a bit of a surprise when corporate America fully endorsed Ali by putting him on a box of Wheaties cereal, "The Breakfast of Champions." The citation on the box credited Ali's impact in sports and beyond: "he was a courageous man who fought for his beliefs" and "became an even larger force outside the ring with his humanitarian efforts."

When Ali, then Cassius Clay, won the heavyweight championship from Sonny Liston in 1964, large portions of white America were uneasy. Although Liston was widely associated with organized crime, and seemed like something of a thug, rumors also circulated about Clay being associated with "Black Muslims." Many people found this truly frightening. And although Ali's wit and boxing skills were extremely entertaining, almost as many were turned off by the talking and bragging of "The Louisville Lip" or "Gaseous Cassius." In short order, some of these people's worst fears were confirmed. Clay turned to Islam and took the name Muhammad Ali. He became a vocal critic of the Vietnam War and was arrested for refusing to be inducted into the armed services.

Ali's resistance to the draft on the grounds that he was a Muslim minister struck many as ludicrous. But he fought in court for his deferment from the army and eventually won in a unanimous Supreme Court decision. However, his legal struggles kept him from boxing for three-and-a-half years, costing him precious time at the peak of his career. But he had proved the depth and sincerity of his beliefs. At the same time, more and more people believed that he was correct to defend African-Americans' rights to their own values and self-respect, and in his opposition to the Vietnamese war.

Eventually Ali got the chance to win back the boxing title he had lost while he was banned from fighting, and that he failed to regain when he met Joe Frazier in 1971. The year was 1974, ten years after he first won the title from Sonny Liston. He fought and won a classic battle against George Foreman in the African nation of Zaire, now called Congo. That year he was named Sportsman of the Year by *Sports Illustrated* and it was clear that most Americans had come to embrace a talented and dedicated athlete who had overcome both racial and cultural barriers and had the courage to define himself and to help and encourage other black Americans to do the same.

After regaining the title from Foreman, Ali fought for several more years. But the numerous punches he had absorbed during his long career made him the victim of Parkinson's syndrome, a neurological disorder which makes motor activity, including walking and talking, extremely difficult. Ali still fights outside the ring for those he regards as his people, and he is a hero to most of America. His skill, his struggle, his commitment, his charm, and his charisma are inspirational. He is one of the most recognized and admired people in the world. Both he and his home nation have come a long way since he burst on the scene as a sassy young fighter who perplexed or repelled much of the country. For many, he remains an important hero.

Christopher Columbus: A Globally Transforming Figure

As Columbus Day approaches each October 12, people are drawn to speculation about Christopher Columbus and his unsurpassed impact on the world we live in today. While almost everyone agrees that Columbus was transforming, people debate whether the transformations he triggered were positive or negative. Regardless of where one stands on this issue, there can be no disagreement about the fact that Christopher Columbus and his 1492 voyage to the Americas left an indelible mark in nearly every corner of the globe.

Transforming events do not take place in a historical vacuum. To understand Columbus's motivation to establish a shipping route to Asia, we must look to the city of Constantinople, now Istanbul, Turkey. For centuries, as the capital of the Orthodox Christian Byzantine Empire, Constantinople had been an important center for trade between Europe and Asia. But in 1453, the Muslim Ottoman Empire conquered Constantinople, forcing Europeans to search for a sea route to Asia that would bypass the Muslims.

Interestingly, Columbus may never have attempted his initial voyage had he not held several misconceptions about global geography. He underestimated the circumference of the earth; he overestimated the size of the Asian landmass; and he believed that Japan lay much farther east of China than in reality. He did, however, have an accurate understanding of the prevailing easterly trade winds that would propel his ships from the Canary Islands to lands far to the west. With about 90 men and sailing under the flag of Spain, Columbus's three ships were fortunate to avoid both tropical storms and the "doldrums"—pockets of sea where there is neither current nor wind.

Most of us know the rest of the story. On October 12, 1492, Columbus and his men landed on the island of Guanahani, and called it San Salvador. Although he failed to reach Asia, Columbus made the western hemisphere known to Europeans, forever altering human history on a global scale. Until very recently, generations of Americans grew up learning that Columbus "discovered" America—a Eurocentric notion that ignored the presence of 50 million indigenous people inhabiting the Americas in 1492. Moreover, other Europeans, such as the Norsemen, had ventured to America 500 years earlier. "Columbus's claim to fame isn't that he got there first," explains historian Martin Dugard, "it's that he stayed" (Dugard, 2005).

The heroic interpretation of Columbus is that his daring voyage into unknown waters required courage and conviction. In 1989 U.S. President George H.W. Bush said that Columbus "set an example for us all by showing what monumental feats can be accomplished through perseverance and faith." Extraordinary changes resulted from Columbus's voyages. The *Columbian Exchange* was established, referring to the two-way transfer of culture, foods, plants, and animals between the continents of Europe and the Americas. The Americas were introduced to crops such as wheat, rice, coffee, bananas, and olives, and animals such as horses, cows, pigs, and chickens. Europeans also received from America many important crops, such as corn, potatoes, tomatoes, lima beans, squash, peanuts, cassava, cacao, and pineapple.

The past few decades have also seen Columbus cast into the role of villain. Deadly European diseases were introduced into the Americas, including diphtheria, measles, smallpox, and malaria. The Americas, in turn, contributed a virulent form of syphilis to Europe. All told, Native American populations suffered to a much greater degree than did Europeans. Epidemics wiped out 80 to 90 percent of the native populations in Hispaniola, and European settlers enslaved many Native Americans. In fairness to Columbus, the worst of these problems occurred after he died, under the watch of later European governors and colonists.

In preparing this profile, we googled *"Christopher Columbus hero villain"* and obtained over 100 websites debating Columbus's status as hero or villain. It's clearly a muddied picture. All we can say with certainty is that Columbus's voyages had a permanently transforming effect on the world. "Every hero is somebody else's villain," said Felipe Fernández-Armesto, a scholar and author of several books related to Columbus, including *1492: The Year the World Began*. "Heroism and villainy are just two sides of the same coin" (Fernández-Armesto, 1991).

Mahatma Gandhi: The Hero of Truth and Peace

Elsewhere in this book, we've noted the tendency of the very best among us to be vulnerable to assassination. John F. Kennedy, Anwar Sadat, Harvey Milk, and Martin Luther King, Jr., are prominent examples of heroes who were killed because their vision, courage, and skills threatened the status quo. To this pantheon of fallen heroes we add the name of Mohandas Karamchand Gandhi, commonly known around the world as Mahatma Gandhi.

As with many heroes of social movements, Gandhi's wisdom was acquired through his personal experience with turmoil and pain. While a young man in South Africa in the 1890s, Gandhi was thrown off buses, beaten by stagecoach drivers, and barred from hotels, simply because he was Indian. These incidents inspired him to form a philosophy of social justice he called *satyagraha*, which encourages the use of non-violent resistance. "The Satyagrahi's object is to convert, not to coerce, the wrong-doer," said Gandhi. Satyagraha is a combination of two Sanskrit words: *satya* meaning truth and *agraha* meaning pursuit of. Thus, satyagraha captures Gandhi's belief that non-violence is an honest and diligent quest for truth.

After using satyagraha successfully in South Africa, Gandhi returned to British-controlled India in 1915 and led the greatest anti-colonial struggle in world history. He urged Indians to boycott all things British, also using fasting as a method of protest. True to his principles, Gandhi was critical of any violence directed toward the British. "When I despair," he said, "I remember that all through history the way of truth and love has always won. There have been tyrants and murderers and for a time they seem invincible, but in the end, they always fall."

Gandhi also aimed to heal the many ethnic rifts in his country. He opposed any plan to carve up India into smaller nations; doing so contradicted his vision of religious unity. He was saddened by the formation of Pakistan because "Islam stands for unity and the brotherhood of mankind, not for disrupting the oneness of the human family. Those who want to divide India into possibly warring groups are enemies alike of India and Islam." Gandhi urged his fellow Hindus to love and befriend Muslims. He played a central role in bringing about the *miracle of Calcutta*—a miraculous peace between the city's warring Hindus and Muslims.

Throughout his life, Gandhi encouraged respect for all religions, equality of all people, and non-violence in thought, speech, and action. Indians referred to him as *Bapu* (Father) and *Mahatma* (Great Soul). In his famous attire of loincloth and shawl, Gandhi traveled throughout India, usually on foot, inspiring hundreds of millions of people with his message of peace. One of Gandhi's lasting legacies to India is a multi-party democracy that to this day functions peacefully.

Gandhi's assassination in 1948 was followed by an enormous outpouring of grief throughout the world. Most Indians still regard Gandhi, along with Buddha, as one of the towering figures of Indian history. Martin Luther King, Jr., who later used satyagraha in his American civil rights movement, said that "Christ gave us the goals and Mahatma Gandhi the tactics." Albert Einstein noted that "generations to come will scarce believe that such a one as this ever in flesh and blood walked upon this earth."

Nelson Mandela: The Ultimate Underdog Hero

Our studies of heroism have shown that there is nothing more inspirational to us than an underdog who triumphs over adversity (Kim et al., 2008). When we've asked people to list their most inspirational underdog heroes, the name of Nelson

Mandela invariably appears more often than any other. No one has suffered and sacrificed more for his country than Mandela, who endured 27 years as a political prisoner before assuming his nation's highest office. "In my country," he quipped, "we go to prison first and then become President."

The classic underdog script consists of the following sequence of events: A disadvantaged person, or underdog, is the target of disrespect or oppression by others who hold greater power. The underdog seeks to achieve a noble goal but is repeatedly thwarted by the established power. There is great struggle and pain along the underdog's journey. Courage and persistence are the keys to the underdog's ultimate success. Like *The Little Engine That Could*, the underdog eventually prevails, and in the process he or she wins over the hearts and minds of nearly all observers.

Mandela's life closely follows this narrative. As a young man, he was a leading member of the African National Congress (ANC), which opposed South Africa's policy of racial separation, known as apartheid. During the 1950s he was repeatedly banned, arrested, and imprisoned. He recalls:

> When I was first banned, I abided by the rules and regulations of my persecutors. I had now developed contempt for these restrictions. To allow my activities to be circumscribed my opponent was a form of defeat, and I resolved not to become my own jailer.

After the government outlawed the ANC in 1960, Mandela was captured, convicted of treason, and sentenced to life in prison. His trial attracted worldwide attention and sympathy. At his trial he uttered the famous words,

> I have cherished the ideal of a democratic and free society in which all persons live together in harmony and with equal opportunities. It is an ideal which I hope to live for and to achieve. But if need be, it is an ideal for which I am prepared to die.

While imprisoned, he and other inmates performed hard labor in a lime quarry. Prison conditions were harsh; prisoners were segregated by race, with black prisoners receiving the least rations. Political prisoners such as Mandela were kept separate from ordinary criminals and received even fewer privileges. Mandela has described how, as a D-group prisoner (the lowest classification), he was allowed one visitor and one letter every six months. But he did not suffer in vain. His long imprisonment propelled him to international fame and adoration as a worldwide symbol of racial equality.

Released in 1990, Mandela became President of South Africa and took steps to abolish apartheid. He also earned international respect for his efforts to reconcile relations between black and white South Africans. When his country hosted the 1995 Rugby World Cup, Mandela encouraged citizens of all colors to support the mostly white South African national rugby team, which historically had been loathed by the nation's black majority. The team was a heavy underdog going into the competition, but miraculously it won the cup. Wearing a team jersey, Mandela presented the trophy to captain Francois Pienaar, who claimed victory for all of South Africa's 45 million citizens. This event was a pivotal moment in healing the rift between white and black South Africans.

Nelson Mandela's triumph as an underdog certainly makes him a hero in the eyes of millions. He also fits the image of an ideal hero with other qualities such as charisma, intelligence, thoughtfulness, humor, optimism, good height (6' 4"), and good looks. This fact has not escaped the attention of Hollywood movie producers. Mandela has been portrayed by Morgan Freeman (*Invictus*, 2009), Sidney Poitier (*Mandela and de Klerk*, 1997), and Danny Glover (*Mandela*, 1987).

Martin Luther King, Jr.: The Hero of Interracial Peace

Sometimes exactly the right person for the right situation emerges to help resolve a seemingly impossible problem. To succeed, the American civil rights movement of the 1950s and 1960s required a charismatic leader who championed the cause, who commanded respect, who practiced what he preached, and who could stir the hearts of millions of followers. The Reverend Martin Luther King, Jr., was the ideal man for the job.

In our research, we've found that special iconic moments can forever define a hero. Martin Luther King, Jr.'s *I Have a Dream* speech, delivered in 1963 from the steps of the Lincoln Memorial in Washington, is indelibly linked to his passion and eloquence as a transforming hero. Below is a brief excerpt of the speech; note the power of his words:

> I have a dream that one day on the red hills of Georgia the sons of former slaves and the sons of former slave owners will be able to sit down together at a table of brotherhood.
>
> I have a dream that one day even the state of Mississippi, a state sweltering with the heat of injustice, sweltering with the heat of oppression, will be transformed into an oasis of freedom and justice.
>
> I have a dream that my four little children will one day live in a nation where they will not be judged by the color of their skin, but by the content of their character.

Martin Luther King, Jr., is forever associated with the noble goal of achieving a color-blind society. He is a hero to millions of people because he promoted goodwill and freedom for all people of all backgrounds. Much of the sympathy and support he drew to the cause stemmed from his embracing Mahatma Gandhi's principles of non-violent protest. King also had the unsurpassed gift of establishing an emotional connection to his listeners. His *I Have a Dream* speech is punctuated by a very stirring use of repetition and soaring rhetoric as he inspires the world to share his vision:

> Let freedom ring. And when this happens, and when we allow freedom to ring—when we let it ring from every village and every hamlet, from every state and every city, we will be able to speed up that day when all of God's children—black men and white men, Jews and Gentiles, Protestants and Catholics—will be able to join hands and sing in the words of the old Negro spiritual: "Free at last! Free at last! Thank God Almighty, we are free at last!"

With this last line, the crowd listening to King erupts in a frenzy of support, love, and hope. The entire speech is a moving, mesmerizing masterpiece. The unsurpassed beauty of its message is combined with a passionate, charismatic delivery. There is no doubt that it is the speech of a legendary hero.

Our research on heroes reveals that people associate the greatest of heroes with eight specific traits: intelligence, strength, compassion for others, selflessness, charisma, inspiration, reliability, and resilience. There is no doubt that Martin Luther King, Jr., embodied all of these "Great Eight" traits. He was exactly the hero that America needed to guide it through painful but necessary social changes. King was indeed a hero who overcame great obstacles to achieve a beautifully noble goal. The only thing he couldn't overcome was the assassin's bullet that killed him in Memphis in April of 1968. The world still mourns the loss.

Thomas Jefferson: We Hold These Truths to Be Self-Evident

Most Americans know that the fireworks and hoopla of the Fourth of July are tied to meaningful history. July 4, in the year 1776, was the day that the nation's founding fathers signed the Declaration of Independence in Philadelphia. That date has been celebrated consistently every year thereafter. Many individuals could be considered heroes of American independence, but most people give Thomas Jefferson credit for authoring the Declaration. That document has inspired people all over the world for well over 200 years. Although Thomas Jefferson was the third President of the United States, he didn't mention that when he dictated the words to appear on his tombstone. He wanted credit for the Declaration, the Statute of Virginia for Religious Freedom, and for founding the University of Virginia.

We think Jefferson's words make him one of the most important heroes of America's founding. He persuaded the Continental Congress that "a decent respect to the opinions of mankind" required a statement of reasons for separation from Great Britain. In articulating those reasons, he deftly stated the most fundamental American principles: "We hold these truths to be self-evident, that all men are created equal, that they are endowed by their creator with certain unalienable rights, that among these are life, liberty and the pursuit of happiness." The reach of these ideas can be heard ringing years later in the opening of one of America's most famous speeches, Lincoln's Gettysburg Address: "Four score and seven years ago our fathers brought forth on this continent, a new nation, conceived in liberty, and dedicated to the proposition that all men are created equal."

Although Thomas Jefferson is widely considered a leading hero of American independence, he did not, of course, operate alone. John Adams was the member of the Continental Congress who most consistently pushed and prodded for independence, and he was one of the five men on the committee assigned to draft a declaration. Adams arguably deserves more credit than Jefferson. But heroism and history work in complicated ways, and it is the story of Jefferson's eloquent writing that most powerfully captures the spirit of the founding.

One of the great ironies of U.S. history is that Thomas Jefferson and John Adams both died on the same day. The date was July 4, 1826, the 50th anniversary of the Declaration of Independence. Jefferson died early in the morning. Adams died later in the afternoon, and it is said that his last words were "Thomas Jefferson still lives." Historian Joseph Ellis argued that Adams was wrong for the moment—Jefferson had already died—but right for the ages—people remember what Jefferson wrote much more than what Adams achieved (Ellis, 2000).

In addition to the Declaration, Thomas Jefferson is known for other acts that served his country well, such as the Louisiana Purchase in 1803, completed during his first term as president. He is also known in less favorable ways, such as for what some scholars consider his hypocrisy regarding slavery. Nevertheless, his ringing articulation of the fundamental values of liberty and equality make him an American Transforming Hero.

Albert Einstein: The Hero Synonymous With Genius

Heroes change the way we think about the world. They challenge conventional thinking or traditional ways of conceiving everyday phenomena. Perhaps no individual reshaped our thinking about the fundamental laws of nature more than Albert Einstein. So transforming was Einstein's work that *Time* magazine in 1999 named him the "Person of the 20th Century".

In science, the set of assumptions from which scientists work is called a *paradigm*, a term coined by Thomas Kuhn (1962). Any rapid change in assumptions that takes place within the scientific community is called a *paradigm shift*. One example of such a dramatic shift in thinking is Copernicus' proposal in 1543 that the earth rotates around the sun, a view that represented a radical departure from the old notion that the earth was the center of the solar system. Copernicus' new paradigm challenged the established and entrenched way of thinking by completely re-framing the way the universe works.

Einstein's paradigm shift was no less groundbreaking. Einstein proposed that space and time are woven into a single fabric, called space-time. He suggested that matter causes space-time to curve and that the motion and properties of matter are, in turn, altered by that curvature. In 1905, at the tender age of 26, Einstein published four seminal research papers on the special theory of relativity, the Brownian motion theory, the photon theory of light, and the equivalence of mass and energy. A decade later, in 1915, Einstein published his famous paper on *general relativity*, unifying Newton's law of gravity and special relativity. The theory spawned some of the greatest and strangest research results in the history of astronomy.

Reinforcing Einstein's status of hero was his unique physical appearance. His image was the perfect embodiment of the quirky mad scientist stereotype. Einstein's hair was long and unkempt, and he sported a walrus mustache. He paid little attention to clothing or fashion. *Time* magazine noted that he was a cartoonist's dream come true. Much to Einstein's dismay, he was instantly recognizable in public. When fans approached him as he took walks near the Princeton campus, Einstein would tell them, "Pardon me, always I am mistaken for Professor Einstein."

In addition to his prodigious scientific achievements, Einstein wrote extensively on topics relating to philosophy (e.g., "The life of the individual has meaning only insofar as it aids in making the life of every living thing nobler and more beautiful"), religion ("Science without religion is lame, religion without science is blind"), war ("Peace cannot be kept by force; it can only be achieved by understanding"), and humor ("Any man who can drive safely while kissing a pretty girl is simply not giving the kiss the attention it deserves").

Einstein's impact on the world was phenomenal, even outside the realm of science. In 1939 he wrote a letter to President Roosevelt, warning him of the possibility of Nazi Germany developing an atomic bomb. This letter is said to have mobilized the United States to create the bomb before Germany did. Einstein was offered the Presidency of Israel in 1952 but declined the honor. Also in 1952 a new element named *einsteinium* was discovered and named in his honor.

Einstein also helped transform our perceptions of the role of scientists in society. From his writings it is clear that he believed that scientists have a moral responsibility to improve the human condition. He was an outspoken advocate of pacifism, international cooperation, democracy, and improving the quality of human life. Einstein helped reshape the image of the scientist from a private specialist to a public personality deeply committed to improving the fate of humanity. His heroic leadership was indirect, yet profound.

TRANSFORMING-SPECIFIC HEROES

John Lennon: The Hero Who Gave Peace a Chance

Heroes move us and inspire us. They do so by offering a noble vision, and by overcoming whatever obstacles stand in their way of fulfilling that vision. Moreover, our greatest heroes die in the service of achieving their dreams. In our research we have found that people show the greatest reverence for heroes of great talent who die in the pursuit of a virtuous cause.

The life of John Lennon fits this template nicely. Lennon played a pivotal role in revolutionizing popular music during the 1960s; he was a tireless advocate of peaceful solutions to world conflict; he overcame adversity of many types along his journey; and he was tragically gunned down in the prime of his life by a crazed fan. John Lennon is best known as a founding member of the Beatles, believed by many to be the greatest rock band in history. At first, Lennon's vision was simply to make money by making good music. But in doing so, he pushed the envelope artistically. In an era when nearly all musicians donned short "crew-cuts," the four Beatles dared to wear long "mop-top" haircuts. The young Beatles defied convention by composing their own songs rather than covering the works of established artists. Under Lennon's leadership, they were the first to create music videos as seen in the movies *A Hard Day's Night*, *Help!*, and *Magical Mystery Tour*.

Most impressively, Lennon encouraged his fellow Beatles to compose song lyrics that would do far more than mindlessly tell stories of teenage love. Lennon wanted to use his music to tell meaningful stories and to effect change in the world. Beginning in the mid-1960s, his lyrics often had a dark edge to them. They revealed his anger, insecurities, infidelities, and painful childhood memories. His famous songwriting partner, Paul McCartney, was clearly influenced by Lennon and began composing songs of equal force.

In many other songs, Lennon's message was clearly one of peace and love. He was an innovative instrumentalist who took artistic risks. Lennon and the Beatles pioneered the practice of multi-tracking their songs, overdubbing their vocals and guitars to produce uniquely rich sounds. They experimented with unusual mid-song tempo changes, 40-piece orchestras, animal noises, vocal cacophonies, backward guitar riffs, and thunderous doom-laden chords. In an era when violent wars and demonstrations were commonplace, Lennon composed song lyrics that urged peaceful solutions. His 1968 song "Revolution" encouraged social change "but," sang Lennon, "when you talk about destruction, don't you know that you can count me out."

As with many great heroes, Lennon overcame significant obstacles. Chief among them was a turbulent childhood in which his mother and father each abandoned him in different ways. Lennon revealed this pain with great artistic success, using primal scream vocals in his 1970 song "Mother." He courageously overcame drug addiction and marital problems with his wife Yoko. In the early 1970s, the Nixon administration targeted his anti-war behavior as an excuse for deporting him back to England. Lennon fought and won his battle to stay in America.

But it was in America that a mentally disturbed individual shot and killed Lennon in 1980 outside the musician's home near Central Park. Over half a million people gathered in the park three days later to honor their hero, many of them singing his anthems of "Give Peace a Chance" and "Imagine". Decades after his death, Lennon remains a pop-cultural icon who symbolizes the enduring themes of love and peace. Countless musicians today have been immeasurably influenced by Lennon's artistic gifts, along with his vision that one day, as he sung in "Imagine", "the world will be as one."

Buddy Holly: The Day the Music Died

Generations of rock fans are familiar with the haunting opening lyrics of Don McLean's classic song, "American Pie": "February made me shiver, with every paper I'd deliver," and "I can't remember if I cried, when I read about his widowed bride, but something touched me deep inside, the day the music died." These words refer, of course, to Buddy Holly, one of the icons of 1950s rock 'n' roll. Our research shows that the dead are often elevated in our esteem and turned into heroes. Holly illustrates this phenomenon as well as anyone. He, and the men killed with him on February 3, 1959, are frozen in time. The images of those three young rock stars endure in American pop culture history. But Holly is also a hero for what he did in life, not the way he died.

Buddy Holly was an ambitious young musician from Lubbock, Texas. In 1957, at the age of 20, Holly released one of the greatest records in rock 'n' roll history, "That'll Be The Day." One of the legends about that song is that a disk jockey in Buffalo locked the studio door and played the song over and over again, for over an hour. True or not, the song was an instant and lasting hit. That tune was followed by many others, most notably perhaps "Oh Boy," "Peggy Sue," and "Maybe, Baby."

Although Holly's recordings were extremely successful, money problems forced him to join a rock 'n' roll tour in the winter of 1959. The tour bus often broke down in freezing weather, and on the night of February 2, the disgusted Holly hired a single-engine airplane to fly him from Clear Lake, Iowa to Moorhead, Minnesota. With him were rock legends Ritchie Valens ("La Bamba") and J.P. Richardson, a.k.a. "The Big Bopper" ("Chantilly Lace"). The plane crashed shortly after takeoff, and the three rockers and the pilot were killed. Other rock stars of the time were fading or retiring, and in some ways the music did die, until the Beatles and others transformed it in the 1960s.

Holly was one of the first rock stars to write, record, and produce his own music. And that music has had enduring influence. The young Bob Dylan saw Holly perform in Duluth, Minnesota a few days before he was killed, and remains indebted to his music to this day. The Beatles chose that name for their band as a nod to Holly's group, The Crickets. The Grateful Dead performed his classic "Not Fade Away" more than any other single tune. Holly's guitar playing, his innovative use of various instrumentations, and his unique blending of a variety of musical traditions were models for other singers, songwriters, musicians, and bands.

Holly himself said that none of what he did would have been possible without the breakthrough performances of Elvis Presley, but Holly's music has had much greater lasting impact. The visual image of Buddy Holly in his thick black-framed glasses, the sound of his guitar, the distinctive hiccup opening the song "Rave On," and his buoyant optimism about making good music will endure. In that respect, the music never died. Rave on.

Bill Cosby: The Hero Who Broke Racial Barriers

People tend to love heroes who come from humble origins, overcome obstacles, and achieve unprecedented success. Bill Cosby is one such hero. Raised in a housing project in north Philadelphia, Cosby grew up in poverty and has joked about the influence of his often-absent father: "Because of my father, I thought my name was Jesus Christ. My brother Russell thought that his name was Dammit" (Cosby, 2011, p. 16).

Cosby held so many jobs while in high school that he was forced to drop out. He later earned an equivalency diploma and earned an athletic scholarship to Temple University, but he left college to pursue a career as a stand-up comic. Cosby's humor, focusing on his childhood experiences and family issues, became immensely popular. He often had to explain why he never injected racial issues into his material:

> A white person listens to my act and he laughs and he thinks, "Yeah, that's the way I see it too." Okay. He's white. I'm Negro. And we both see things the same way. That must mean that *we are alike. Right?* So I figure this way I'm doing as much for good race relations as the next guy.
>
> (p. 36)

In 1965 Cosby became the first African-American to co-star in a dramatic television series. The show was called *I Spy*, and it earned him three consecutive Emmy Awards for Best Actor. When the series ended, Cosby finished his bachelor's degree and then earned a master's degree in education from the University of Massachusetts. Throughout the 1970s, Cosby enjoyed great success with a Saturday morning cartoon series called *Fat Albert and the Cosby Kids*. His doctoral degree dissertation, written in 1976, focused on the role of this cartoon in promoting learning among elementary school children.

Cosby's greatest artistic success came when he starred in the highest-rated comedy television sitcom of all-time, *The Cosby Show*, which aired from 1984 to 1992. Cosby has said that he developed this series in response to his disdain for television programming that predominantly focused on vulgarity and violence to attract viewers. *The Cosby Show* was a throwback to a time when TV shows were wholesome and family oriented. It defied racial stereotypes by portraying an African-American family as affluent and well educated. The series won dozens of Emmy, People's Choice, and Golden Globe awards.

Cosby has been known for expressing some controversial ideas on racial issues confronting America. He has absorbed considerable criticism for urging African-Americans to take more personal responsibility for their economic well-being, to make better moral choices, and to focus on good parenting. Critics have attacked Cosby for ignoring many of the structural impediments to African-American prosperity, but Cosby insists that his ideals are consistent with the healthy development of any child, regardless of race.

Heroes take courageous steps to defy the status quo, even at great risk to their lives or careers. Bill Cosby has devoted his life to making people laugh, and he has achieved this goal by breaking racial barriers and by daring to be different. "Civilization had too many rules for me," he said, "so I did my best to rewrite them." As with most heroes, Cosby achieved success because he risked failure. "I don't know the key to success," he once said, "but the key to failure is trying to please everybody" (Cosby, 2011, p. 125).

Myriam Merlet: The Lost Hero

Sadly, many of our most powerful heroes perish at a young age. Some are assassinated (e.g., John F. Kennedy and John Lennon); some are killed in accidents (Princess Diana and Buddy Holly); and some self-destruct (e.g., John Belushi and Heath Ledger). It is unusual to hear of a hero dying at a young age in a natural disaster. But that is exactly what happened recently to Myriam Merlet, who was killed at the age of 53 when her home collapsed on her during the Haitian earthquake on January 12, 2010.

Who was Myriam Merlet? She was a champion of women's rights in a country, Haiti, that desperately needed such a champion. Until 2005 it was not illegal for a man to rape a young girl or woman in Haiti. By Haitian law, rape was considered a crime against honor—a squandering of virginity that was often settled with a payment to the victim's family. Sometimes judges suggested as reparation that the rapist marry the victim. All this changed in Haiti because of the collective efforts of women activists such as Myriam Merlet, Magalie Marcelin, and Anne Marie Coriolan—all of whom perished in the quake.

In an essay written in 2001, Myriam Merlet explained her calling to help Haitian women. Merlet lived and was educated abroad until the age of 29, when she felt "the need to be part of something. This couldn't be the black cause in the United States or the immigration cause in Canada. It could only be the cause of the Haitian people." Merlet was especially interested in remedying arbitrarily defined differences in power and status among different groups of people: "I look at things through the eyes of women, very conscious of the roles, limitations, and stereotypes imposed on us." Merlet wanted everyone, men and women, to reach their full potential as human beings:

> The idea is to give women the opportunity to grow so that we may end up more complete human beings who can really change things. Individuals should have the opportunity to be complete human beings, women as well as men, youth as well as old people, the lame as well as the healthy.

As with most heroes, Merlet was not deterred by the challenges of achieving her vision of an egalitarian society.

> Of course it's a utopian dream. The more people share in the same dream, as in Martin Luther King's *I Have a Dream* speech, the more likely we'll achieve it collectively. Often I ask myself if it's possible to make this dream a reality when it's not shared by others. More people must be willing to take a different course, though some might call them crazy.
>
> It's hard and frustrating because you find yourself alone. I don't mean to say that I'm responsible for the problems [of Haiti]. But still, as a Haitian woman, I must make an effort so that all together we can extricate ourselves from them.

In Haiti, a hero has been lost. Although there is concern in Haiti about the future of the rights of women and girls, we are optimistic that someone will fill the void. We have found that heroes such as Merlet leave an indelible mark on the societies they change, and one of those marks is the seed of heroism that they plant in others. We eagerly await the future fruits of Merlet's great vision and labors.

Chapter 11

Transcendent Heroes
Influence at its Deepest Level

In reading about other heroes up to this point, you may have wondered whether we actually placed particular individuals into the right category or type. You may have questioned, for example, whether Gabrielle Giffords is a Transitory Hero, rather than, perhaps, a Traditional Hero. Is Traditional Hero Pat Tillman better regarded as a Transitory Hero? We have named him a Traditional Hero because we don't feel that the U.S. military's partial fabrications of his story diminish his genuine heroism. But people can disagree. Indeed, we indicated earlier that the two of us did not see eye to eye on whether *Star Trek*'s Captain Kirk is a Transitional or Traditional Hero. And, as we have written many times, eyes of beholders are where heroes rise, reside, and fall.

In many cases, placing someone into one category rather than another is difficult, and finally, it seems, somewhat arbitrary. Furthermore, you may have wondered why certain heroes who would seem to fit a specific category were not found in that chapter. Abraham Lincoln, for example, is on the cover of this book, and would certainly seem to be a Transforming Hero. But he hasn't been profiled thus far. The reason is that we are saving the best for last. Some heroes transcend the categories of our taxonomy. They illustrate more than one kind of heroism and more than one kind of heroic influence. For example, we discussed U.S. President Woodrow Wilson as a Trending Hero. However, he can easily be seen as a Traditional Hero. We profiled UCLA basketball coach John Wooden when we discussed Transparent Heroes, because many of his efforts to emphasize education and academics as much as athletic achievement were not publicized. But given the way he and his teams changed the way college basketball is played, he could easily be regarded as a Transforming Hero.

Jesus of Nazareth: A
Transcendent Hero

We think it's important to recognize the differing and significant kinds of influence some individuals have had by treating them as *Transcendent Heroes*. Abraham Lincoln, as suggested above, is one of our favorite examples. He seems clearly to fit the Transforming Hero category. In accomplishing the abolition of slavery and pointing the way toward equal rights for all Americans, few people have had more impact on U.S. history. Yet Lincoln was also transfigured, during his lifetime and after his assassination. He was, he admitted himself, quite ugly. Yet when a young soldier in the Union army met Lincoln on a visit to a battlefield, he transformed the President's visage so as to perceive heroism in Lincoln's face. He wrote that the President's countenance was "strong yet tender" and that in it "the agony of the life and death struggle of the hour was revealed as we had never seen it before." This transfiguration of Lincoln's face inspired and aroused the motives of this young man. His narrative continued, "With a new understanding, we knew why we were soldiers" (Foote, 1958, p. 803). Thus we see that not only can Lincoln be considered both Transfigured and Transforming, but the psychological process of transfiguring Lincoln had an elevating and transforming effect. One kind of heroic influence led to another. While this transfiguration happened during Lincoln's life, his tragic assassination accelerated the construction of his heroic image. Daniel Chester French's iconic sculpture in the Lincoln Memorial in Washington, D.C. creates an unforgettable heroic image of the 16th President. That sculpture, along with Lincoln's own words carved into the sides of the Memorial, completes the heroic transfiguration.

In highlighting Lincoln as a Transcendent Hero we want to signal that we have decided to restrict the label "transcendent" to heroes who are clearly Transforming as well as having other kinds of influence. The individuals we consider here as Transcendent Heroes have had an exceptional impact on a significant aspect of world society, and warrant being singled out. One clear example is Jesus of Nazareth. Undoubtedly a Transforming Hero, centuries of iconography have also transfigured him. For some people, Jesus also served as a Transitional Hero. Former U.S. President George W. Bush completely transformed his life just after his 40th birthday by quitting drinking and becoming an evangelical Christian. For him, Christ was a transforming figure at a transitional point in his life.

Throughout our study of heroism, we have been struck by how many heroes are fictional. Roughly one-third of heroes named in our surveys are characters from fiction, whether it be film, literature, or mythology. One such figure who fits the Transcendent Hero category is Harry Potter. We will see that Potter transformed Hogwarts School and also the realm of witchcraft and wizardry. He is also a Transitional Hero. He served as an inspiring hero for many young people who have since left him behind as an influential figure. And in fitting the template of the heroic journey discussed so eloquently by Joseph Campbell in *The Hero with a Thousand Faces*, Harry Potter is a Traditional Hero. His journey included such elements from Campbell as a born calling, help from a wise old man, and struggles with an evil villain.

In sum, we end our study of heroes by profiling those we regard as transcendent. They have had a remarkable influence on our culture.

Harry Potter: The Archetypal Hero

In June of 1997, when the first Harry Potter book appeared in bookstores, no one could have predicted that the character was destined to become one of the greatest heroes in literary history. Author J.K. Rowling was a complete unknown, and the lead character of Harry Potter had an appearance that hardly fit the image of a hero. He was described as "small and skinny for his age" with "a thin face" and "knobbly knees". He also wore round eyeglasses and had a scar on his forehead. Harry was alone, vulnerable, and lacking in confidence. All of these qualities made him an unlikely hero.

Or did they?

We argue that the genius of Rowling was her recognition that people are drawn to stories in which homeliness blooms into greatness, the weak prevail over the strong, and the young outwit the old. Stories of triumphant underdogs pervade all of literature, from the biblical account of David and Goliath to Hans Christian Andersen's *The Ugly Duckling*. There is something powerful and striking about unexpected heroism. A number of investigators have now documented the compelling allure of underdogs who overcome significant odds on their journey to greatness (Goldschmied and Vandello, in press; Kim et al., 2008; Vandello et al., 2007).

We suggest that a triumphant underdog derives its appeal from its ability to tap into a Jungian hero *archetype*. The underdog archetype is but one of many heroic elements with which J.K. Rowling endowed her Harry Potter novels. The series owes its immense popularity to Rowling's use of additional archetypes such as *orphan, sidekick, adolescent, bigot, lover, executioner*, and *shape-shifter*. Our hero Harry Potter must cope with the tragic death of his parents, who were slain by the story's villain, Lord Voldemort. As an 11-year-old orphan, Harry discovers he has special powers that need cultivating at the Hogwarts School of Witchcraft and Wizardry, where he encounters a sidekick, Ron Weasley, who will help him in his adventures.

Harry Potter's journey through the turbulent period of adolescence is also archetypically important. It is during adolescence that people experience some of the greatest pains and greatest joys of life, a time when we are transformed physically and emotionally, and when we discover some of our greatest talents. Harry Potter is the symbol of both the tumult and triumph of adolescence. Other archetypical images in the *Harry Potter* series include Ginny Weasley as the maiden, Professor Dumbledore as the wise old man, Professor McGonagall as the mother figure, Fred and George Weasley as the tricksters, Hagrid as the eternal child, and Severus Snape as the shifting individual whose goodness or badness is unclear.

But first and foremost, *Harry Potter* tells the classic story of good versus evil. Rowling has said that the moral significance of the tale seems "blindingly obvious". Her characters are often forced to choose between what is right and what is easy, "because that is how tyranny is started, with people being apathetic and taking the easy route and suddenly finding themselves in deep trouble." Harry's encounters with his nemesis, the evil Lord Voldemort, set the stage for timeless archetypal conflicts such as virtue versus vice, young versus old, and life versus death. As Carl Jung would say, these conflicts are as old as the human race itself, ensuring our endless fascination with how our hero Harry Potter resolves them.

Jesus of Nazareth: The Born Hero

As with leaders, people often ask whether heroes are born or made. In our studies of heroism we have found that the "born hero" is a rare breed. Extraordinary situations typically bring out the heroes among us. Every Christmas and Easter, much of the world honors the most powerful story of the born hero in the western world. It is, of course, the story of Jesus of Nazareth.

Few people dispute that Jesus was an actual historical figure. He was born about the year 5 BCE in what is now Israel. The events of his life have been verified by several Roman historians and other non-Christian figures. Moreover, few people deny that he died by crucifixion around the year 33 AD. His death is described in all four gospels, documented by other contemporary sources, and regarded as a historical event. We also know that during his lifetime Jesus was a *transforming leader*, inspiring people and elevating them to new levels of morality.

Jesus was, and is, a polarizing figure. During his lifetime, his followers witnessed him perform miracles, and they believed in the new morality that he preached: a message of love, generosity, and forgiveness. But in his day Jesus was also a revolutionary who violated Jewish customs and defied Roman law. Although he did not make the claim explicitly, many biblical passages imply strongly that Jesus was the son of God. Like Socrates of ancient Greece, Jesus could have spared his own life by offering some defense of the social disruptions he caused. But he did not. His threat to the status quo was deemed too great by Roman authorities, and he was gruesomely executed.

The circumstances surrounding the death of Jesus are largely responsible for the formation of the Christian faith. The gospels tell us that three days after he died, Jesus rose from the dead and was lifted to heaven. The story of the resurrection is a central part of Christianity because it signifies to Christians that God approved Jesus' work on earth and that Jesus lives forever. After Jesus died, many of his followers were burned, stoned, or crucified by Roman authorities. This persecution backfired. As martyrs, these Christians were the source of inspiration for millions of people who began practicing the faith. Today there are roughly two billion Christians worldwide, and Christianity appears to be growing in some parts of the world, such as Asia and Africa. But over the past half-century, Europe has witnessed a significant drop in Christian believers. North America, too, is experiencing a similar albeit slower decline. It is also true that some atheists have become emboldened in their condemnation of religion.

Whether or not you believe that Jesus was the son of God, there is no denying his unparalleled impact on western thought and culture. Historian and author H.G. Wells wrote, "I am an historian, I am not a believer, but I must confess as a historian that this penniless preacher from Nazareth is irrevocably the very center of history. Jesus Christ is easily the most dominant figure in all history." Mahatma Gandhi, a Hindu, had nothing but praise for Jesus, describing him as "a man who was completely innocent, offered himself as a sacrifice for the good of others, including his enemies, and became the ransom of the world." Referring to Jesus' sacrifice on the cross, Gandhi said, "It was a perfect act."

Will Jesus still be worshipped as a hero 2,000 years from now? We cannot even begin to conjecture. As with many transforming heroes, the legend is compelling, the message is powerful, and there are iconic institutions in place to ensure significant staying power.

Abraham Lincoln: A Transcendent Hero

We are now in the midst of the sesquicentennial of the American Civil War. That war produced many people who are regarded as heroes. In some ways, its losers are regarded as heroes more than the winners. It is hard to find as much adulation in the North for Abraham Lincoln, Ulysses S. Grant or William T. Sherman as there is in the South for Stonewall Jackson and Robert E. Lee.

Still, Lincoln towers above them all in illustrating the different types of heroes that we have identified. We think that Lincoln is certainly a Traditional Hero. We also hold that he is a Transforming Hero more than is routinely recognized, and that in interesting ways he helps us understand the concept of Transfigured Heroes. Since he embodies so many aspects of heroism, he illustrates our overarching type, the *Transcendent Hero*, one who combines the features of several different kinds.

First, Lincoln is a Traditional Hero. He appears on America's penny and five-dollar bill. High-school students in many parts of the country still memorize the Gettysburg Address. We are taught that he saved the Union. More important perhaps, is the way Lincoln was transforming. Prior to the Civil War, slavery was rooted deeply in American society and American politics. Despite the Declaration of Independence claim that the idea that "all men are created equal" was a "self-evident" truth, slavery was built into and protected by the U.S. Constitution. Although the South seceded because it feared the ways that Lincoln might restrict slavery, he did not enter the presidency to abolish slavery. His goal was to preserve the Union, and bring the rebel states back.

But the war had its own dynamic, and by the time of Lincoln's second inauguration, on March 4, 1865, slavery was finished. In his inaugural address that day

Lincoln summarized the struggle's evolution perfectly: "Neither party expected for the war, the magnitude, or the duration, which it has already attained." And he went on to underline how transformed the country was: "Each looked for an easier triumph, and a result less fundamental and astounding." Historian Eric Foner has called our attention to that last word, *astounding*. In ending slavery, the war, through its own vicissitudes, changed the country in a way that is, if one thinks about it, simply astounding. Lincoln's central role in that transformation makes him a Transforming Hero.

Most interesting, perhaps, is Lincoln as a Transfigured Hero. Many Americans have constructed a charismatic, almost God-like image of Lincoln. The irony is that while we are drawn to so many aspects of Lincoln, including his appearance, he was, as he very readily admitted, an unattractive person. When a political adversary accused him of being two-faced, Lincoln asked whether anyone could really believe he would display the face they saw if he had another one.

Yet Civil War historian Shelby Foote, who gained fame during Ken Burns' television miniseries on the war, quotes a soldier who did cognitive work with Lincoln's appearance, and saw in it quite heroic qualities. As mentioned earlier, after Lincoln visited the army, the soldier wrote of Lincoln's face:

> None of us to our dying day can forget that countenance. Concentrated in that one great, strong yet tender face, the agony of the life and death struggle of the hour was revealed as we had never seen it before. With a new understanding, we knew why we were soldiers.

This young man was transformed by the transfiguration he had done himself. Heroism of various kinds is clearly in the eye of the beholder. Of those kinds, transfigured individuals have the most to teach us about how human cognition creates its heroes.

Conclusion
Leadership, Heroism, and Heroic Leadership

Abraham Lincoln was both a leader and a hero. He led the United States during the Civil War, and in doing so succeeded in both saving the Union and ending American slavery. He is consistently ranked by historians, along with George Washington and Franklin Roosevelt, as one of the greatest of all U.S. Presidents. He was also a hero—to many during his presidency, and to many more after his assassination. Among those who revered Lincoln as a hero while he was alive was an African-American woman Lincoln encountered when he toured Richmond, Virginia two days after the Confederate government abandoned its capital. She touched the President's arm as he walked the city's streets and shouted, "I know that I am free, for I have seen Father Abraham and felt him." The moment Lincoln died his near apotheosis and transformation into a more widely recognized hero began almost instantaneously. Standing at the bedside of the slain President, Secretary of War Edwin Stanton proclaimed, "Now he belongs to the ages." Millions of people soon saw Lincoln as a martyr (Harris, 2004, p. 205).

There are many other examples of people who have been both leaders and heroes. Alexander the Great was a military leader transformed into a hero. Military historian John Keegan (1987) offers Alexander as an example of "heroic leadership." The name he is known by in itself attests to his status as hero. His heroic transformation, like Lincoln's, was most likely facilitated by his early death. Another example we described earlier is Irena Sendler. A leader of Polish resistance to the Nazis, Sendler became a hero to those she saved and to those who admired her bravery, ingenuity, and sacrifice.

The purpose of our book is to develop an understanding of the relationship between leadership and heroism. Noting that many individuals are both leaders and heroes is only a start. Earlier we argued that all heroes are leaders, but that not all leaders are heroes. John Keegan once again is useful. He describes Ulysses

Seabiscuit: An Unconventional Hero

S. Grant as an example of "unheroic leadership." While Grant was as effective a commander as Alexander, his manner was not at all heroic. He eventually defeated Robert E. Lee, but Lee, fighting for the "lost cause" dear to many Southerners, is more widely regarded as a hero. While there are many examples of leaders who are heroes and leaders who are not heroes, these instances by themselves do not sustain the argument that all heroes are leaders, but not the other way around. To make the case in what follows, we consider definitions of leadership and heroism, and how different kinds of heroes in our taxonomy further clarify the argument.

What is Leadership?

Leadership scholars have proposed many different definitions of leadership. Like our undergraduates' responses discussed earlier, they converge on several central ideas: The five factors of *persona*, *vision*, *ethics*, *actions*, and *influence*. Considering a number of scholars' approaches in more detail, we see that there is most agreement regarding the importance of influence, and least consensus on the importance of ethics or morality in understanding leadership. Specifically, scholars differ radically on whether leadership only applies to influence toward moral thought or behavior. Ronald Heifetz (1998) argues that leadership is a term saturated in values, and that when we speak of leadership—for example, saying that the country needs more leadership—we reveal that we understand leadership to be a good thing, something that is moral. On the other hand, Barbara Kellerman (2004) argues that to call immoral leadership something other than leadership, for example, "power wielding," is to blind ourselves to instances of leadership, such as Hitler's, that we desperately need to understand. She makes the point that writers have not always treated leadership as something moral. Machiavelli, for example, regarded it as far from anything ennobling. Leaving the moral dimension aside, in other respects there is much overlap in the way scholars define leadership.

A good starting point is Hogan, Curphy and Hogan's (1994) view that "leadership involves persuading other people to set aside for a period of time their individual concerns and to pursue a common goal that is important for the responsibilities and welfare of a group" (p. 493). They add that their definition is "morally neutral" and that "leadership is persuasion, not domination." It "occurs when others willingly adopt, for a period of time, the goals of a group as their own." The idea that leadership is not domination and that followers willingly go along is consistent with other definitions stating that all leaders have power but that not all power holders are leaders (Burns, 1978; Magee, Gruenfeld, Keltner, and Galinsky, 2005). Some people with power wield it coercively to get people with less power to do their bidding. That, scholars argue, is not leadership.

Heifetz (1998) defines leadership "as an activity … mobilizing people to do something" (p. 18). We think this is a useful approach. Heifetz goes on to focus on "something" he calls "adaptive work," that is, addressing "conflicts in the values people hold" or diminishing "the gap between the values people stand for and the reality they face." Such work typically involves "a change in values, beliefs, or behavior" (p. 22). Leaders must find ways of helping people clarify and perhaps change their values, and think through how they can act to further their values, given reality.

Many scholars choose to offer definitions of leaders as well as or instead of leadership, mostly because defining the latter is a little more complicated. For example, Michael Hogg (2001) defines leaders as "people who have disproportionate influence, through possession of consensual prestige or the exercise of power, or both, over the attitudes, behaviors, and destiny of group members." He adds that leadership is about having "disproportionate power and influence to set agenda, define identity, and mobilize people to achieve collective goals" (p. 188).

Howard Gardner (1995) offers the broadest definition of a leader. He says that leaders are "persons who, by word and/or personal example, markedly influence the behaviors, thoughts, and/or feelings of a significant number of their fellow human beings" (pp. 8–9). Gardner also cites Harry Truman's marvelous quote that "a leader is a man who has the ability to get other people to do what they don't want to do and like it." Most important, as noted previously, Gardner greatly extends our understanding of leadership by contrasting *direct* leadership—as exercised, for example, by Winston Churchill, who spoke to his followers in person or through the radio—and *indirect* leadership—for example, that of Albert Einstein, who generally led through his published work rather than through face-to-face contact. Indirect leadership can be exerted through a range of scholarly or artistic products, such as music, dance, science, political treatises, or literature. Some leaders lead both directly and indirectly, at different times to different groups of followers, or audiences. For example, Martin Luther King led directly when he gave his *I Have a Dream* speech in Washington, D.C. in 1963. That same year he led indirectly with his "Letter from Birmingham Jail." Both King's ideas and his persona were important elements of his leadership.

The ideas that stories, poems, paintings, performances, and scholarship can influence, and that those who generate these products are leaders, greatly expand our understanding of leadership. It is particularly relevant for linking heroism to leadership. Many heroes influence us through their impersonal works, for example, their words and music, rather than through their personal presence or *persona*. This influence would be defined by Gardner as indirect leadership.

In extending the idea of leadership to examples, products, and accomplishments rather than personally directed influence, the question arises as to whether people who are no longer alive can be considered leaders. When Lincoln gave his Gettysburg Address, urging that Americans work to ensure that "government of the people, by the people, for the people shall not perish from the earth," he was clearly exercising leadership at that moment. To the extent that Lincoln's exhortation influences people today, is Lincoln a dead leader? We readily grant hero status to people who are dead, but calling them leaders may seem to stretch the definition too far. However, in some of our earlier work on people's tendencies to "deify the dead and downtrodden" (Allison and Eylon, 2005; Allison and Goethals, 2008) we argued that leaders are often most inspiring and therefore most influential when they are, in fact, dead. In a number of studies we provide support for the idea that some leaders inspire us the most when they are dead. They lead indirectly.

From the authors quoted above, we can distill a working definition of leadership. It is an activity or product which influences or persuades, but not coerces, other people to think, feel or act in particular ways, very often ways that advance the interests or goals of the group to which both the leader and followers belong. Leaders, then, are the individuals who perform the influencing activities or fashion the influencing products. We think that all heroes can be shown to be leaders in accordance with this definition. To make this case we need to outline further how we define heroes and heroism.

What is Heroism?

Heroism is the activities or products of individuals judged to be heroes on account of their activity or product being regarded as heroic. More simply, heroes are people who are judged to have behaved heroically. This somewhat circular definition reflects our belief that heroism is in the eye of the beholder, and that people decide for themselves who is worthy of being called a hero. Some individuals, for example the late Princess Diana of Great Britain, are regarded as heroes by many people the world over. Others, for example favorite teachers or coaches, or family members, are regarded as heroes by just a few, perhaps only one other person. And our research shows that heroes are often fictional characters, such as Wonder Woman, or animals, such as the racehorse Seabiscuit, or even inanimate but personifiable objects such as "The Little Engine That Could."

Thus a very wide range of real persons, fictional characters, animals, etc. are regarded as heroes. But who or what people regard as heroes is not totally arbitrary. We have shown that people have mental lists of the defining characteristics of heroes and that when one's understanding of a person matches one's mental lists of heroes' defining characteristics, that person is deemed a hero. Furthermore, we can specify what those mental lists look like. They include the dimensions of great achievement or accomplishment, or in a word competence. They also include moral behavior, particularly moral behavior that is difficult to perform, that puts one at risk, and may even involve self-sacrifice to the point of death and martyrdom. Prototypical heroes such as Superman are both highly competent and extremely virtuous. As described on the 1950s television show, the Man of Steel was "faster than a speeding bullet, more powerful than a locomotive" and "able to leap tall buildings in a single bound." Furthermore, he fought for "truth, justice, and the American way." At the time, "the American way" was unquestionably moral to the TV audience. And people such as Gandhi illustrate the idea that people who give their lives for what is regarded as a noble cause are viewed as heroes.

Still, on what basis can we assert that all heroes are leaders? We believe that heroes provide exemplars of admirable behavior that provide behavioral models for people to emulate, or at least aspire to. They help us define how we should or want to live our lives, and often provide specific instruction in how to lead those ideal lives. Like leaders, their "word and/or personal example" markedly influences "the behavior, thoughts, and/or feelings of" others (Gardner, 1995, p. 8). Furthermore, we can see a closer connection between leadership and heroism when we explore the ways the influence of both leaders and heroes stems from their role in satisfying important human motives.

Leadership, Heroism, and Motivation

Several theorists give human motivation a central place in their understanding of leadership. James MacGregor Burns (1978) argues that leadership happens "when persons with certain motives and purposes mobilize, in competition or conflict with others, institutional, political, psychological, and other resources so as to arouse, engage, and satisfy the motives of followers" (p. 18). He also states that by gratifying followers' motives, the leader can change them. That is, once followers' current motives are satisfied, a leader can engage new ones. Nicholas Warner (2008) suggests Captain Ahab in Herman Melville's novel *Moby Dick* as a brilliant example of a rather sinister leader engaging new motives after satisfying more basic ones. Ahab realizes that he can use his charismatic authority to get the *Pequod*'s crew excited about chasing the white whale once he has taken care of their more mundane needs for income from a successful voyage.

Van Vugt (2006) argues that leadership evolves from the very basic human need to coordinate efforts to achieve both individual and group goals. In order for a group to function effectively it must have a good mix of leaders and followers, and groups that have found ways to devise a good mix will be evolutionarily successful. He further suggests that there are three ways in which leadership is particularly important. First, leaders must decide what to do and where and when to do it. Second, leaders must keep peace within the group. Third, leaders must protect the group from outside threats, whether from other groups or from non-human threats. Van Vugt's account is similar to Heifetz's assertion in *Leadership Without Easy Answers* that followers expect leaders to satisfy their needs for direction, protection and order (1998, p. 177).

The role of motivation is also underlined in the work of David Messick (2005). He suggests that leaders and followers participate in an exchange in which each party satisfies needs of the other. Leaders, for example, provide followers with vision and direction, protection and security, inclusion and belongingness, and achievement and effectiveness. Followers engage with leaders for the satisfaction of these needs, and in return work hard to achieve the objectives set out by the leader. Messick notes that the motives that leaders satisfy correspond to several of the five broad need categories made famous in Maslow's (1954) motive hierarchy. For example, "protection and security" corresponds to Maslow's Safety needs, "inclusion and belongingness" corresponds directly to Maslow's Love/Belonging needs, and "achievement and effectiveness" corresponds to Malsow's Esteem needs. There is a weaker correspondence between "vision and direction" and Self-Actualization, but there is some. The most useful implication of the connection between Messick's work and Maslow's theory is that human beings have a considerable manifold of motives, and that leadership is important in satisfying many of them.

Messick's category of "vision and direction" resonates with our earlier finding of the centrality of *vision* in both lay and scholarly understandings of the nature of leadership. Followers' need for vision can be seen as an aspect of a more fundamental motive or need emphasized by Howard Gardner. Gardner's theory emphasizes the stories that leaders relate, and puts considerable focus on the idea that leaders' most effective stories are about identity. That is, leaders help people define where they have come from, where they are going, what obstacles they will face along the way, and, more generally, who they are. Identity gives people a sense of meaning, an important aspect of Maslow's self-actualization. Terror management theory also emphasizes the idea that charismatic leaders provide people with meaning and self-affirmation (Greenberg, Solomon, and Pyszczynski, 1997).

They make followers feel that they are a valued part of something great (Cohen et al., 2006) and arouse followers' motives to help their group achieve and maintain that greatness.

The importance of followers' sense of value is central to Tyler and Lind's (1992) theory of procedural justice. They argue that voluntary compliance with the directives of authority depends on the perceived legitimacy of both the authority and the directive, and legitimacy, in turn, depends on whether the authority treats the follower in a procedurally just manner. Is the leader fair in her or his decision-making? If the leader treats one fairly, he or she, as a representative of the group, signals that one has value. When leaders affirm followers' value by behaving fairly, followers will work hard to do as directed by the leader (see also Riggio, Chaleff, and Lipman-Blumen, 2008).

Many of the motivational themes above are also seen in Kellerman's (2004) book on *Bad Leadership*. She argues that sometimes people follow bad leaders because of the needs such leaders satisfy. These include the individual needs for safety, simplicity, and security as well as group needs for order, cohesion, and identity.

In sum, motivation is a central aspect of leadership. Leaders have the potential to gratify a range of human motives. That range is best illustrated using Maslow's motivational hierarchy. Depending on the circumstances, leaders can help people satisfy basic physiological motives, their need for safety, their need for inclusion, belongingness and love, their need for self-esteem, and their need for meaning and identity, or what Maslow calls self-actualization. When they do, they can then engage followers in activity toward other goals. In many such cases, the leaders' goals and motives and those of the followers merge, at least for a period of time.

James MacGregor Burns (1978) alerted us to the fact that when leaders and followers engage in the pursuit and satisfaction of mutual goals, the possibility of transforming leadership arises. The transforming leader can then take the initiative in focusing followers' attention on new goals, goals which can raise both leader and follower to higher levels of motivation and morality. This idea is nicely captured in a letter by America's second president, John Adams, who wrote to the effect that he must study politics and war so that his children could study mathematics and philosophy, so that their children in turn could study "painting, poetry, music [and] architecture" (May 12, 1780). In other words, once peace is achieved, leaders can help people understand the physical world, and that understanding in turn enables people to develop their finer sensibilities. While the range of motives that leaders can address is wide, transforming leaders focus on engaging higher motives once lower ones are satisfied, and helping followers fashion more moral identities.

Is motivation as relevant for heroes as it is for leaders? Our research suggests that it is. One-third of the heroes mentioned in our surveys of a wide cross-section of people are immediate family members or perhaps teachers or coaches. These individuals have provided satisfaction of both basic needs, such as needs for protection, love, or esteem, and higher needs for growth and development toward self-actualization. They have also provided moral guidance and inspired those who admire them to higher levels of motivation and morality. We can see this same range of needs satisfied, directly or vicariously, by fictional heroes. Superman protects the world, including us, from evil villains. Sherlock Holmes uses his highly developed skills of reasoning and deduction to solve crimes, often in ways that are unconventional and even unlawful but clearly moral. Like many other heroes he has flaws, but he contributes to the common good, and models intellectual engagement and development. In this way he offers an element of identity that is relevant to many readers. Actual persons who are heroes also satisfy needs and provide inspiring moral examples. Golda Meir protected her country from enemies, and modeled decisive, reasoned decision-making under the most stressful circumstances. Pretty Boy Floyd, as portrayed in Woody Guthrie's song, gave money to starving farmers and Christmas dinners to poor families in Oklahoma City.

In short, heroes satisfy a wide range of needs and motives, just as leaders do. They particularly satisfy our need for meaning and identity by providing models of high levels of achievement and creative moral solutions.

Reviving Heroic Leadership

Textbook treatments of leadership typically outline trait theories, situational theories, and contingency theories, followed by considerations of leaders' behaviors, newer emphases on transformational and charismatic leadership, and then a consideration of leader–follower relations. The idea of the "great man," considered in many seminal studies of leadership (e.g., Bales, 1958) has been left by the wayside, consigned to the dustbin of history, as have most trait theories. At the same time, some newer approaches (Hogan, Curphy, and Hogan, 1994; Zaccaro et al., 2008) have revived the trait approach by placing it in fresh contexts. For example, Hogan et al. discuss the trait approach using the Big Five personality dimensions that are prominent in many contemporary approaches to understanding persons. We believe that the heroic aspects of leadership, and the many similarities between leaders and heroes, should tip the balance back toward recognizing that leadership is often heroic. Because of our need for heroes, rooted in heroes' satisfaction of our needs for inspiring models of identity, many leaders are regarded as heroes by their followers, or by their distant admirers. To many, Abraham Lincoln is more than an effective leader. He is celebrated as a "political genius" and as a man who pointed his nation toward "a way [that] is plain, peaceful, generous, just…" in ending slavery (Goodwin, 2006, p. 37). In short, he became a hero as well as a leader.

Seabiscuit became more than a great racehorse. He was an inspiration to persistent effort and high achievement against great odds for millions of Americans during the depression. Irena Sendler became more than a resistance leader against Nazi tyranny during World War II. She became a selfless and inspiring model for courageous and creative opposition to overwhelming evil, in short, a hero. Many originally ordinary leaders achieve the status of heroes for their transforming visions and models, and many people who become heroes for their selfless sacrifice or exceptional achievement become indirect leaders who influence our thoughts, feelings, and behaviors. Leaders and heroes do many of the same things, and we should realize how central heroism is to many forms and instances of leadership. Although the study of leaders and leadership has taken us well beyond simple notions of the great man or of hero worship, we should recognize that heroes are an important category of leaders, and they often have the most profound effect.

Similarities and Differences Between Leaders and Heroes

Although we believe that leadership and heroism have much in common, we do not at all believe they are the same thing. For example, we have argued that not all leaders are heroes. There are non-heroic leaders as well as heroic ones. What then are some of the differences between heroes and leaders, especially when we consider non-heroic leaders? First, the fact that heroes are leaders but not vice versa means that there are more leaders than heroes. The number of heroes in our lives may be quite small. Second, there are differences in the value we place on leaders versus heroes. All of our heroes are good, in one way or another. That good quality makes them heroes. However, not all leaders are good. Some, asserts Kellerman (2004), are simply evil, or they may be ineffective, or bad in some other way. Bad heroism would seem an oxymoron.

Third, heroes are more likely to be indirect leaders than direct leaders. Most leaders, especially non-heroic leaders, are direct. There are many direct leaders we interact with on a regular basis, at work or at play, or in our local communities. Although we may admire and like them, we do not regard them as heroes. Part of this may be because we see them up close, and realize shortcomings as well as strengths and virtues. This makes sustaining a heroic view of them difficult or impossible. In contrast, heroes are often viewed from afar, in many cases after their deaths. They lead indirectly, and the indirect nature of their leadership makes it easier for us to continue thinking about them in heroic terms. This point suggests a related difference between leaders and heroes. The influence of heroes often takes place solely in our heads. We imagine them and what they have accomplished, and these images in turn influence and guide our thoughts, aspirations, and behavior. The influence of leaders sometimes takes place in our heads as well, but very often they influence us through interpersonal contact. They are, so to speak, in our faces as well as in our minds.

Another difference is that the influence of heroes is almost always inspirational. Heroes provide models for being persistent, for being courageous, for caring about others, and, most importantly, for doing what we know is right, even when it is difficult. They move us toward following up moral thought with moral behavior. Leaders sometimes have this kind of impact, but it is less frequent.

Another consideration involves motives. While we have emphasized that both leaders and heroes satisfy a range of motives, there are likely some differences in the kinds of motives that each typically gratifies. Leaders of various sorts address almost all of Maslow's motive categories at different times. Heroes, on the other hand, may often satisfy basic needs for physical sustenance and safety but not so often needs for belongingness and esteem. On the other hand, heroes may provide models for identity, meaning, and self-actualization more than typical leaders. These possibilities are highly speculative. They suggest that more work needs to be done in conceptualizing the similarities and differences in how leaders and heroes exert influence, and the motives addressed by leaders and heroes.

We see more similarities than differences when we consider the overlap in the images that people have of leaders and heroes. Our research revealed that there is a set of eight traits (the so-called Great Eight Traits of Heroes) that people perceive as defining heroes. Heroes are thought to be strong, smart, selfless, caring, charismatic, reliable, resilient, and inspiring. Many of these traits are also part of people's leader schemas or "implicit theories of leadership." For example, Simonton (1987) suggests that our prototypical image of leaders defines them as strong, active, and good. He further suggests that this image of leaders might be "archetypical" and have "transhistorical, even cross-cultural relevance," and "may even possess a sociobiological substratum" (pp. 238–240). Strong, active, and good sounds a lot like a hero. Thus there may be leader archetypes just as there are hero archetypes, and the two archetypes might be very similar. Of course many of the actual leaders we routinely encounter may not fit a leader prototype that represents leaders in a way that closely aligns them with heroes. In Freud's terms, they may not represent their group in a "particularly clearly marked and pure form" (Freud, 1921, p. 129).

In sum, there are many points of similarity and difference between heroes and leaders. Exploring both will be an important challenge for scholars in the future.

Heroes and Heroic Leadership in Perspective

We originally came to the study of heroism quite apart from our interest in leadership. Our research on rooting for underdogs and admiring people who have passed away led us to think about the range of ways we come to admire people.

That led us to focus on the widespread phenomenon of judging people to be heroes. Still, exploring heroes and heroism initially was far removed from our studies of leadership. However, when we considered why people create heroes and the impact that heroes have, we were struck by what we called *shaping* (Allison and Goethals, 2011). That is, heroes influence or shape us, much like leaders. The idea that all heroes are leaders gained traction from Howard Gardner's concept of indirect leaders. Very often heroes have an indirect influence, and the idea that leaders can influence other people indirectly powerfully added to our belief that all heroes are leaders. Perhaps, however, the bulk of leadership is more mundane than heroic. While that may be so, we remain confident that focusing on heroes and heroism contributes to a broader and more refined understanding of leaders and leadership.

References

Adler, J. (2006). Freud in our midst. Retrieved from www.myspace.com/32661578/blog/101412768 on May 18, 2012.

Allison, S.T., and Eylon, D. (2005). The demise of leadership: Death positivity biases in posthumous impressions of leaders. In D. Messick and R. Kramer (Eds.), *The Psychology of Leadership: Some new approaches* (pp. 295–317). New York: Erlbaum.

Allison, S.T., and Hensel, A. (2012). Sensitivity to the changing fortunes of others. *Personality and Social Psychology Connections*. Retrieved from spsptalks.wordpress.com on June 15, 2012.

Allison, S.T., and Goethals, G.R. (2008). Deifying the Dead and Downtrodden: Sympathetic Figures as Exceptional Leaders. In C.L. Hoyt, G.R. Goethals, and D.R. Forsyth (Eds.), *Leadership at the Crossroads: Psychology and leadership*. Westport, CT: Praeger.

Allison, S.T., and Goethals, G.R. (2011). *Heroes: What They Do and Why We Need Them*. New York: Oxford University Press.

Allison, S.T. and Goethals, G.R. (2012). *Wesley Autrey and Dave Hartsock: Heroes who seized the heroic moment*. Retrieved from blog.richmond.edu/heroes on June 15, 2012.

Allison, S.T., Messick, D.M., and Goethals, G.R. (1989). On being better but not smarter than others: The Muhammad Ali effect. *Social Cognition, 7*, 275–296.

Allison, S.T., Eylon, D., Beggan, J.K., and Bachelder, J. (2009). The demise of leadership: Positivity and negativity in evaluations of dead leaders. *The Leadership Quarterly, 20*, 115–129.

Allport, G.W. (1985). The historical background of social psychology. In G. Lindzey and E. Aronson (Eds.), *The Handbook of Social Psychology*. New York: McGraw Hill.

Aronson, E., and Linder, D. (1965). Gain and loss of esteem as determinants of interpersonal attractiveness. *Journal of Experimental Social Psychology, 1*, 156–171.

Augustine of Hippo (1998; original written in A.D. 398). *Confessions*. New York: Oxford University Press.

Bales, R.F. (1958) Task Roles and Social Roles in Problem-solving Groups. In E.E. Maccoby, T.M. Newcomb, and E.L. Hartley (Eds.) *Readings in Social Psychology*. New York: Holt, Rinehart, and Winston, pp. 437–447.

Bass, B.M. (1998). *Transformational Leadership: Individual, military, and educational impact*. Mahwah, NJ: Lawrence Erlbaum.

Bass, B.M., and Riggio, R.E. (2006). *Transformational Leadership*. Hillsdale, NJ: Lawrence Erlbaum.

Baumeister, R.F., and Tierney, J. (2011). *Willpower*. New York: Penguin Books.

Baumeister, R.F., Bratslavsky, E., Finkenauer, C., and Vohs, K. (2001). Bad is stronger than good. *Review of General Psychology, 5*, 323–370.

Becker, G.K. (2009). Moral leadership in business. *Journal of Business Ethics, 2*, 7–21.

Bloch, N. (2009, March 26). Top ten actresses past their expiration date. Retrieved from www.spike.com on October 29, 2011.

Bocchiaro, P., Zimbardo, P., and Van Lange, P.A.M. (2012). To defy or not to defy: An experimental study of the dynamics of disobedience and whistle-blowing. *Social Influence, 1*, 1–16.

Bradley, M. (2010, July 8). LeBron goes from Cleveland to Miami, from hero to villain. Retrieved from http://blogs.ajc.com/mark-bradley-blog on October 30, 2011.

Bruner, J. (1989a). *Actual Minds, Possible Worlds*. Cambridge, MA: Harvard University Press.

Bruner, J. (1989b). Essay in K. Nelson (1989), *Narratives From the Crib*: Cambridge, MA: Harvard University Press. Quoted in M. Gladwell (2000), *The Tipping Point*. Boston: Little, Brown, p. 118.

Bruner, J. (1991). *Acts of Meaning*. Cambridge, MA: Harvard University Press.

Burgess, C. (2000). *Teacher in Space: Christa McAuliffe and the* Challenger *legacy*. Lincoln: University of Nebraska Press.

Burns, J.M. (1978). *Leadership*. New York: Harper & Row.

Burns, J.M. (2003). *Transforming Leadership: A new pursuit of happiness*. New York: Atlantic Monthly Press.

Buss, D. (1994). *The Evolution of Desire: Strategies of human mating*. New York: Basic Books.

Butler, S. (1999). *East to the Dawn: The life of Amelia Earhart*. Da Capo Press.

Campbell, J. (1949). *The Hero with a Thousand Faces*. Bollingen Series 17. Princeton, NJ: Princeton University Press.

Campbell, W.J. (2012). The Military's "Fabrication"? No, Jessica Lynch was WaPo's story. Retrieved from http://mediamythalert.wordpress.com/2012 on June 10, 2012.

Carruthers, P., Laurence, S., and Stich, S. (2005). *The Innate Mind: Structure and contents*. New York: Oxford University Press.

Chomsky, N. (1986). *Knowledge of Language: Its nature, origin, and use*. New York: Greenwood.

Cialdini, R.B., Borden, R.J., Thorne, A., Walker, M.R., Freeman, S., and Sloan, L.R. (1976). Basking in reflected glory: Three (football) field studies. *Journal of Personality and Social Psychology, 34*, 366–375.

Cohen, G.L., Garcia, J., Apfel, N., and Master, A. (2006). A self-affirmation intervention to reduce the racial achievement gap. *Science, 313*, 1307–1310.

Conger, J.A., and Kanungo, R.N. (1998). *Charismatic Leadership in Organizations*. Thousand Oaks, CA: Sage.

Cook, E.T. (2012). *The Life of Florence Nightingale*. Berkeley: University of California Libraries.

Cosby, B. (2011). *I Didn't Ask to be Born (but I'm glad I was)*. Center Street Press.

Davies, H. (2004). *The Beatles*. New York: W.W. Norton Publishers.

Dehaene, S. (1997, October 27).What are numbers, really? A cerebral basis for number sense. Retrieved from www.edge.org/3rd_culture/dehaene/dehaene_p2.html on March 5, 2010.

DeLalla, A. (2012). How Meryl Streep inspires me. Retrieved from www.youtube.com/user/FaithJacobsen on June 14, 2012.

Dugard, M. (2005). *The Last Voyage of Columbus*. New York: Little Brown & Company.

Ellis, J.J. (2000). *Founding Brothers: The revolutionary generation*. New York: Knopf.

Emrich, C.G. (1999). Context effects in leadership perception. *Personality and Social Psychology Bulletin, 25*, 991–1006.

Erikson, E.H. (1959). *Identity and the Life Cycle*. New York: International Universities Press.

Eylon, D., and Allison, S.T. (2005). The frozen in time effect in evaluations of the dead. *Personality and Social Psychology Bulletin, 31*, 1708–1717.

Fernández-Armesto, F. (1991). *Columbus*. New York: Oxford University Press.

Festinger, L. (1954). A theory of social comparison processes. *Human Relations, 7*, 117–140.

Foote, S. (1958). *The Civil War: A narrative, Fort Sumter to Perryville*. New York: Random House.

Franco, Z.E., Blau, K., and Zimbardo, P.G. (2011). Heroism: A conceptual analysis and differentiation between heroic action and altruism. *Review of General Psychology, 15*, 99–113.

Freud, S. (1921). *Group Psychology and the Analysis of the Ego*. London: Hogarth.

Gardner, H. (1995). *Leading Minds: An anatomy of leadership*. New York: Basic Books.

Gini, A. (1998). Moral leadership and business ethics. In J.B. Ciulla (Ed.), *Ethics, the Heart of Leadership*. Westport, CT: Greenwood Publishing.

Goethals, G.R., and Allison, S.T. (2012). Making heroes: The construction of courage, competence and virtue. *Advances in Experimental Social Psychology, 46*, 183–235.

Goethals, G., and Hoyt, C. (2011). What makes leadership necessary, possible, and effective: The psychological dimensions. In R. Riggio and M. Harvey (Eds.) *Leadership Studies: The dialogue of disciplines*. Northampton, MA: Edward Elgar, pp. 101–118.

Goethals, G.R., and Wren, J.T. (Eds.). (2009). *Leadership and Discovery*. New York: Palgrave Macmillan.

Goldschmied, N., and Vandello, J.A. (2009). The advantage of disadvantage: Underdogs in politics. *Basic and Applied Social Psychology, 31*, 24–31.

Goldschmied, N., and Vandello, J.A. (in press). The future is bright: The underdog label, availability, and optimism. *Basic and Applied Social Psychology*.

Goodwin, D.K. (2006). *Team of Rivals: The political genius of Abraham Lincoln*. New York: Simon & Schuster.

Greenberg, J., Solomon, S., and Pyszczynski, T. (1997). Terror management theory of self-esteem and social behavior: Empirical assessments and conceptual refinements. In M.P. Zanna (Ed.), *Advances in Experimental Social Psychology*. New York: Academic Press, vol. 29, pp. 61–139.

Greenleaf, R.K. (1977). *Servant Leadership: A journey into the nature of legitimate power and greatness*. Mahwah, NJ: Paulist Press.

Harris, W.C. (2004). *Lincoln's Last Months*. Cambridge, MA: Harvard University Press.

Harvey, M., and Riggio, R.E. (2011). *Leadership Studies: The dialogue of disciplines*. Northampton, MA: Edward Elgar.

Heifetz, R.A. (1998). *Leadership Without Easy Answers*. Cambridge, MA: Harvard University Press.

Hemphill, J.K., and Coons, A.E. (1957). Development of the leader behavior description questionnaire. In R. Stogdill and A. Coons (Eds.), *Leader Behavior: Its description and measurement*. Columbus, Ohio: Bureau of Business Research.

Hogan, R., Curphy, G., and Hogan, J. (1994). What we know about leadership: Effectiveness and personality. *American Psychologist, 49*, 493–504.

Hogg, M.A. (2001). A social identity theory of leadership. *Personality and Social Psychology Review, 5*, 184–200.

House, R.J., Spangler, W.D., and Woyke, J. (1991). Personality and charisma in the U.S. presidency: A psychological theory of leader effectiveness. *Administrative Science Quarterly, 36*, 364–396.

Hunt, J.G. (1991). *Leadership: A new synthesis*. Newbury Park, CA: Sage.

Johnson, M.H., and Morton, J. (1991). *Biology and Cognitive Development: The case of face recognition*. Oxford: Blackwell.

Jung, C.G. (1969). *Collected Works of C.G. Jung, Volume 9 (Part 1): Archetypes and The Collective Unconscious*. Princeton, NJ: Princeton University Press.

Jung, C.G., and von Franz, M.L. (1964). *Man and his Symbols*. Garden City, New York: Doubleday and Co., Inc.

Kahneman, D., and Tversky, A. (1979). Prospect theory: An analysis of decision under risk. *Econometrica, 12*, 263–291.

Kantabutra, S. (2009). Toward a behavioral theory of vision in organizational settings. *Leadership and Organization Development Journal*, 30, 319–337.

Kassin, S.M., Fein, S., and Markus, H.R. (2010). Social Psychology (8th edn.). Boston, MA: Houghton Mifflin.

Keegan, J. (1987). *The Mask of Command*. New York: Viking.

Kellerman, B. (2004). *Bad Leadership: What it is, how it happens, why it matters*. Boston: Harvard Business School Press.

Kim, J., Allison, S.T., Eylon, D., Goethals, G., Markus, M., McGuire, H., and Hindle, S. (2008). Rooting for (and then abandoning) the underdog. *Journal of Applied Social Psychology, 38*, 2550–2573.

Kinsella, E.L., Ritchie, T.D., and Igou, E.R. (2010, April). Essential features and psychological functions of heroes. Poster session presented at the Northern Ireland British Psychological Society Annual Conference, Enniskillen, Co. Fermanagh, UK.

Kinsella, E.L., Ritchie, T.D., and Igou, E.R. (2011, July). Characteristics of persons of influence: A look at heroes, role models, and leaders. Poster session presented at the 16th Annual General Meeting, Stockholm, Sweden.

Kinsella, E.L., Ritchie, T.D., and Igou, E.R. (2012, July). Superman, Mother Teresa and Mom: What psychosocial functions are provided by our heroes? Poster session presented at the 13th Annual Meeting of the Society for Personality and Social Psychology, San Diego, California.

Klinnert, M., Campos, J.J., Sorce, J., Emde, R.N., and Svedja, M. (1983). Emotions as behavior regulators: Social referencing in infancy. In R. Plutchik and H. Kellerman (Eds.), *Emotions in Early Development, Vol. 2: The emotions.* New York: Academic Press.

Kramer, R.M., and Cook, K.S. (2004). *Trust and Distrust in Organizations: Dilemmas and approaches.* New York: Russell Sage Foundation.

Kramer, R.M., and Pittinsky, T.L. (2012). *Restoring Trust in Organizations and Leaders: Enduring challenges and emerging answers.* New York: Oxford University Press.

Kuhn, T. (1962). *The Structure of Scientific Revolutions.* Chicago: University of Chicago Press.

Kurzban, R. (2010). *Why Everyone (Else) is a Hypocrite: Evolution and the modular mind.* Princeton: Princeton University Press.

Leary, M. (2012). John Edwards' modular mind. *Personality and Social Psychology Connections.* Retrieved from http://spsptalks.wordpress.com/2012/05/03/john-edwards-modular-mind on December 4, 2012.

Lee, J., and Hancocks, P. (2011). Workers endure astere conditions in averting nuclear disaster. *CNN World*, March 29. Retrieved from articles.cnn.com/2011-03-29/world/japan.nuclear.workers_1_nuclear-power-plant-radioactive-water-tokyo-electric-power?_s=PM:WORLD on March 1, 2012.

Lindqvist, E. (2011). Height and leadership. *The Review of Economics and Statistics.* Retrieved from mitpressjournals.org/doi/abs/10.1162/REST_a_00239 on May 28, 2012.

Loeb, V. (2003). She was fighting to the death. *The Washington Post*, April 3.

Magee, J.C., Gruenfeld, D.H., Keltner, D.J., and Galinsky, A.D. (2005). Leadership and the psychology of power. In D. Messick and R. Kramer (Eds.), *The Psychology of Leadership: Some new approaches.* New York: Erlbaum, pp. 287–306.

Marcus, G.F. (2005). What developmental biology can tell us about innateness. In P. Carruthers, S. Laurence, and S. Stich (Eds.) *The Innate Mind: Structure and contents.* New York: Oxford University Press.

Maslow, A. (1954). *Motivation and personality.* New York: Harper.

McGrath, C. (2010). The 50th Anniversary of Ted Williams' Last Game—and "Hub Fans Bid Kid Adieu". *The New York Times*, September 28.

McNamara, M. (2009). Muhammad Ali's new fight: Literacy. Retrieved from www.cbsnews.com/stories/2006/11/22/eveningnews/main2207050.shtml on June 15, 2012.

McPherson, J.M. (1988). *Battle Cry of Freedom.* New York: Oxford University Press.

Meindl, J.R. and Ehrlich, S.B. (1987). The romance of leadership and the evaluation of organizations. *Academy of Management Journal, 30,* 91–110.

Meltzoff, A.N., and Moore, M.K. (1995). Infants' understanding of people and things: From body imitation to folk psychology. In J.L. Bermudez, A. Marcel, and N. Eilan (Eds.), *The Body and the Self.* Cambridge, MA: MIT Press, pp. 43–69.

Messick, D.M. (2005). On the psychological exchange between leaders and followers. In D. Messick and R. Kramer (Eds.), *The Psychology of Leadership.* Mahwah, NJ: Lawrence Erlbaum Associates, pp. 83–98.

Mio, J.S., Riggio, R.E., Levin, S., and Reese, R. (2005). Presidential leadership and charisma: The effects of metaphor. *The Leadership Quarterly, 16,* 287–294.

Monin, B., Sawyer, P.J., and Marquez, M.J. (2008). The rejection of moral rebels: Resenting those who do the right thing. *Journal of Personality and Social Psychology, 95,* 76–93.

Monroe, I. (2012). Bayard Rustin: One of the tallest trees in our forest. *Huffington Post,* March 22. Retrieved from www.huffingtonpost.com/irene-monroe/bayard-rustin_b_1371165.html on June 14, 2012.

Murphy, C. (2006). Looking for fame in all the wrong places. *Chicago Tribune,* August 25, p. 34.

Myers, D.G. (2010). *Social Psychology* (10th edn.). New York: McGraw-Hill.

Nelson K., (1989). *Narratives from the Crib.* Cambridge, MA: Harvard University Press.

Piaget, J. (1952). Autobiography. In E. Boring (Ed.), *History of Psychology in Autobiography.* Worcester, MA: Clark University Press.

Pinker, S. (1991). Rules of language. *Science, 253,* 530–535.

Powell, A. (2011). Can we apply the Peter Principle to politics? Retrieved from www.herald-mail.com on June 15, 2012.

Richards, D., and Engle, S. (1986). After the vision: Suggestions to corporate visionaries and vision champions. In J.D. Adams (Ed.), *Transforming Leadership.* Alexandria, VA: River Press, pp. 199–215.

Riggio, R.E., Chaleff, I., and Lipman-Blumen, J. (Eds.). (2008). *The Art of Followership: How great followers create great leaders and organizations.* San Francisco: Jossey-Bass.

Schein, E.H. (1992). *Organizational Culture and Leadership.* San Francisco, CA: Jossey-Bass.

Schulz, C. (1956). *Good Grief, More Peanuts,* 25. New York: Rinehart & Co. Cartoon caption: "This is a 'security and happiness' blanket ... All little kids carry them."

Simonton, D.K. (1987) *Why Presidents Succeed: A political psychology of leadership.* New Haven, CT: Yale University Press.

Sophocles (2001; 429 BCE). *Oedipus The King.* New York: Simon & Schuster. (B. Knox, trans.).

Sorenson, G. and Hickman, G.R. (2002). Invisible leadership: Acting on behalf of acommon purpose. In C. Cherry and L.R. Matusak (Eds.), *Building Leadership Bridges.* College Park: James MacGregor Burns Academy of Leadership, pp. 7–24.

Stogdill, R.M. (1974). *Handbook of Leadership: A survey of theory and research.* New York: Free Press.

Sternberg, R. (2011). Leadership and education: Leadership stories. In R. Riggio and M. Harvey (Eds.) *Leadership Studies: The dialogue of disciplines.* Northampton, MA: Edward Elgar. pp. 161–170.

Taylor, S.E., Peplau, A.L., and Sears, D.O. (2006). *Social Psychology* (12th edn.). Englewood Cliffs, NJ: Prentice Hall.

Treviño, L.K., Weaver, G.R., and Reynolds, S. (2006). Behavioral ethics in organizations: A review. *Journal of Management, 32,* 951–990.

Tyler, T.R., and Lind, E.A. (1992). A relational model of authority in groups. *Advances in Experimental Social Psychology, 25,* 115–191.

Updike, J. (1960). Hub Fans Bid Kid Adieu. *The New Yorker,* October 22.

Vandello, J.A., Goldschmied, N.P., and Richards, D.A.R. (2007). The appeal of the underdog. *Personality and Social Psychology Bulletin, 33*, 1603–1616.

Van Vugt, M. (2006). Evolutionary origins of leadership and followership. *Personality and Social Psychology Review, 10*, 354–372.

Warner, N.O. (2008). Of Gods and Commodores: Leadership in Melville's *Moby-Dick*. In C.L. Hoyt, G.R. Goethals, and D.R. Forsyth (Eds.), *Leadership at the Crossroads: Psychology and leadership*. Westport, CT: Praeger.

Weir, T. (2012). LeBron James expresses regret about "The Decision". *USA Today*, June 12. Retrieved from content.usatoday.com/communities/gameon/post/2011/12/lebron-james-expresses-regrets-about-the-decision/1#.UKFHCIevF99 on June 15, 2012.

White, T.H. (1978). *In Search of History: A personal adventure*. New York: Harper & Row.

Yammarino, F.J. (1994). Indirect leadership: Transformational leadership at a distance. In B.M. Bass and B.J. Avolio (Eds.), *Improving Organizational Effectiveness Through Transformational Leadership*. Thousand Oaks, CA: Sage, pp. 26–47.

Yukl, G. (2013). *Leadership in Organizations*. Boston, MA: Pearson.

Yukl, G., and Lepsinger, R. (2004): *Flexible Leadership: Creating value by balancing multiple challenges and choices*. San Francisco, CA: Jossey-Bass.

Zaccaro, S.J. (2007). Trait-based perspectives of leadership. *American Psychologist, 62*, 6–26.

Zaccaro, S.J., Gulick, L.M.V., and Khare, V.P. (2008). Personality and leadership. In C. Hoyt, G.R. Goethals, and D. Forsyth (Eds.), *Social Psychology of Leadership*. New York: Praeger.

Zimbardo, P. (2012). Heroic imagination project. Retrieved from http://heroicimagination.org on October 31, 2011.

Author Index

Adler, J. 33
Allison, S.T. 4, 8–10, 14, 16, 20, 29, 75,
    79, 84, 89, 96, 101, 147, 163, 191,
    198
Allport, G.W. 16
Aronson, E. 21
Augustine of Hippo 23

Bachelder, J. 147
Baer, G. 116
Bales, R.F. 195
Bass, B.M. 5–6, 164–5
Baumeister, R.F. 34, 81
Becker, G.K. 7
Beggan, J.K. 147
Blau, K. 18
Bloch, N. 20
Bocchiaro, P. 16, 42
Bradley, M. 22
Bratslavsky, E. 81
Brown, R. 143
Bruner, J. 12
Burgess, C. 51–2
Burns, J.M. 1, 25, 164–5, 190, 192, 194
Buss, D. 10
Butler, S. 152

Campbell, J. 13–15, 24–6, 96, 183
Campbell, W.J. 24
Campos, J.J. 15
Carruthers, P. 15
Chaleff, I. 194
Chomsky, N. 15
Cialdini, R.B. 16
Cohen, G.L. 194
Conger, J.A. 5
Cook, E.T. 133

Cook, K.S. 6
Coons, A.E. 7
Cosby, B. 178–9
Curphy, G. 190, 195

Davies, H. 17–18
Dehaene, S. 15
DeLalla, A. 8
Dugard, M. 169

Ellis, J.J. 174
Emde, R.N. 15
Emrich, C.G. 9
Engle, S. 7
Erikson, E.H. 22
Eylon, D. 29, 147, 191

Fein, S. 16
Fernández-Armesto, F. 169
Festinger, L. 29
Finkenauer, C. 81
Flexner, J.T. 141
Foote, S. 11, 183, 187
Franco, Z.E. 18
Freud, S. 197
Franz, M.L. von 14

Galinsky, A.D. 190
Gardner, H. 8, 12, 132, 190–3, 198
George, E. 89
Gini, A. 6
Goethals, G.R. 4, 7–10, 14, 16, 29, 75,
    84, 89, 96, 101, 147, 163, 191, 198
Goldschmied, N. 29, 184
Goodwin, D.K. 195
Greenberg, J. 193
Greenleaf, R.K. 10

Gruenfeld, D.H. 190
Guralnick, P. 86

Hancocks, P. 44
Harris, W.C. 188
Harvey, M. 5
Heifetz, R.A. 189–90, 193
Hemphill, J.K. 7
Hensel, A. 20
Hickman, G.R. 82
Hirsch, J. 149–50
Hogan, J. 190, 195
Hogan, R. 190, 195
Hogg, M.A. 14, 190
House, R.J. 7
Hoyt, C. 9
Hunt, J.G. 8
Hutchins, R. 41, 57

Igou, E.R. 10

Johnson, M.H. 15
Jung, C.G. 14, 145

Kahneman, D. 20
Kanfer, S. 124
Kantabutra, S. 6
Kanungo, R.N. 5
Kassin, S.M. 16
Keegan, J. 188–9
Kellerman, B. 189, 194, 196
Keltner, D.J. 190
Kim, J. 6, 29, 170, 184
Kinsella, E.L. 10
Klinnert, M. 15
Kramer, R.M. 6
Kuhn, T. 17, 175
Kurzban, R. 76–7

Laurence, S. 15
Leary, M. 76–7
Lee, J. 44
Lepsinger, R. 7
Levin, S. 5
Lind, E.A. 194
Linder, D. 21
Lindqvist, E. 12
Lipman-Blumen, J. 194
Loeb, V. 24

Magee, J.C. 190
Marcus, G.F. 15
Markus, H.R. 16
Marquez, M.J. 16
Maslow, A. 193–4
McGrath, C. 159
McPherson, J.M. 83
Meindl, J.R. 9
Meltzoff, A.N. 15
Messick, D.M. 193
Mio, J.S. 5
Monin, B. 16
Monroe, I. 93
Moore, M.K. 15
Morton, J. 15
Murphy, C. 21
Myers, D.G. 16

Nelson K. 12

Peplau, A.L. 16
Piaget, J. 145
Pinker, S. 15
Pittinsky, T.L. 6
Powell, A. 37
Pyszczynski, T. 193

Reese, R. 5
Reynolds, S. 6
Richards, D. 7
Richards, D.A.R. 29
Riggio, R.E. 5, 194
Ritchie, T.D. 10

Sawyer, P.J. 16
Schein, E.H. 5
Schulz, C. 55
Schultz, J. 82
Sears, D.O. 16
Simonton, D.K. 3, 70, 163, 197
Solomon, S. 193
Sophocles 68
Sorce, J. 15
Sorenson, G. 82
Spangler, W.D. 7
Sternberg, R. 12
Stich, S. 15
Stogdill, R.M. 5
Svedja, M. 15

Taylor, S.E. 16
Tierney, J. 34
Treviño, L.K. 6
Tversky, A. 20
Tyler, T.R. 194

Updike, J. 159–60

Van Lange, P.A.M. 16, 42
Van Vugt, M. 9, 193
Vandello, J.A. 29, 184
Vohs, K. 81

Warner, N.O. 192

Weaver, G.R. 6
Weir, T. 73
Wertheim, J. 122
White, T.H. 66
Winnicott, D. 55
Woyke, J. 7
Wren, J.T. 7

Yammarino, F.J. 8
Yukl, G. 5–7

Zaccaro, S.J. 5, 195
Zimbardo, P. 16, 18, 42, 76

Subject Index

3:10 to Yuma 23, 74
9/11 44, 94–5, 154

Aaron, Hank 138, 150
Abdul-Jabbar, Kareem 85
Abrams, J.J. 46
Adams, John 174, 194
Addison, Joseph 107–8
Aguilera, Christina 35
alcoholism 106–7, 122–4
Ali, Muhammad 89, 166–8
Alou, Moises 54
Anderson, Daniel 98, 122–4
archetypes 14–15, 96, 145–6, 162, 184–5, 197
Arnaz, Desi 129
Auden, W.H. 33
Autrey, Wesley 1–8, 16, 45, 49, 102, 113

"Big Iron" (song) 147–9, 152
Backstreet Boys 21
Bailey, George (character in *It's a Wonderful Life*) 98, 102–3, 134
Ball, Lucille 98, 129–30
Barrymore, Drew 30, 34–5, 134
Bartman, Steve 41, 54
Batman (superhero) 13, 22, 24, 34–5, 74–6
Beach Boys 18, 22, 55
Beatles 17–18, 133, 135, 161, 176, 178
Beckham, David 23
Bieber, Justin 19, 57–8
bin Laden, Osama 101, 147, 154–5
Black, Hugo 53
Bloomberg, Michael 3
Bogart, Humphrey 98, 124–5, 144
Bogert, Carroll 42
Brown, Bundini 89

Bruner, Jerome 12
Bryant, Kobe 69
Buchanan, James 32
Buckner, Bill 22–3
Burns, Ken 187
Burton, LeVar 59
Bush, George H.W. 140, 169
Bush, George W. 84, 183
Butler, Benjamin "Beast" 41, 48–9

Cambers, Elizabeth 102
Capra, Frank 102–3
Carver, George Washington 98, 139–40
Casablanca (film) 124, 144, 152, 158
Cash, Johnny 35, 134
Cervantes, Miguel de 88
Challenger disaster 41, 51–2
charisma 5–6, 9–12, 16, 105, 193, 195, 197; Ahab and 193; Ali and 168; Autrey and 6; Churchill and 136; Clemente and 137; Clinton and 22; Downey and 63; Edwards and 76; Kennedy and 147, 163; King and 25, 172–3; Mandela and 172; Palmer and 78; Robin Hood and 148; Shatner and 62; Winfrey and 135
Chilean miners 19, 147, 156–7
Churchill, Winston 98, 136–7
Clay, Cassius *see* Ali, Muhammad
Clayton, Grace Golden 90
Clemente, Roberto 98, 137–8
Cline, Patsy 56
Clinton, Bill 22, 53, 59, 67
Clinton, Hillary 135
Closer, The (television series) 89, 148
collective unconscious 14
Columbus, Christopher 166, 168–9

Conard, Norm 102
Confucius 16, 98, 103–4, 124
Conners, Phil (character in *Groundhog
    Day*) 98, 110–11
Coolidge, Calvin 11
Coons, Sabrina 102
Cooper, John Milton 36
Copernicus, Nicolaus 17, 33, 124, 175
Cosby, Bill 134, 166, 178–9
Costner, Kevin 146, 148, 157
Cowen, Scott 118
Cox, James 11
Crowe, Russell 23, 74, 119, 148
Cumberbatch, Benedict 152
Curie, Marie 98, 115–16
Curie, Pierre 115–16

Dalai Lama 17, 50, 98–100, 124
Darby, Joe 41–3
Darwin, Charles 17, 33
Daugherty, Harry 10–11
DeGeneres, Ellen 98, 117–18
Dent, Harvey *see* Two-Face (superhero)
DiMaggio, Joe 140
Dion, Celine 24
Dirty Harry (film) 128, 145, 157
Doby, Larry 18, 150
Dodd, Sonora Smart 90
Downey, Jr., Robert 63
Doyle, Arthur Conan 88, 126, 146, 151,
    157; *see also* Holmes, Sherlock (fic-
    tional character)
Durocher, Leo 13
Dylan, Bob 161, 178

Earhart, Amelia 147, 152–3
Eastwood, Clint 98, 127–8, 145, 157
Edwards, John 69, 74, 76–7
Ehrlich, S.B. 9
Einstein, Albert 8, 17, 19, 25, 33, 115,
    166, 170, 174–6, 190
Elder, Lee 18
Eliach, Yaffa 111
Emerson, Ralph Waldo 124
Enberg, Dick 85
Ephraim, Gotthold 37
Erickson, Keith 85–6

Fairbanks, Douglas 148

fairy tales 74
Father's Day 90–1
Fey, Tina 98, 116–17
Field of Dreams (film) 146, 157
fire, prehistoric makers 82, 87–8
Fisher, Carrie 13
Floyd, Charles Arthur "Pretty Boy" 53,
    147–8, 161–2, 195
Flynn, Errol 148
Fonda, Henry 98, 144
Ford, Harrison 13
Ford, Henry 17, 87
Fox, Terry 98, 130–1
Frank, Anne 101
Freud, Sigmund 14, 17, 30, 33–5, 41, 91,
    197
Fukushima power plant disaster 41, 44–5

Gandhi, Mahatma 1, 8, 19, 22, 53, 112,
    134, 186, 192; non-violence and 17,
    93, 124, 173; as Transforming-Global
    Hero 25, 164, 166, 169–70
Geffen, David 24
Gibson, Althea 98, 120–1
Giffords, Gabrielle 39–41, 47–8, 181
Gladwell, Malcolm 10–11
Glenn, John 8
Gorbachev, Mikhail 98, 142–3
Grant, Ulysses S. 48, 83, 186; as Trending
    Hero 20, 29, 31–3, 36; as unheroic
    leader 188–9
Great Eight Traits of heroism 9–10, 12,
    16, 105, 136, 173, 197
Greene, Nathanael 83
Groundhog Day (film) 110–11
Guinness, Alec 13
Guthrie, Woody 147, 161–2, 195
Gyatso, Tenzin *see* Dalai Lama

Hale, Nathan 98, 107–8, 150, 157
Hamill, Mark 13
Harding, Warren G. 10–11, 32
Havel, Vaclav 50
Hernandez, Daniel 47
Hernandez, Rudy 138
heroes and heroism; compared with leader-
    ship 196–7; defined 4, 9, 191–2; Great
    Eight Traits of 9–10, 12, 16, 105, 136,
    173, 197; monomyth and 13–14,

24–5, 96; motivation and 192–5; shaping and 198; social influence and 16–26; taxonomy of 18–26
Hillary, Sir Edmund 34, 119
Hitler, Adolf 15, 54, 115, 136–7, 189
Hogg, Michael 14, 190
Hollopeter, Cameron 1–2, 6–7
Holly, Buddy 17, 166, 177–9
Holmes, Sherlock (fictional character) 86, 88–9, 126, 146, 148, 151–2, 157, 195
Howe, William 107
Hunt, Helen 20

indirect leadership 8–9, 52, 125, 132, 176, 190–1, 196, 198
Iron Man (superhero) 57, 63–4
It's a Wonderful Life (film) 102–3

Jackson, Andrew 90
James, LeBron 19, 22, 72–3
Jarvis, Anna 89
Jarvis, Gregory B. 51
Jefferson, Thomas 173–4
Jemison, Mae 43–4
Jennings, Peter 42, 86
Jesus of Nazareth 16, 19, 26, 98–100, 183, 185–6
Joan of Arc 8, 83
Jobs, Steve 17, 25
Johnson, Lyndon B. 32, 113
Johnson, Walter 120, 140
Jordan, Michael 19, 21, 133
Jung, Carl 14–15, 96, 145, 162, 184–5

Keisker, Marion 82, 86–7
Keller, Helen 1, 3–8
Kennedy, Jacqueline 66
Kennedy, John F. 66, 70, 89, 133, 147, 152, 159, 162–3, 169, 179
Kennedy, Robert F. 89
Key Largo (film) 124–5
Kilmer, Val 20
King, Jr., Martin Luther 1, 8, 19, 22, 26, 83, 113, 124–5; charisma of 25; "I Have a Dream" speech 172–3, 180, 190–1; non-violence and 17, 93; Rustin and 93; social influence of 16; as Transforming-Global Hero 166, 169–70

Kirk, Captain James T. (*Star Trek* character) 46, 57, 61–3, 158, 181
Korematsu, Fred 41, 52–3
Krakauer, Jon 47
Kuhn, Bowie 137
Kwasnica, Christina 47

Lady Gaga 19, 29–31, 53, 58
Lawton, Marcia J. 123
leadership: actions and 7; compared with heroism 196–7; defined 4–5, 189–91; ethics and 6–7; five factor model 5–9; indirect 8–9, 52, 125, 132, 176, 190–1, 196, 198; influence and 7–9; as mental construction 9–15; motivation and 192–5; narrative and 12–13; persona and 5–6; traits of effective 9–10; transactional 164–5; vision and 6; *see also* Traditional Heroes; Tragic Heroes; Transcendent Heroes; Transfigured Heroes; Transforming Heroes; Transitional Heroes; Transitory Heroes; Transparent Heroes; Transposed Heroes; Trending Heroes
Lee, Robert E. 32, 84, 186, 189
Lee, Sook-Yin 130
Lennon, John 17, 35, 134, 176–7, 179
Lewis, Ray 69
Lincoln, Abraham 1, 8, 22, 31–2, 84, 126, 142; charisma 12; Emancipation Proclamation 48–9; Gettysburg Address 13, 174, 191; as leader and hero 188, 195; on his mother 89; narrative and 12–13; patience of 124; physical appearance 11–12, 183; as Traditional Hero 24; as Transcendent Hero 181, 183, 186–7
Liu Xia 50
Liu Xiaobo 41, 49–50
Lohan, Lindsay 57–8
Lynch, Jessica 24, 155

McAuliffe, Christa 41, 51–2
McCartney, Paul 176
McClellan, George B. 11
McIlroy, Rory 20
McMurtry, Larry 162
McNair, Ronald E. 51
McPherson, James 48

Mandela, Nelson 1, 8, 25, 34, 53, 112, 125, 128, 165–6, 170–2
Marshall, George 98, 101, 132–3
Martin, George 18
Mays, Willie 13, 22, 55, 83, 138, 141, 149–50
Meigs, Montgomery 82–3
Merlet, Myriam 166, 179–80
Merlin 147, 153–4
Miller, Jonny Lee 152
Minogue, Kylie 30–1
monomyth 13–14, 24–5, 96
Moses 13
Mother's Day 90
Moynihan, Daniel Patrick 70
Muhammad 16
Murray, Bill 110–11
Musial, Stan 140

narratives 12–13
Nash, John 98, 119–20, 134
Navy SEALs 147, 154–5
negativity bias 81
Nichols, Nichelle 43
Nicklaus, Jack 69, 74, 77–8
Nightingale, Florence 98, 133–4
Nixon, Richard 67, 70–1, 91, 163, 177
Noonan, Fred 153
Norgay, Tenzing 34, 119

Obama, Barack 17, 24, 40, 57, 135, 140, 154–5
Odyssey 13
Oedipal Complex 14
Oedipus, King 65, 67–8
One Flew Over the Cuckoo's Nest (film) 144
Onizuka, Ellison S. 51
Oppenheimer, Robert 115

Palmer, Arnold 77–8
Panza, Sancho (fictional character) 13, 86, 88–9
parents as heroes 82–3, 89–91
Parks, Rosa 52, 93, 98, 112–14
Paterno, Joe 74–5, 78–80
Patrick, Saint 158–9
Pausch, Randy 41, 45–6, 62
persona 5–6
Picasso, Pablo 8

Poe, Edgar Allan 98, 125–6
polymaths 43, 92–3
Potter, Harry (fictional character) 19, 24, 98, 183–5
Power Rangers 19, 21
Presley, Elvis 17, 25, 56–7, 82, 86, 152, 166, 178
Pretty Boy Floyd 53, 147–8, 161–2, 195
prototypes 10, 14, 23, 61, 75, 83, 96
Putnam, George 153

Quixote, Don (fictional character) 13, 86, 88

Ramis, Harold 110–11
Reagan, Nancy 13
Reagan, Ronald 13, 31–2, 51, 128, 143
Reeve, Christopher 108–9
Reeve, Dana 98, 108–9, 134
Rescorla, Rick 83, 94–5
Rescorla, Susan 95
Resnik, Judith A. 51
Richards, Reed (Mr. Fantastic) 57, 60–1, 134
Richardson, J.P. 178
Richmond, Jeff 117
Robbins, Marty 147, 149
Robbins, Tim 128
Robin Hood 19, 147–8, 159
Robinson, Edward G. 125
Robinson, Jackie 13, 18, 120–1, 150
Roddenberry, Gene 62
Rogers, Fred 57–60
Roosevelt, Franklin D. 11, 140, 188; civil rights and 93, 120; Einstein's letter to 175; Executive Order No. 9066 52, 93; World War II and 52, 132
Roosevelt, Theodore 140
Rose, Reginald 98, 144–5
Ross, Betsy 147, 160–1
Rowling, J.K. 24, 184
Rumsfeld, Donald 42
Russell, Bill 140
Rustin, Bayard 83, 92–4
Ruth, Babe 133, 150, 160

Sandusky, Jerry 79
schemas 9–12, 14–15, 17, 23, 70, 96, 145–7

Schlesinger, Arthur 20, 36
Schwarzenegger, Arnold 30, 37–8
Scobee, Francis R. 51
Scully, Vin 138
Secretariat 98, 126–7
Seles, Monica 98, 121–2
Sendler, Irena 98, 101–2, 188, 196
September 11, 2001; terrorist attacks of
    44, 94–5, 154
servant leadership 10
Shakespeare, William 22, 65
Shatner, William 62
Shelton, Jessica 102
sidekicks 82, 88–9
Sifford, Charlie 18
Simonton, Dean Keith 3, 70, 163, 197
Slater, Steven 19, 21, 40–1, 54
Smith, Michael J. 51
social influence 16–26
Sollers, Wick 79
Sorensen, Theodore 89
Spahn, Warren 98, 140–1
Spears, Britney 57–8
Spira, Israel 98, 111–12, 114, 134
Spitzer, Eliot 69
Springsteen, Bruce 161
Star Trek (television and film franchise)
    43–4, 46, 57, 61–3, 158, 181
Star Wars (film) 13–14, 24
Steinbeck, John 162
Stengel, Casey 141
Stewart, James 102–3
Stewart, Mary 154
Stewart, Megan 102
stories and storytelling 12–13
Streep, Meryl 1, 3–8
Sullenberger, Chesley "Sully" 19, 21,
    39–40
Sullivan, Anne 1, 4–8

ten Boom, Corrie 98, 114–15
Teresa, Mother 98, 105–6
Tillman, Pat 98, 100–1, 155, 181
Traditional Heroes 23–4, 96–8; *see also*
    Traditional-Competent Heroes; Tradi-
    tional-Complete Heroes; Traditional-
    Moral Heroes
Traditional-Competent Heroes; Anderson,
    Daniel 98, 122–4; Ball, Lucille 98,

129–30; Bogart, Humphrey 98, 124–5;
Curie, Marie 98, 115–16; DeGeneres,
Ellen 98, 117–18; Eastwood, Clint 98,
127–8; Fey, Tina 98, 116–17; Gibson,
Althea 98, 120–1; Nash, John 98,
119–20; Poe, Edgar Allan 98, 125–6;
Secretariat 98, 126–7; Seles, Monica
98, 121–2
Traditional-Complete Heroes; Carver,
George Washington 98, 139–40;
Churchill, Winston 98, 136–7;
Clemente, Roberto 98, 137–8; Fox,
Terry 98, 130–1; Gorbachev, Mikhail
98, 142–3; Marshall, George 98, 132–3;
Nightingale, Florence 98, 133–4; Spahn,
Warren 98, 140–1; *Twelve Angry Men*
(Henry Fonda's character in) 98, 144–5;
Washington, George 98, 141–2; Win-
frey, Oprah 98, 134–6
Traditional-Moral Heroes; Bailey, George
98, 102–3; Confucius 98, 103–4;
Conners, Phil (character in *Groundhog
Day*) 98, 110–11; Dalai Lama 98–100;
Hale, Nathan 98, 107–8; Parks, Rosa
112–14; Reeve, Dana 98, 108–9;
Sendler, Irena 98, 101–2; Spira, Israel
98, 111–12; ten Book, Corrie 98,
114–15; Teresa, Mother 98, 105–6;
Tillman, Pat 98, 100–1; Wilson, Lois
98, 106–7
Tragic Heroes 22, 65–7; Nixon, Richard
67–71; Oedipus, King 67–8; Woods,
Tiger 67–9
transactional leadership 164–5
Transcendent Heroes 25–6, 181–3; Jesus
of Nazareth 183, 185–6; Lincoln,
Abraham 181, 183, 186–7; Potter,
Harry 183–5
Transfigured Heroes 24–5, 145–7; "Big
Iron" 147–9; Chilean miners 147,
156–7; Earhart, Amelia 147, 152–3;
Floyd, Charles Arthur "Pretty Boy"
147–8, 161–2; Holmes, Sherlock
146, 151–2; Kennedy, John F. 147,
162–3; Mays, Willie 149–50; Merlin
147, 153–4; Navy SEALs 147, 154–5;
Patrick, Saint 158–9; Robin Hood
147–8; Ross, Betsy 147, 160–1;
Williams, Ted 159–60

Transforming Heroes 25, 164–6; *see also* Transforming-Global Heroes; Transforming Specific Heroes
transforming leadership 1, 25, 164–5, 185, 194
Transforming-Global Heroes; Ali, Muhammad 166–8; Columbus, Christopher 166, 168–9; Einstein, Albert 166, 174–5; Gandhi, Mahatma 25, 164, 166, 169–70; Jefferson, Thomas 173–4; King, Jr., Martin Luther 166, 172–3; Mandela, Nelson 166, 170–2
Transforming-Specific Heroes; Cosby, Bill 166, 178–9; Holly, Buddy 17, 166, 177–9; Lennon, John 176–7; Merlet, Myriam 166, 179–80
Transitional Heroes 21–2, 55–7; Bieber, Justin 57–8; Iron man 57, 63–4; Kirk, Captain James T. 57, 61–3; Richards, Reed 57, 60–1; Rogers, Fred 57–9
transitional objects 55–6
Transitory Heroes 21, 39–41; Bartman, Steve 41, 54; Butler, Benjamin "Beast" 41, 48–9; Darby, Joe 41–3; Fukushima power plant workers 41, 44–5; Giffords, Gabrielle 41, 47–8; Jemison, Mae 41, 43–4; Korematsu, Fred 41, 52–3; Liu Xiaobo 41, 49–50; McAuliffe, Christa 41, 51–2; Pausch, Randy 41, 45–6; Slater, Steven 40–1, 54; Sullenberger, Chesley "Sully" 39–40
Transparent Heroes 23, 81–3; Keisker, Marion 82, 86–7; Meigs, Montgomery 82–3; parents 82–3, 89–91; prehistoric makers of fire 82, 87–8; Rescorla, Rick 83, 94–5; Rustin, Bayard 83, 92–4; sidekicks 82, 88–9; Wilson, Edith 83, 91–2; Wooden, John 82, 84–6
Transposed Heroes 22–3, 72–3; Edwards, John 74, 76–7; Nicklaus, Jack 74, 77–8; Paterno, Joe 74–5, 78–80; Two-Face (Harvey Dent) 22, 74–6
Travolta, John 20
Trending Heroes 20–1, 28–30; Barrymore, Drew 34–5; Freud, Sigmund 33–4; Grant, Ulysses S. 31–3; Lady Gaga 30–1; Schwarzenegger, Arnold 37–8; Wilson, Woodrow 35–7
Truman, Harry 32, 66, 120, 132–3, 190
Tutu, Desmond 17, 50
Twelve Angry Men (film) 98, 144–5
Two-Face (superhero) 22, 74–6

Urzua, Luis 156

Valens, Ritchie 178
Van Roekel, Dennis 52
Vick, Michael 69

Wahlen, George 101
Walsh, John 106
Walters, Barbara 31
Warhol, Andy 21, 39
Washington, Booker T. 139
Washington, George 83, 89–90, 98, 141–2, 147, 160, 188
Watson, Dr. John (Sherlock Holmes) 86, 88–9, 146, 151, 157
Waugh, Joan 32
Weathers, Beck 47
Welles, Orson 132
West, Jerry 22
Westen, Drew 33–4
whistleblowers 18, 41–3
Wilentz, Sean 32
Williams, Ted 140, 150
Wilson, Bill 106–7
Wilson, Edith 83, 91–2
Wilson, Ellen Axson 91
Wilson, Lois 98, 106–7, 134
Wilson, Woodrow 32, 83, 91–2, 160; as Trending Hero 19–20, 30, 35–7, 181
Winfrey, Oprah 8, 17, 24–5, 35, 46, 98, 134–5
Wooden, John 19, 25, 82, 84–6, 134, 181
Woodfill, Jerry 52
Woods, Tiger 9, 18–19, 67–9, 78, 122

Yeltsin, Boris 142
Young, Andrew 76

Zellweger, Renée 20